Corporations and Partnerships in Ireland

Corporations and Partnerships in Ireland

Third Edition

Irene Lynch Fannon

This book was originally published as a monograph in the International Encyclopaedia of Laws/Corporations and Partnerships.

Founding Editor: Roger Blanpain
General Editor: Frank Hendrickx
Volume Editors: Koen Geens

Wolters Kluwer

Published by:
Kluwer Law International B.V.
PO Box 316
2400 AH Alphen aan den Rijn
The Netherlands
E-mail: lrs-sales@wolterskluwer.com
Website: www.wolterskluwer.com/en/solutions/kluwerlawinternational

Sold and distributed by:
Wolters Kluwer Legal & Regulatory U.S.
920 Links Avenue
Landisville, PA 17538
United States of America
E-mail: customer.service@wolterskluwer.com

ISBN 978-94-035-0058-4

e-Book: ISBN 978-94-035-0068-3
web-PDF: ISBN 978-94-035-0078-2

The Author

Professor Dr Irene Lynch Fannon is a graduate of *University College Dublin, Oxford University* and the *University of Virginia*. She is a qualified Solicitor specialising in the law relating to corporate insolvency, restructuring and rescue in Ireland. She also researches in the area of corporate law theory. She taught Company Law, Corporate Insolvency Law and Corporate Law Theory in the School of Law, at *University College Cork* from 1987 until 2021. She is now a Professor Emeritus. She is the author (with Gerard Murphy BL) of *Corporate Insolvency and Rescue* (Second Edition, Bloomsbury, Dublin 2012), having co-authored the first edition with Rory O'Ferrall and Jane Marshall in 1996. She has published articles in a range of journals on corporate law, corporate insolvency and corporate governance. She has served on a number of government bodies including the Audit Review Committee (2000), the Business Regulation Forum (2005–2007), and the High-Level Group on Business Regulation (2007–2011). She is currently the Chairperson of the Corporate Insolvency Sub Committee of the Irish Company Law Review Group (www.clrg.org), having been appointed for the periods 2016–2018, 2018–2022 and 2022–2026 by the Minister of the relevant Irish Government department. She was a Visiting Professor at Cleveland Marshall College of Law and then Baker Hostetler Chair at that law school for the academic year 2003/2004. She was a Visiting Academic at Oxford Law Faculty in 2014. She is currently the Head of Knowledge Management at Matheson LLP.
Any errors in the text are the responsibility of the author.

The Author

Table of Contents

List of Abbreviations

ADR	American Depository Receipts
ADS	American Depository Securities
AGM	Annual General Meeting
AIM	Alternative Investment Market
CEA	Corporate Enforcement Authority (formerly the Office of the Director of Corporate Enforcement)
CJEU	Court of Justice of the European Union
CLRG	Company Law Review Group
CPT	Cuideachta Phoibli Theoranta
CRO	Companies Registration Office
CSO	Central Statistics Office, Ireland
DAC	Designated Activity Company
ECHR	European Convention on Human Rights
EEA	European Economic Area
EEIG	European Economic Interest Grouping
EGM	Extraordinary General Meeting
ESRI	Economic and Social Research Institute (Ireland)
EU	European Union
FDI	Foreign Direct Investment
GDP	Gross Domestic Product
IDA	Industrial Development Authority
IEX	Irish Enterprise Exchange
ILP	Investment Limited Partnership
LTD	Private Company Limited by Shares
NAMA	National Asset Management Agency
ODCE	Office of the Director of Corporate Enforcement (now the Corporate Enforcement Authority)
OECD	Organisation of Economic Co-operation and Development
PLC	Public Limited Company
SAP	Summary Approval Procedure

List of Abbreviations

UCITS	Undertakings for Collective Investment in Transferable Securities
VAT	Value-Added Tax

General Introduction

§1. THE GENERAL BACKGROUND OF THE COUNTRY

I. Geography

1. The island of Ireland is situated in the northwest of Europe between 51.5 and 55.5°N latitude and between 5.5 and 10.5°W longitude. The total area of the island of Ireland is 84,421 km^2 (32,595 sq. mi) with the Republic of Ireland covering 70,282 km^2 (27,136 sq. mi) and Northern Ireland, 14,139 km^2 (5,459 sq. mi). The greatest length (N/S) is 486 km (302 mi), the greatest width (E/W) is 275 km (171 mi), and the total coastline measures 3,172 km (1,970 mi). The island comprises a large central lowland of limestone with a relief of hills surrounded by a discontinuous border of coastal mountains that vary greatly in geological structure. Influenced by the Gulf Stream and with the prevailing winds predominantly from the southwest, the climate is equable and temperatures are fairly uniform over the whole country. The coldest months are typically January and February, with mean daily air temperatures of between 4°C and 7°C, while July and August are the warmest (18°C–20°C on average inland). Extremes of air temperature, below –10°C or above 30°C, have rarely been recorded. Average annual rainfall in the lowlands varies between 750 mm and 1,250 mm, with higher figures (up to 2,000 mm). The State of Ireland is not coterminous with the island of Ireland, in that one-sixth of the territory (in the northeast corner) is known as Northern Ireland and is part of the United Kingdom.[1] In effect, there are four different legal jurisdictions in the British Isles – the Republic of Ireland (the State of Ireland), Northern Ireland, Scotland and finally, England and Wales. In relation to the Republic of Ireland (the State of Ireland), there is a completely separate legislative framework and court system whereas this is not the case in relation to all matters within the United Kingdom. It should be noted that post the Brexit Referendum in 2016, the Republic of Ireland remains a full Member State of the European Union (EU). The United Kingdom including Scotland, England and Wales, and Northern Ireland, are now no longer members of the EU. However, the position of Northern Ireland is different in that it remains part of the single market under the Northern Irish Protocol. As of March

1. Unless the context indicates the contrary, all information in this monograph concerns the State of Ireland, described in cases of ambiguity as the Republic of Ireland, although its official name is Ireland. ('The name of the state in English is Ireland and is Éire in the Irish language … ' Bunreacht na hÉireann (Constitution of Ireland), Art. 4).

2023, issues pertaining to this matter but also pertaining to the body of European law still in force in the UK are, as yet, unresolved.

II. Cultural Composition

2. Under the Constitution (*Bunreacht na hÉireann*), '[t]he Irish language as the national language is the first official language. The English language is recognised as a second official language'.[2] The predominantly spoken first language is English. In 2011, 1.77 million people said they could speak Irish, but just 77,185 persons spoke Irish daily outside the education system.[3] In 2022, the figure of individuals reporting that they could speak Irish was 1.9 million. Most interesting, however, is that in Census 2022, 751,507 Irish residents spoke a language other than Irish or English at home, an increase of 23% since 2016. Of these, the top languages spoken were Polish, Lithuanian Romanian and Portuguese (16,737) – the latter by a mostly Brazilian population. Hindi has also become a significant minority language spoken at home.

3. The Constitution of Ireland guarantees '[f]reedom of conscience and the free profession and practice of religion', subject to public order and morality, to every citizen, and guarantees that the State will neither 'endow any religion' nor 'impose any disabilities nor make any discrimination on the ground of religious profession, belief or status'.[4] The stated religion of most people in Ireland (Republic) is Roman Catholic. According to the 2011 census, 84.1% of the population were Roman Catholics. In 2022, this figure declined to 69%. The remainder were members of the Church of Ireland (Anglican), which represented an increase in figures from 2011, Presbyterian, Methodist, Jewish, Muslim or other faith, along with minorities who either stated they had no religion or declined to say.[5] The number of persons who identified as Muslim again increased in 2022 and the number of Hindus doubled to 33,043.

III. Political System

A. *The Constitutional Framework*

4. Ireland is a parliamentary democracy, and as such, operates under the second constitution passed since independence, namely the 1937 Constitution (*Bunreacht na hÉireann*). The national parliament (in the Irish language, *Oireachtas*) consists of the President (*an tUachtarán*) and two Houses: a House of Representatives (*Dáil*

2. Bunreacht na hÉireann (Constitution of Ireland), Art. 8.
3. Census 2016. Note that there has been a more recent Census in 2022 (delayed due to COVID-19) The Publication Schedule for the results of the Census 2022 indicates that various reports will be published throughout 2023. Extensive summaries are available at www.cso.ie at present.
4. Bunreacht na hÉireann (Constitution of Ireland), Art. 44.2.
5. Census 2022, *supra* n. 3.

Éireann) and a Senate (*Seanad Éireann*). In October 2013, a referendum was held which considered abolishing the second house, i.e., the Senate (*Seanad Éireann*) but this was rejected by the population. The executive power of the State is 'subject to the provisions of [the] Constitution,' exercised 'by or on the authority of the Government', which is to consist of not less than seven and not more than fifteen members.[6] The Prime Minister (*Taoiseach*), Deputy Prime Minister (*Tánaiste*) and Minister for Finance must be members of the Dáil. The other members of the Government may be members of the Dáil or Seanad, but not more than two may be members of the Seanad. The Government acts collectively and is responsible to the Dáil. The Taoiseach is appointed by the President on the nomination of the Dáil. He or she must resign on ceasing to retain the support of a majority in the Dáil. The Taoiseach nominates one member of the Government to be Tánaiste. The Tánaiste acts in place of the Taoiseach, if the Taoiseach is temporarily absent or becomes incapacitated.

5. The Attorney General is 'the adviser to the Government in matters of law and legal opinion', and, though s/he 'shall not be a member of the Government', may (and in practice does) attend Cabinet meetings.[7] The Attorney General's tenure of office is normally coterminous with that of the Taoiseach. The Taoiseach assembles a Government and assigns Departments of State to Ministers. Usually, each member of the Government heads one Department, but occasionally, a Minister is responsible for more than one Department. Ministers of State, or 'junior ministers', who are not members of the Government, assist Government Ministers in their Parliamentary and Departmental work. The maximum number of Ministers of State is fixed by law at twenty.

B. Political Parties

6. Ireland is a constitutional democracy. Elections are based on a system of voting known as proportional representation. At the time of writing (2023), following an election held in early 2020, the Government was composed of a coalition between *Fine Gael* (loosely translated from Irish as 'tribe of the Irish'), *Fianna Fail* (which, loosely translated, means 'Soldiers of Destiny') and the Green Party. This coalition is of historical interest and significance in that it involves a coalition of what would have been considered the two main political parties whose divisions derived from Civil War Politics post the Anglo-Irish Treaty signed in 1921 and described below. The opposition parties are currently *the Labour Party* and *Sinn Féin* ('ourselves alone'), together with a range of independent members of parliament. All elected members of parliament are referred to as TDs, an abbreviation of the Irish term, *Teachta Dála*. Apart from the Green Party, the two main government parties Fine Gael, and Fianna Fáil and one of the opposition parties, Sinn Fein, have their historical roots in the armed struggle for Irish independence and in the stance

6. Bunreacht na hÉireann (Constitution of Ireland), Arts 28.2 and 28.1, respectively. The rest of this paragraph is a brief summary of Art. 28.
7. *Bunreacht na hÉireann* (Constitution of Ireland), Art. 30.

taken by these parties in relation to republicanism and later the Anglo-Irish Treaty of 1921, the subsequent Civil War and the establishment of the Free State in 1922 pursuant to the Treaty. Historically speaking, Fianna Fáil would have been regarded as more conservative on social issues than Fine Gael and Sinn Féin, but this categorisation is no longer apt. Fianna Fáil and Fine Gael are often similarly positioned on fiscal issues, although the latter are generally regarded as more fiscally conservative and pro-business, with Sinn Féin a more socialist party on issues such as distributive justice. Following the global financial crisis and subsequent economic crash in Ireland which began in 2008, the 2011 general election heralded a period of significant political change with the then-dominant party Fianna Fail suffering considerably from populist opinion which blamed the government for continuing with policies which contributed to a period of economic crisis. Consequently, the previous government (consisting of a Fine Gael/Labour coalition) was returned with a significant majority. The current government formation reflects this ongoing political shift in changing attitudes. Although the Labour Party's fortunes have continued to decline, there is a significant shift towards fiscally left-wing politics evidenced by continuing growth in support for Sinn Fein, but this party remains somewhat controversial because of its perceived failure to deal with legacy issues arising from its association with the IRA and the violent activities of the latter in Northern Ireland, the United Kingdom and indeed, the Republic of Ireland from the 1970s–1990s. Nevertheless, Sinn Fein continues to gain support in Northern Ireland also and is a significant 'all-island' party in that context.

IV. Population and Employment Statistics

7. Preliminary results from the 2022 Census indicate a population increase to 5,123,536 from 4,761,865 for the Republic of Ireland with the increase attributed to a natural increase of 171,338 and to a net migration figure of 190,333. This is the first time the population has exceeded 5 million since a census was taken in 1851.[8]

V. Enterprise, Corporation and Partnership Statistics

A. *Economic Context*

8. Ireland is a member of the Eurozone, joining the EU currency system in 1999. Between 2008 and 2011, Ireland experienced a significant period of economic change following the global financial crisis. The years following recovery from the financial crisis was a period of prosperity and economic recovery which was surprisingly robust. Most recently the economy has been effected by COVID-19, but again, economic resilience seems to have been a hallmark of the economy.

8. CSO Census 2022. Press Release on preliminary results, 23 Jun. 2022. A full set of results with accompanying reports, will be published during 2023. www.cso.ie.

9. Ireland is a small, modern, trade-dependent, open economy that experienced unprecedented economic growth between 1994 and 2004. However, by the end of the following summer, in 2009, it became clear that Ireland's problems were not linked to the global financial crisis alone and that the economic downturn would be more serious and likely to be more sustained in Ireland. Effectively, the Irish banking sector had become overexposed to the property market with significant risks emerging that the banking sector would collapse. In response, the Government executed a bank guarantee in 2008, effectively turning a banking crisis into a sovereign debt crisis. The Committee of Inquiry into the Banking Crisis, colloquially known as the Banking Inquiry,[9] was a joint committee of the Houses of the Oireachtas. It was formally established in November 2014 under the Houses of the Oireachtas (Inquiries, Privileges and Procedures) Act 2013. The purpose of the Inquiry was to inquire into the reasons Ireland experienced a systemic banking crisis, including the political, economic, social, cultural, financial and behavioural factors and policies which impacted on, or contributed to, the crisis and the preventative reforms implemented in the wake of the crisis.

10. These events led to an austerity programme overseen by the IMF, the European Central Bank and the European Commission which provided funds to Ireland to support the guarantee. From 2015 onwards, there were significant signs of economic recovery which have continued to the current period. Nevertheless, a significant personal debt problem, again linked to the property bubble, continues to be problematic. Because of the economic effects of COVID-19 experienced across Europe, the Eurozone and indeed other economies significant to Ireland, such as the US and the UK, it is difficult to really predict what will occur in the coming years. It is difficult to predict what the current situation is as regards the personal debt problem due to the unemployment effects of COVID-19 but on the other hand, the effects of significant state supports seem to be important.

11. That said, in the insolvency area, it was predicted that growth in corporate and business insolvencies would occur in the two years following 2021 as far out as 2024. This will be further considered in the relevant section on insolvency law provisions but to date has not materialised (April 2023) in Ireland.

12. One of the most significant features of the Irish recovery from the Great Recession was the creation of an Irish 'bad bank', the National Assets Management Agency (NAMA) under the legislation of the same name. This organisation took over non-performing loans from the bailed-out banks, managed these loans and in some cases, the underlying securities which included parcels of real property, with a view to realising the securities on an open market. During the period of its operation from 2009 to the present, NAMA has been largely successful in this strategy recovering significant sums for the Irish exchequer through the sale of assets.

9. Report of the Joint Committee of Inquiry into the Banking Crisis 2016 https://inquiries.oireachtas.ie/banking/about-the-inquiry/.

B. Statistics

13. As of 2022 (the date of the last Annual Report published by the Companies Registration Office, there were 261, 967 private companies registered with the Registrar of Companies (CRO); 2% of these companies were private limited companies registered as Designated Activity Companies (DACs). In addition, there were near to 1050 companies registered as Public Limited Companies (PLCs), nearly 5,000 unlimited companies and over 16,000 companies limited by guarantee.[10] Interestingly a significant number of companies are registered as external companies, the figure is currently near 3,000. Thus, it can be seen that private limited companies continue to make up the vast majority of companies. In 2020, 2021 and 2022, there was a significant rise in the number of businesses registering as companies. Even though there are views that this may be attributable to BREXIT with companies registered in the UK seeking to register companies in Ireland (within the EU), there has been no similar rise in external registered companies. There were 336 Limited Partnerships registered in 2022.

VI. Social and Cultural Values

14. The last three decades from 1996 – present have witnessed significant impacts on the Irish economy and in turn changes in Irish society. Growth in Ireland's Gross Domestic Product (GDP) in the decade from 1996 to 2000 averaged about 9% year on year with a turning point around the year 2000, but, thereafter, the economy averaged growth of around 4% from 2000 to 2005. By 2005, the Organization of Economic Co-operation and Development (OECD) estimated that in terms of GDP per capita, based on Purchasing Power Parities, Ireland was ranked fifth in the world. In 2005, Ireland's GDP growth rate averaged 5% for that year but in 2009, within a period of four years, the GDP rate of decline averaged –9%. In the Euro Zone 15, the figures for the same years are just under 2% growth rate in 2005 and –4% decline in 2009 showing a much less significant 'swing' than that of Ireland. Following the financial crisis and the Great Recession, in 2010, the Euro Zone 15 showed a small overall growth rate, whereas the figures were still negative for Ireland for 2010. Household indebtedness, as a percentage of gross disposable income, also began to grow remarkably from 2002 and continues to be problematic, barring assessment of COVID-19 effects on household saving figures. This has led to significant growth in disparity between wealthier sections of Irish society and less well-off. However, significant social welfare provisions and supports are in place. By 2014, the shock of the financial crisis seemed to recede with unemployment figures continuing to improve year on year from 2015 onwards. By early 2020, unemployment was at 4.7% but post-COVID-19, the Central Statistics Office (CSO) began the practice of providing two figures, the first a 'traditional unemployment rate' and the second a 'COVID-19 rate' which includes figures based on individuals receiving government unemployment supports related directly to COVID. Thus, the traditional unemployment rate for mid-2021 was 5.8% and the COVID-adjusted rate

10. https://www.cro.ie.

was 22.4%.[11] By the end of 2021, the CSO stated that the traditional unemployment rate stood at 4.9% with the COVID-adjusted rate standing at 7.5%. This is effectively full employment with severe labour shortages being experienced. These robust figures continue to improve at the time of writing despite the threats of a global recession.

15. When considered in the overall European context, the figures from 1996 onwards illustrate that Ireland and its people have experienced significant economic and related cultural changes during the last two and half decades in terms of GDP growth, decline and regrowth, compared even with its closest European neighbours. Much of this is now due to external factors. A significant factor in this ongoing pattern of change includes developments in relation to regulation of corporate taxation matters and international responses to this matter.

16. One factor which has remained constant throughout the cycle of boom and bust is that agriculture, once the most important sector, is now dwarfed by industry and services. Industry accounts for 46% of GDP and about 80% of exports and employs 28% of the labour force. The food industry is however an important sector. The Census figures for 2011 and 2016 (in addition to summaries of the 2022 census) show that there has been a significant and continued move to urban areas. Again, this illustrates the close connection between economic shifts and changes in cultural patterns.

17. The period of apparently spectacular economic growth from the mid-1990s onwards and post the banking and economic crisis of 2008, was preceded by periods of stagnation that, on balance, commentators are now agreed should not have occurred. For example, during the period 1977–1984, the Government pursued fiscal and economic policies that had a damaging effect on overall economic performance.[12] In addition, Ireland's relatively poor economic performance in the 1950s and particularly in the 1960s[13] meant that some part of the initial growth in the 1990s involved an element of catch-up with its European neighbours, although commentators are divided as to the significance of this catch-up point. There is a broad consensus in relation to factors that fed into the period of growth and which continue to contribute to growth. Relying on information available from government agencies such as the Economic and Social Research Institute (ESRI),[14] these factors include the following:

- pursuit of pragmatic and innovative government policies;
- an emphasis on education and technological innovation;
- a youthful population and rapidly expanding labour supply;
- an openness to international trade in goods and services and to new ideas;

11. https://www.cso.ie/en/releasesandpublications/er/mue/monthlyunemploymentapril2021/.
12. Brian Nolan et al., *Bust to Boom? The Irish Experience of Growth and Inequality* (Institute of Public Administration 2000); Kieran A. Kennedy et al., *The Economic Development of Ireland in the Twentieth Century* 87–90 (Routledge 1988).
13. Joe Lee, *Ireland, 1912–1985: Politics and Society* (Cambridge University Press 1989).
14. Economic and Social Research Institute. www.esri.ie.

- substantial inward investment inflows, encouraged by (among other factors) a low rate of corporation tax and the work of agencies such as Enterprise Ireland[15] and the Industrial Development Authority (IDA);[16]
- the strategic deployment of EU Structural and Cohesion Funds; and
- a 'social partnership' approach to economic development.

These factors continue to be present in the Irish economic and political framework.

18. In addition to economic development and related cultural and social changes, Ireland has also experienced a period of secularisation. As described in the earlier section on Cultural Composition, Ireland was traditionally a predominantly Catholic country. However, over the four decades from the 1990s onwards, significant social changes have occurred beginning with increased availability of contraception in the 1980s, the decriminalisation of homosexual activity between consensual male adults in 1993, the legalisation of divorce in 1996 and more recently the legalisation of abortion in 2018. In 2015, Ireland became the first country to legalise same-sex marriage through a referendum in 2015.[17]

19. In terms of political identity, post-BREXIT, the Republic of Ireland remains a member state of the EU sharing a land border with Northern Ireland which is part of the UK. Therefore, the island of Ireland has two jurisdictions, one within the EU and one outside it. Yet, the Ireland/Northern Ireland Protocol to the BREXIT Treaty means that Northern Ireland remains within the EU Customs Union. It is difficult to predict the difficulties in terms of trade which BREXIT and this Protocol will cause. In early 2021, the European Commission sought to invoke Article 16 of the Ireland/Northern Ireland Protocol to the Brexit Treaty in response to a controversy surrounding the supply of COVID-19 vaccinations by AstraZeneca to the EU. The fear seemed to be that the preservation of Northern Ireland in the customs union would lead to a leakage of vaccinations into the UK. Article 16 concerns 'safeguards' and the mechanism for putting them in place. As explained by Hayward and Phinnemore, such safeguards are 'often found in trade agreements and allow each party to take unilateral measures in response to an unexpected negative effect arising from the agreement. A similar provision is included, for example, in Article 112 of the Agreement on European Economic Area. Such measures are rarely used'.[18]

20. This purported action was considered to be extremely controversial at the time and the many issues surrounding this Protocol remain unresolved.

---

15. www.enterprise-ireland.com.
16. www.idaireland.com.
17. In the words of the Irish Taoiseach (Prime Minister) at the time: 'In the privacy of the ballot box, the people made a public statement. With today's vote we have disclosed who we are. We are a generous, compassionate, bold and joyful people who say yes to inclusion, yes to generosity, yes to love, yes to gay marriage', a statement which more than any other illustrates the changes which have occurred in Ireland in three decades.
18. https://blogs.lse.ac.uk/brexit/2021/01/11/article-16-of-the-ireland-northern-ireland-protocol-offers-no-quick-fix/.

VII. Privatisation Efforts and Golden Shares

21. In Ireland, significant enterprises remain state-owned where a commercial business is beneficially owned, either completely or through a majority shareholding, by the Irish Government. Usually, the body has a sponsor (hence the term 'state-sponsored body') who will be the relevant Minister who acts as a shareholder, either independently, or in conjunction with the Minister of Finance. State-sponsored bodies may either be statutory corporations or incorporated companies. Statutory corporations are officially non-profit and do not formally have shareholders, but have a board or other authority appointed by the sponsor Minister. Corporations of this type include public service broadcasting companies,[19] corporations significant to Irish trade[20] and some utilities such as the Electricity Supply Board.

22. In addition, there are a significant number of corporations with significant state shared ownership. These can be privately owned companies or companies incorporated as PLCs and include an array of businesses from airport and port authorities, utility companies and transport companies. Since the Great Recession, a number of banks were bailed out and became state-owned with the State eventually aiming to sell shares in these companies at future dates. This has occurred with some success as described in the following paragraph.

23. A programme of privatisation of previously state-owned enterprises has progressed since the 1990s with mixed success. Some privatisations have attracted considerable controversy. For example, in 1991, the chief executive of Greencore (Irish Sugar PLC created following the privatisation of the Irish sugar industry) was forced to resign immediately prior to the company's flotation when it was discovered he was a shareholder in a company which had been purchased by Irish Sugar prior to its flotation. Similarly, the initial privatisation of the Irish telecommunications body caused considerable concern when following a highly publicised public flotation, a significant drop in the public company's – Eircom – share price following the company's flotation caused a loss to ordinary shareholders/ investors that many became opposed to future privatisations. That said the privatisation of state-owned banks (ACC, ICC and AIB) following the bailout in 2008 and recovery in recent years seem to have been successful. Depending on the nature of the business, provision is made for the retention of golden shares in accordance with particular conditions set out by agreement within the general framework of company law. The issue of, and the terms surrounding, 'golden shares' is purely a matter of contract law in this jurisdiction.

19. Raidió Teilifís Éireann (Radio and Television of Ireland) and Teilifís na Gaeilge (the Irish language television channel).
20. Bord Bia (Food Board) and the IDA Ireland (Industrial Development Authority).

§2. The Historical Background of Corporations and Partnerships

I. The Development of the Common Law

24. Ireland was part of the British Empire until the declaration of independence in 1916 and the subsequent establishment of the Irish Free State in 1922. The Irish law of companies and partnerships reflects that history, and as a consequence, this body of law shares the same historical provenance as the law of England and Wales and many other common-law countries. In understanding the regulatory framework, it is important to recognise that Irish company law is still today a combination of statute law and judicially developed principles derived both from common law and equity. For example, two fundamental principles underpinning the success and significance of the limited liability corporation are the concepts of limited liability, a statutory invention, and the concept that the corporation or company is a separate legal person, a judicial doctrine developed and refined in case law.[21] Thus, statute and judicial doctrine continue to combine to create the body of Irish company law.

25. The Partnership Act of 1890, is still the primary relevant legislation, concerning Irish partnership law. However, the 1890 Act was itself a distillation of pre-existing principles developed by the courts at common law and in equity. These principles continue in force to the extent that they are not inconsistent with, the 1890 Act.[22] The Investment Limited Partnership (ILP) Act 2020 came into force in 2021 and this has provided a new framework for equity funds to operate in Ireland.[23]

II. The Genesis of Company Law

A. The Common Law Period

26. The limited liability company is a relatively recent legal invention that came into existence towards the end of the nineteenth-century as a result of statutory intervention. Until 1844, there were only two means by which a company could be legally incorporated. First, the Crown granted charters and letters patent authorising the creation of companies, often for purposes related to overseas colonies (e.g., facilitating trade with these colonies).[24] Second, private Acts of Parliament were enacted, creating companies for specific objects or purposes, such as the completion of infrastructure projects, sometimes with a lifespan limited in time or by the

21. These are discussed in detail *infra* Part 1, Ch. 1 §3.
22. *See infra* Part II on Partnerships.
23. *See infra* Part II on Partnerships.
24. The East India Company ('the grandest society of merchants in the universe') is a well-known example. Elizabeth I granted its charter in 1600, initially allowing the company a twenty-one-year monopoly on trade in the East Indies. Over time, the company acquired auxiliary governmental and military functions, and for a time (ending in 1858) virtually ruled India and several other Asian colonies.

particular project.[25] These early 'joint-stock companies' had several of the attributes of modern companies, including perpetual succession and power to act and transact in the corporate name (including in litigation). However, Royal Charters, letters patent and private Acts of Parliament were difficult and expensive to obtain. Over time, it became clear that there was greater demand for the corporate form amongst business people: 'the privilege of limited liability was precisely that of which [practical men] were most desirous, and without which mere incorporation was of little importance'.[26]

27. In 1844 and 1855, Parliament moved to provide an alternative legal structure to facilitate the operation of businesses and, in particular, to facilitate groups of merchants investing in a collective business scheme. Statutes enacted in those years laid the foundations of modern company law in Ireland and in England and Wales.[27] Considerable similarities remain between these jurisdictions. The result was that investors were now free, firstly, to incorporate companies for their own purposes (subject to registration with a State official), and, secondly, to limit their liability to the amount of their investment. The introduction of these concepts – incorporation by registration and limited liability – provided the foundations of a legislative framework for the modern company, which, though consolidated on several occasions,[28] has remained in place ever since. At the time, the idea of limited liability was received with distaste by some commentators, who feared it would amount to 'a rogue's charter'.[29] This concern, surviving in various degrees, has led over the ensuing century and a half to the accretion of a body of statutory law aimed at minimising abuse or misuse of limited liability – to reduce the rogue's freedom to do harm or, as the economist would say, to reduce externalities. The mid-Victorian legislatures that enacted these reforms appear to have maintained a distinction between partnerships and companies on the basis of the number of members. Thus, the 1844 Act provided that, where twenty-five or more persons associated together for the purpose of business, they could not form a partnership, only a company. The 1855 Act then provided that twenty-five persons was the minimum number of members required before a limited liability company could be

25. Many examples of the latter type of companies are found in the case law, including the Irish case of *Hutton v. West Cork Railway Company* (1883) 23 Ch D 654; *Bagshaw v. Eastern Union Railway Co.* (1849) 7 Hare 114, 68 ER 46; and *Preston v. Grand Collier Dock Company* (1840) 10 L.J.Ch. 73, 11 Sim. 327, 59 ER 900. On the formation of companies by Royal Charter and Letters Patent, *see* F.W. Clark, *A Treatise on the Law of Partnership and Joint-Stock Companies, According to the Law of Scotland* 96–102 (books.google.com 1866).
26. F.W. Clark, *A Treatise on the Law of Partnership and Joint-Stock Companies,* 1, 76 (Forgotten Books 2013).
27. *See* the Companies Act 1844 (7 & 8 Vict. c. 110) and the Limited Liability Act 1855 (18 & 19 Vict. c. 133), respectively.
28. The Joint Stock Companies Act 1856 (19 & 20 Vict. c. 47), the Companies Act 1862 (25 & 26 Vict. c. 89) and the Companies (Consolidation) Act 1908 were the chief instances applicable to pre-independent Ireland. Palmer described the 1862 Act as 'the *Magna Carta* of co-operative enterprise'. G. Morse et al., *Palmer's Company Law* 1 (25th edn., Sweet & Maxwell 1992).
29. (1854) 24 *Law Times* 142; (1855) 25 *Law Times* 116 and 210. Others saw the 1855 Act rather differently: 'This Act was no sooner in operation, than it gave great and general satisfaction, and the prognostications made by the opponents of limited liability were found to have been purely imaginary.' (Clark, *Treatise on the Law of Partnership*, 9).

incorporated. Today this numerical framework of minimum and maximum members has more or less vanished from the law. The 1856 Act reduced the minimum number of members in a limited liability company to seven, the Irish Companies Act 1963 reduced this number to two, and in 1989, the Member States of the European Community agreed to permit the creation of single-member companies in a Directive that was transposed into Irish law in 1994.[30] This is now re-enacted in the Companies Act 2014.[31] This result had, of course, been substantially achieved a century before, due to the decision of the House of Lords in *Salomon v. Salomon & Co.* (interpreting the 1862 Act, which had maintained the seven-member minimum) that a sole trader could validly incorporate his business, along with six bare nominees (in that instance, the appellant's wife and children). The House of Lords refused to imply into the statute a legislative requirement that all seven members need to take an active part in the affairs of the company, nor that there was any requirement that the members would be independent of each other.[32] More importantly, the number of directors required in an Irish company had been reduced to two by 1990 and has now been further reduced to one by virtue of implementation of the EU Directive referred to above. It is clear that recognition of the benefits of what are sometimes termed the 'privileges' of limited liability and corporate personality must be counterbalanced by the need for regulation to prevent abuse of these doctrines. In modern Ireland, as in other jurisdictions, debate continues as to the proper balance to be struck in this regard. Recent changes to the regulatory structure have been of sufficient significance to have raised the question as to whether the burden of legal compliance is now too heavy. This concept of incorporation as a privilege has a clear historical provenance, in that, as noted above, prior to the general availability of incorporation to all kinds of businesses, only certain kinds of business ventures were granted the privilege of incorporation. The grand trading companies such as the English East India Company were early examples. In the nineteenth-century, railways were granted corporate status, but they were tightly controlled by the State granting the privilege; the corporation was confined to specific objects and purposes, such as infrastructural projects, and often confined to survival for a specified lifespan. Although corporation is today readily available to all kinds of business people, this availability has historically been coupled with a desire on the part of the courts and legislature to address excesses.

B. Post-1937 Constitution

28. Following the passage in 1937 of *Bunreacht na hÉireann* (the Constitution of Ireland) and the establishment of independent Irish courts, the development of an independent Irish corporation and partnership legal framework began in earnest.

---

30. EC Directive 89/667, [1989] O.J. L395/40 (transposed into Irish law by the European Communities (Single-Member Private Limited Companies) Regulations of 1994 (S. I. 275 of 1994)). Note that the UK Parliament had moved to this position earlier: Companies Act 1985, s. 1(3A).
31. Companies Act 2014, s. 128
32. *Salomon v. Salomon & Co.* [1897] AC 22. Lord Halsbury remarked that the legislature had 'enact[ed] nothing as to the extent or degree of interest which may be held by each of the seven [members] or as to the proportion of interest or influence possessed by one or the majority over the others'.

The original legislation was the 1908 Companies Act. In 1963, the Companies Act was passed, which up until 2014, was referred to as the 'Principal Act'. Significant amendments and changes to the 1963 legal framework were made in subsequent legislation from the 1980s onwards. Most noteworthy of these legal enactments were the two pieces of legislation passed in 1990, the 1990 Companies Act and the 1990 Companies (Amendment) Act. This latter Act introduced a statutory corporate rescue process known as 'Examinership'.[33] In addition, the 2001 Company Law Enforcement Act made a significant difference in the enforcement of and compliance with Company Law in Ireland.[34]

29. However, following a major process of review and consolidation of all existing company law, conducted under the auspices of the Company Law Review Group (CRLG), a draft Companies Consolidation Bill, which would consolidate and update all prior company law legislation was published in 2007.[35] Following extensive consultation and debate, this legislation was passed by the legislature in late 2014, signed into law by the President on 23 December 2014 and was, in large part, commenced in June 2015. It is the largest single statute passed in the history of the State and is designed to present the body of Irish company law in a 'single comprehensible code.' Between 2014 and the present date (2023), a number of amending statutes have been passed, not least the Companies (Miscellaneous Provisions COVID-19) Act 2020 addressing matters during the COVID-19 pandemic such as the holding of virtual creditor and shareholder meetings. A new rescue process for micro and small companies was introduced under the Companies (Rescue Process for Small and Micro Companies) Act 2021. This monograph has been re-written to take account of these developments and has been updated accordingly. For further updates on reform projects, the CRLG provides information on ongoing issues at www.clrg.org.

III. Development of Irish Company Law and Membership of the EU

A. *Introduction*

30. Ireland acceded to the European Community in 1972 and since that time has enacted Directives relevant to Company Law in the legislation indicated *infra*. In terms of affecting the landscape of Irish law, some of the EU Directives have had more impact than others, in particular, the Directives concerning minimum capital requirements and accounting and the Directives in relation to the regulation of the capital markets, such as the Directives on Prospectuses, Insider Dealing and Market Manipulation. In some cases more than others, the process of harmonisation of company law at EU level is marked by a notable difference between the common law

33. *See infra*, Part I, Ch. 1 §5, IV.
34. *See infra*, Part I, Ch. 1 §4, III, F.
35. *See* www.clrg.org.

origins of Irish and UK company law and the civil law origins of the corporation systems of other Member States. The significance of the legislative changes deriving from Europe is summarised below:

- The First Company Law Directive (68/15/EEC) was enacted through the European Communities (Companies) Regulations 1973, which provided a statutory notification framework regarding officers and others with the authority to deal on behalf of the company and a notification framework regarding the filing of other company documents. The most significant changes emanating from this legislation, ameliorating the doctrine of constructive notice regarding outsiders dealing with the company and the registration of individuals with authority to act on behalf of the company are now contained in sections 39 and 40 of the Companies Act 2014. See also an additional regulation which enacts an obligation to deal in good faith imposed on third parties dealing with the company.[36]
- The Second Directive (77/91/EEC) regarding the formation of PLCs, minimum capital requirements for PLCs, and important capital maintenance and alteration rules was enacted by the Companies (Amendment) Act 1983, which also set out the requirements that private limited companies would be denominated by the term 'Limited' or 'Ltd' or the Irish language equivalent 'Teoranta' or 'Teo'. For PLCs, the term used is PLC or in Irish 'cuideachta phoibli theoranta' (CPT). See further obligations imposed by Directive 2006/68/EC, which amends these provisions. Under the Companies Act 2014, these provisions are now contained in Part 17. The abbreviation PLC or CPT is retained for public limited companies, but private companies limited by shares are now categorised into LTD or DAC, depending on whether the private company limited by shares has opted to have no specific designated activity or has opted for a designated activity structure.[37]
- The Third Directive (78/855/EEC), which dealt with the mergers of public companies, and the complementary Sixth Directive (82/891/EEC) on demergers were enacted in Ireland by the European Communities (Mergers and Divisions of Companies) Regulations 1987. Now enacted as Regulation 5 of the European Communities (Mergers and Division of Companies) (Amendment) Regulations 2011 (S.I. No. 306 of 2011).[38]
- The Fourth Directive (78/660/EEC) related to the preparation of annual accounts was enacted by the Companies (Amendment) Act 1986. In enacting the legislation, the Irish Government provided for the inclusion of the exemptions available in the Directive to small and medium-sized private companies. These companies can accordingly present their accounts in an abbreviated format. These provisions are now contained in Part 6 of the Companies Act 2014.
- The Seventh Directive (83/349/EEC) provided for the preparation of consolidated accounts in the group context and was enacted in Ireland by the European Communities (Companies) (Group Accounts) Regulations 1992 (S.I. 201 of 1992). See also the European Communities (Accounts) Regulations 1993 (S.I.

36. Regulation 6(3) of EC Regulations 1973, (S.I. 163 of 1973).
37. *See* Companies Act 2014, Part 2 s. 38, Part 16 ss 972, 973.
38. Considered *infra* Part 1, Ch. 1 §6, III.

369 of 1993) and the European Communities (International Financial Reporting Standards and Miscellaneous Amendments) Regulations 2005 (S.I. 116 of 2005).

Directive 2006/46/EC consolidates and amends these Directives. These provisions are now contained in Part 6 of the Companies Act 2014:

- The Eighth Directive (84/253/EEC) deals with the qualifications, professional standing and independence of Auditors. This was implemented by Part X of the 1990 Companies Act. See further the Companies (Auditing and Accounting) Act 2003 passed following the Report of the Audit Review Group in 2000. These provisions are now amended and contained in Part 6 of the Companies Act 2014.
- A draft 'Ninth Company Law Directive on the Conduct of Groups containing a Public Limited Company as a Subsidiary' was circulated by the Commission in December 1984 for consultation. According to its Explanatory Memorandum, the Directive was intended to provide a framework in which groups can be managed on a sound basis while ensuring that interests affected by group operations are adequately protected. Such a legal framework, adapted to the special circumstances of groups, was considered to be lacking in the legal system of most Member States. However, in the course of discussions, it became apparent that there was very little support for such a comprehensive framework on group law: such an approach was largely unfamiliar to most Member States, and the business sector viewed it as too cumbersome and too inflexible. Nevertheless, interest in groups is of some relevance to the Irish economy as a result of renewed discussions on the regulation of corporate tax issues. In some respects, matters have moved on from this with initiatives on corporate social responsibility.
- The Prospectus Directives – 80/390/EEC, 79/279/EEC and 82/121/EEC – which have now been consolidated in Directive 2003/58/EC, were transposed in the Investment Funds, Companies and Miscellaneous Provisions Act 2005 and 2006. These provisions are now amended and contained in Part 23 of the Companies Act 2014.
- The European Economic Interest Grouping (EEIG) Regulation (EEC/2137/85) was further implemented by the European Community (EEIG) Regulations 1989 (S.I. 191 of 1989).
- The Twelfth Directive (89/667/EEC), which provided for the single-member private company, was enacted as mentioned by the European Communities (Single-Member Private Limited Companies) Regulations of 1994 (S.I. 275 of 1994). These provisions are now amended and contained in Part 4 of the Companies Act 2014.
- The Takeover Directive (2004/25/EC) was implemented in Ireland by the European Communities (Takeover Bids Directive) Regulations 2006 (S.I. 225 of 2006).
- In light of the increased interest in contributing to the liquidity of capital markets within the EU in recent years, a number of Directives have been passed addressing the preservation of the integrity of such capital markets. These include Directive 2004/109/EC (the Transparency Directive), Directive 2004/39/EC (Markets in Financial Instruments Directive) and Directive 2003/6/EC (the Market Abuse Directive). These were implemented in the Investment Funds, Companies and

Miscellaneous Provisions Acts of 2005 and 2006, as well as the Market Abuse (Directive 2003/6/EC) Regulations 2005 (S.I. 342 of 2005). These provisions are now amended and contained in Part 23 of the Companies Act 2014.

- The EC Council Regulation 1346/2000 on cross-border insolvencies is an important development in the recognition of insolvency processes and orders among the Member States of the EU. This has now been replaced by EC Council Regulation 848/2015 usually referred to as the EIR Recast. This is the subject matter of the JCOERE research project for which the author was the Principal Investigator.[39] This matter has become of increasing relevance in recent years in Ireland. Also of interest in the insolvency space is the recent Preventive Restructuring Directive EU Directive 2019/1023 enacted in June 2019 with an implementation date of June 2021.[40] This implementation period has been extended to June 2022 and was implemented in Ireland by the European Union (Preventive Restructuring) Regulations 2022 with changes to the Examinership procedure discussed below.

There has been further activity in the area of shareholders' rights with Directive 2017/828 on the encouragement of long-term shareholder engagement which amends Directive 2007/36/EC.

The Irish regulations implementing SRD II (the Regulations), which were adopted in March 2020, introduced three new chapters into Part 17 of the Companies Act 2014:

Chapter 8A (Rights of Shareholders) – which covers the identification of underlying shareholders and information flows between underlying shareholders and companies. This chapter is principally addressed to shareholding intermediaries. The obligations in this chapter require these intermediaries, including asset managers, credit institutions and central securities depositories, to transmit information about share ownership. An important underlying policy is to facilitate the exercise of rights attached to shares. The obligations in Chapter 8A take effect in Ireland from 3 September 2020. Chapter 8B (Transparency of institutional investors, asset managers and proxy advisors) – which provides new transparency obligations for these sectors with the objective of encouraging shareholder engagement and the development of long-term investment strategies. Ireland as a jurisdiction has extended the obligations under Chapter 8B to Undertakings for Collective Investment in Transferable Securities (UCITS) and AIFs. Accordingly, for the purposes of the Regulations, the term 'asset manager' covers authorised investment firms, AIFMs, UCITS management companies and self-managed UCITS and the term 'institutional investor' means EU life insurers and EU pension funds. However, the Regulations only apply to asset managers and institutional investors that invest in shares traded on an EU-regulated market. Finally, Chapter 8C (Remuneration Policy, remuneration report and transparency and approval of related party transactions) – covers shareholder approval of directors' remuneration and related party transactions. Traded PLCs are required to

39. EC Council Regulation 848/2015. *See* further the JCOERE Project at www.ucc.ie/en/jcoere. This project also considers the Preventive Restructuring Directive 2019/1023. 'the PRD' which is to be implemented by June 2021.

40. *See* further JCOERE Project www.ucc.ie/en/jcoere.

prepare a remuneration report and remuneration policy on directors' remuneration, both of which must be voted on at general meetings. The remuneration report must be presented every year, and in the case of the remuneration policy, every four years.

Additional Directives which are broadly relevant include the Directive on use of Digital Tools and Processes in Company Law 2019/1151 and the Directive 2019/2121 on Cross Border Conversions, Mergers and Divisions Directive which will be implemented by January 2023. In relation to the former, implementation of this Directive will involve the full availability of online forms on the CRO website. (www.cro.ie)

Directives which are being considered at present by the Commission and European Parliament are the Corporate Sustainability Reporting Directive[41] which is passed and must be implemented in Ireland by June 2024 and the Corporate Sustainability and Due Diligence Directive[42] currently under negotiation, in addition to an ambitious harmonising directive in the area of insolvency law proposed by the European Commission and currently under discussion.[43]

B. *Choice of Law*

31. In terms of choice of law, the importance of the European Court of Justice (CJEU) decisions in the *Centros, Überseering* and *Inspire Art* cases cannot be underestimated.[44] The freedom for nationals of different Member States to form and establish companies in any country of the EU has had a significant impact on the importance of Ireland, along with the UK (prior to Brexit) and the Netherlands, as desirable places of incorporation. A supportive tax structure is considered to be a significant advantage (*see infra* Part I Chapter 1, §9). Given the growth of company formation in Ireland and some concerns regarding abuse of the corporate form during the 1990s, some specific control measures were put in place to ensure the 'authenticity' of business incorporating in Ireland. These include:

(i) a requirement that at least one of the directors must be resident in Ireland which was provided for in section 43 of the Companies (Amendment No. 2) Act 1999. This has been re-enacted in section 137 of the 2014 Act as a requirement that at least one director must be resident in an European Economic Area (EEA) state;
(ii) a limitation was imposed by section 45 of the same Act on the number of directorships that any one particular individual may hold. Section 142 of the 2014 Act provides that a person shall not at any particular time be a director

41. Directive (EU) 2022/ 2464 – published on 16 Dec. 2022 which came into force on 5 Jan. 2023.
42. Directive (EU) 2019/ 1937
43. Proposal for a Directive Harmonising Certain Aspects of Insolvency Law Com (2022) 702/final 2022/0408 (COD).
44. *Infra* n. 148.

of more than twenty-five private companies limited by shares, or in the case of other types of companies, twenty-five in total;

(iii) a requirement that an Irish-registered company must carry on an activity in the state under section 44 of the same Act (now section 18 of the 2014 Act).

IV. The Modern Period

32. 1998 was a significant year in Irish Company Law with the publication of the McDowell Report on Company Law Compliance. This report found that more than 60% of registered Irish companies were non-compliant with many provisions of company law. As a consequence, significant efforts were made to increase enforcement with the enactment of the Company Law Enforcement Act 2001, which accomplished two major initiatives: first establishing the Office of the Director of Corporate Enforcement which has recently been reorganised into the Corporate Enforcement Authority (CEA); (*See* www.cea.gov.ie) and second, establishing the CLRG (*See* www.clrg.org) charged with continuously monitoring company law developments. Since 2001, detection and enforcement of breaches of company law in Ireland has significantly improved, due largely to the efforts of what was then, the Office of the Director of Corporate Enforcement (ODCE) and the CRO (www.cro.ie). Provisions of the 2001 Act have been re-enacted as Part 15 of the Companies Act 2014. Chapter 3 effectively re-enacts sections 7–18 of the Company Law Enforcement Act 2001, which outlines the powers of the ODCE. Chapter 4 deals with the CLRG and re-enacts sections 67–71 of the CLEA 2001. Recently the ODCE has been re-established as a distinct enforcement agency under the Companies (CEA) Act 2021.

V. Reform Proposals for Irish Company Law

33. Once established, the CLRG engaged in a significant consolidation and codification process in addition to reforming certain key areas of Irish company law. In 2007, the CRLG published a draft Companies Consolidation Bill, which was designed to consolidate and update all existing Irish company law legislation. The thematic drivers of this reform project were stated by the CLRG in its 2007 report (Chapter 3) to be as follows:

- to promote enterprise;
- facilitate commerce;
- simplify the operation of the Companies Acts;
- enhance corporate governance; and
- encourage commercial probity.'

The Bill was enacted as the Companies Act 2014 and was commenced (i.e. put into force) in large part in June 2015. Even though the Companies Act 2014 replaced and consolidated all existing Companies Acts from 1963 to 2013 and has, as one of its aims, the goal of consolidating and simplifying the operation of the legislative framework in which companies operate, events and other circumstances have required further amendments in the form of successive statutes. It is therefore not possible to point to this comprehensive piece of legislation as encompassing the current state of Irish company law as there have been additional statutes including the aforementioned Companies (Miscellaneous Provisions) (COVID-19) Act 2020 and others including the Companies (Accounting) Act 2017 and the Companies (Statutory Audits) Act 2018. Other pieces of legislation which are not obviously indicated as relating to company law as such are equally important, for example, the Migration of Participating Securities Act 2019. There have been additional amendments made during COVID (2020), implementing EU Directives (2022) and legislation proposed to address other domestic issues, for example the Plan of Action on Collective Redundancies Bill 2023).

The reforms introduced by the Companies Act 2014 and further reforms from subsequent legislation will be described in this text.[45] Nevertheless, the Companies Act 2014 can properly be regarded as the 'principal legislation' with a particular legislative impetus and with an approach to the regulation of companies which is still dominant. Since the beginning of the original review process in 2007, the idea of 'Think Small First' (possibly inspired by a similar approach in the UK) has been adopted and in fact, this latter theme has refocused the legislation on the private company limited by shares, as distinct from the public limited company (PLC). Accordingly, the structure of the 2014 Act is to provide for the regulation of the private company limited by shares in Parts 1–14 so that the private (or closed company) limited by shares is viewed as the default model, with specific provisions relevant to other types of company being provided for in subsequent particular parts. For example, the PLC is specifically provided for in Part 17. This Part thus begins by providing a Table of relevant sections of Parts 1–14 which are disapplied or altered as they apply to the PLC.[46] The same model is applied to other kinds of companies. Part 16 of the Companies Act 2014 deals with what are called Designated Activity Companies, which are private companies limited by shares with stated activities.[47] Part 18 deals with Guarantee Companies and so on.

VI. The Role of Partnership Law

34. In Ireland, the formation of a limited liability company is relatively cheap because of the fact that, unlike most European countries, there is no minimum capital requirement and formation costs are likewise low. Because of the cheap availability of the limited liability corporate form, there has been a decline in interest among most business people in the types of partnership structures available. As far as partnerships go, the regulatory framework is based on the Partnership Act 1890, the Limited Partnerships Act 1907 and the Limited Partnership Act 1994, which has

45. *See* generally Courtney (gen. ed.), *Bloomsbury Professional's Guide to the Companies Act* (Bloomsbury Professional, Dublin, 2015).
46. *See* Companies Act 2014, s. 1002 and the Table contained therein.
47. *See* Part 1, Ch. 2, §§1–3.

contributed a significant statutory framework in relation to the development of investment funds and the investment fund industry in Ireland. Over 30% of the global hedge fund industry is based in Dublin, Ireland. Dublin is now a world administration centre for hedge funds.[48] The ILP (Amendment) Act was passed in 2020.

§3. Definitions and Structure of Corporations and Partnerships

I. Different Forms of Corporations and Partnerships

35. Several different kinds of corporate forms are available under Irish law. In relation to companies that acquire the privilege of limited liability, companies can be limited by shares or by guarantee. However, private companies limited by shares are the most popular type of incorporated limited companies. It is also possible to incorporate with unlimited liability, which is a popular corporate form used as a holding company in a group situation, particularly where the corporate group is privately held.

36. Partnerships are more commonly used in relation to the operation of particular professions, such as the legal and accounting professions. A statutory impediment imposed on legal firms in Ireland still prevents them from forming private companies. The introduction of the Limited Partnership Act in 1994 added significantly to the range of options in Ireland. Many law firms are now incorporated as LLPs.

A. *Limited Company*

37. There are four types of limited company:

(1) *A private company limited by shares*: In the event that the company is wound up, the members' liability, is limited to the amount, if any, unpaid on the shares they hold. There is no minimum capital requirement in Ireland for private companies, and so it is possible to form a limited liability company cheaply on payment of the registration fee of approximately EUR 100. The usual number of shareholders is two, but it is possible, to form a single-member company, under sections 175(3) and 175(4) of the Companies Act 2014. The maximum number of members for a private company is 149. The single-member private company was introduced as a business form pursuant to an EC Directive of 1989,[49] which was transposed into Irish law in 1994. Originally, even where there was only one shareholder, the company was obliged to have

48. Figures from the Irish Funds Industry Association show that in August 2015 over 6,000 different funds were registered in Ireland with net assets valued at just over EUR 1.8 billion. www.irishfunds.ie.

49. EC Directive 89/667, [1989] O.J. L395/40 (transposed into Irish law by the European Communities (Single-Member Private Limited Companies) Regulations of 1994 (S.I. 275 of 1994)).

at least two directors and a secretary. This is no longer the case under the Companies Act 2014[50] where these companies are permitted to have only one director. The sole member company was permitted to dispense with the holding of general meetings, including Annual General Meetings (AGMs). This exemption still pertains but has been extended under the Companies Act 2014 to other companies in certain circumstances.[51] Accounts and reports that would normally be laid before the AGM of a company still need to be prepared, forwarded to the member(s) and filed in the normal way.[52]

The Companies Act 2014 recognises two different types of private company limited by shares. The first type is a LTD – a private company limited by shares with no specified activities in its constitution. These companies have full capacity to engage in any activity. The second type of private company limited by shares is a DAC-designated activity company, where companies either opt for specifying particular activities in their Constitution or where, in certain cases, the company is obliged to specify an activity. This latter obligation usually arises only in relation to companies which are seeking to trade in debt securities on a market. The Companies Act 2014 requires that where a company wants to list debt securities on a stock exchange or has debt securities listed on a stock exchange, it must register as a DAC.[53] Subject to compliance with Central Bank requirements where a company is operating as a credit institution or insurance undertaking, it will be registered as a DAC.

As regards DACs, these companies are confined to acting within specified purposes. It should be emphasised, however, that the specification of activities does not raise any issue of legal capacity in terms of the old *ultra vires* rule.[54] DACs must be registered with at least two directors.[55]

(2) *A company limited by guarantee not having a share capital*: In the event that this kind of company is wound up, the members' liability is limited to the amount they have undertaken to contribute to the assets of the company, not exceeding the amount specified in the memorandum. If a guarantee company does not have a share capital, the members are not required to buy any shares in the company. Many charitable and professional bodies find this form of company to be a suitable vehicle as they wish to secure the benefits of separate legal personality and limited liability but do not necessarily require any working capital and therefore do not generally raise funds from the members. These companies are now governed by Part 18 of the Companies Act 2014.

(3) *A company limited by guarantee having a share capital*: The members have liability under two headings: firstly, the amount, if any, that is unpaid on the shares they hold, and, secondly, the amount they have undertaken to contribute to the assets of the company, in the event it is wound up. These are now governed by Part 18 of the Companies Act 2014.

50. Companies Act 2014, s. 128.
51. *Infra*. Part 1 Ch. 1, §4, II.
52. Companies Act 2014, s. 175.
53. Companies Act 2014, ss 56, 68.
54. *Infra*. Part 1, Ch. 2, §2, III.
55. Companies Act 2014, s. 985(1).

(4) *A public company limited by shares*: This company type must have a minimum of seven members. The liability of the shareholders is limited to the amount, if any, unpaid on shares held by them. It should be noted that it is unlawful to issue any form of prospectus except in compliance with the Companies Act 2014. The nominal value of the company's allotted share capital must not be less than EUR 25,000,[56] at least 25% of which must be fully paid up before the company commences business or exercises any borrowing powers, as provided for by the Companies Act 2014. This amount has been reduced from previous legislation. This can be changed by Ministerial order (usually by what is referred to as a Statutory Instrument). The essential difference between a private limited company and a PLC is that the shares of the latter must be traded on a public market. Irish PLCs are quoted on the Irish Stock Exchange www.ise.ie, which provides for full listing but also has a market for smaller companies, the Irish Enterprise Exchange (IEX); the IEX is equivalent to the UK alternative investments market (AIM). It is possible to have a dual IEX and AIM listing. Several Irish PLCs are also quoted on the London Stock Exchange and on the New York Exchanges. PLCs are now governed by Parts 1–14 and Part 17 of the Companies Act 2014.

B. Unlimited Company

38. In an unlimited company, no limit is placed on the liability of the members. Recourse may be had by creditors to the shareholders in respect of any liabilities owed by the company that the company has failed to discharge. Such companies must have a minimum of two shareholders. In Irish commercial practice, it is common to convert the holding company of a group into an unlimited company due to the less rigorous disclosure requirements applicable under the accounting provisions. The shareholders may, and often will be, companies with limited liability. These companies are now governed by Parts 1–14 and 19 of the Companies Act 2014.

II. Partnerships

A. Traditional Partnerships

39. The partnership is a traditional form of business dating back centuries, and is defined in section 1 of the Partnership Act 1890 as 'the relation which subsists between persons carrying on a business in common with a view of profit'. It is an alternative form of business organisation to a sole tradership or incorporation. Several factors differentiate a traditional partnership from a limited liability company.

40. The law of partnerships is considered in more detail in Part II.

---

56. Companies Act 2014, s. 1000(1)(a).

B. Limited Partnerships

41. This business form is quite popular, particularly in the investment fund, private equity and venture capital sector in Ireland. As of the end of 2022 there were over 3,000 limited partnerships registered with the CRO.[57] These are called investment limited partnerships. The relevant governing legislation includes the Limited Partnership Act 1907 and rules made under that, the Limited Partnership Rules (S.I. 1020 of 1907), the ILP Act 1994 and subsequent rules (S.I. 402 of 1994 and S.I. 570 of 2001). This latter legislation has been amended by the ILP Act 2020 enacted in response to the growing use of this business format as a vehicle for the operation of investment funds such as private equity funds, private credit, real assets and other private fund strategies.

III. Distinction Between Structures and Consequences

A. Limited Company

42. As noted above, there are a number of variations of a limited company whether limited by shares or by guarantee. The private company limited by shares is by far the most important corporate vehicle in Ireland, and thus is by far the most important and popular business vehicle. The majority of statements in this monograph apply to this corporate form.

B. The Unlimited Corporation

43. The advantages of this form of incorporation lie in reduced disclosure obligations under the legislation as compared with disclosure obligations imposed on limited liability companies. Incorporation is also attractive to non-profit businesses such as charitable corporations.

C. Partnership

44. A partnership is not a separate entity but merely refers to the relationship between partners. In addition, partners, unlike shareholders in a limited liability company, are liable beyond their capital investment to the full extent of the debts owned by the partnership. (Limited partnerships are a more recent statutory creation; *see* infra.) Certain kinds of businesses are not permitted under Irish law to form limited liability companies and usually conduct their business as a partnership, for example, those practising as Solicitors (lawyers).

57. Companies Registration Office Report 2022.

IV. Non-Profit Associations and Other Corporate Legal Persons

A. *Undertakings for Collective Investment in Transferable Securities (UCITS)*

45. A UCITS is a type of PLC formed under the European Communities (UCITS) Regulations of 1989 and 1999, and the Companies Act 2014. The sole object of a UCITS is the collective investment in transferable securities of capital raised from the public that operates on the principle of risk spreading. The competent authority, which must approve all registrations of UCITS that wish to carry on activities within the State, is the Central Bank of Ireland. See additional regulations which have been implemented through the enactment of Chapters 8A – 8C in the Companies Act 2014, but which are outside the scope of this text.[58]

B. *European Economic Interest Grouping*

46. The EEIG is a mechanism through which businesses within the EU can engage in cross-border commerce. This was created as an entity by virtue of the EEIG Regulation (EEC/2137/85), which was implemented in Ireland by the European Community (EEIG) Regulations 1989 (S.I. 191 of 1989). The purpose of an EEIG is to facilitate or develop the economic activities of its members on a cross-border, non-profit model. For example, it could be used to facilitate the development of research or products. An EEIG must have from two to twenty members, who may be companies or natural persons, from different Member States. The manager of an EEIG may be a natural person or a body corporate.

C. *Societas Europaea*

47. A Societas Europaea (SE) is a European public limited liability company formed under EC Council Regulation 2157/2001 and the European Communities (European Public Limited Liability Company) Regulations 2007 (S.I. 21 of 2007). An SE can be formed by merger, as a holding or subsidiary SE or by conversion of a PLC. An SE must have members from different Member States. As there is no pan-European registration system, the SE must be registered in a particular Member State. An interesting feature of this form is that an accompanying Directive (2001/86/EC) provides a model for the involvement of worker representatives on management boards. This has caused some controversy over the period of harmonisation of European company law, for example the discussions surrounding the proposed Fifth Directive on worker representation, which was never enacted. The Societas Europaea is to be regarded as a PLC for the purposes of the Companies Act 2014 and is governed by Part 17 of that Act.[59]

---

58. www.irishstatutebook.ie.
59. Companies Act 2014, s. 1003.

D. Registration of a Business Name

48. It is obligatory to register a business name in Ireland. When individuals or partnerships carry on a business under a name other than their own true names, this business name must be registered with the CRO. This applies to all business formats from sole traders to partnerships to companies where the business name is different from the actual name of the company.[60]

§4. Sources and Hierarchy of the Law on Corporations and Partnerships

I. International Sources

49. Under the provisions of the Irish Constitution (*Bunreacht na hÉireann*) of 1937, the force of international law and Ireland's obligations under internationally agreed treaties is recognised. Of particular interest in this context is that Ireland is a signatory to the European Convention on Human Rights (ECHR) and accordingly recognises the decisions of the European Court of Human Rights; decisions of that court have in recent years acceded to the notion that corporations may be entitled to the protection of at least some of the rights accorded under that Convention.[61] This viewpoint has met with some resistance on the domestic front in relation to constitutionally protected rights.[62] Quite apart from the ECHR, however, Ireland is a Member State of the EU, and the Constitution of Ireland has been amended to recognise the doctrine of supremacy enunciated in the case law of the CJEU. That is, Ireland is bound to apply the laws and regulations necessitated by such membership, even when these are contrary to current or pre-existing domestic law.[63] Accordingly, compliance with EU law is of paramount importance in the hierarchy of sources of Irish law.

50. In addition, the CLRG has considered whether Ireland should follow the UNCITRAL Model Law on Cross Border Insolvency and related matters. A Report which is broadly in favour of this strategy has been published.[64]

A. The European Union

51. As regards sources of law, it is important to note that as with other Member States, the passing of a Directive requires implementation into domestic legislation, normally with some provisions in the Directives being a matter of choice for the

60. Registration of Business Names Act 1963; www.cro.ie.
61. *Pine Valley Developments Ltd v. Ireland* (1992) 14 EHRR 319; *National & Provincial Building Society v. UK* (1997) 25 EHRR 127.
62. *See infra*, paras 90–91 and 92–93.
63. *Bunreacht na hÉireann* (Constitution of Ireland), Art. 29.4.10.
64. http://www.clrg.org/publications/clrg-uncitral-model-law-on-cross-border-insolvency-recommendations.pdf.

particular jurisdiction. However, Regulations emanating from the EU have a direct effect. It is worth mentioning that failure to implement a particular Directive in a proper and timely manner may lead to the possibility of its provisions being directly enforceable against that Member State.[65] In addition, once implemented, Directives may be relied upon and enforced by individuals against public bodies; this is known as the 'vertical direct effect' of EU law.[66] It is usually the case that Directives, unlike Treaty provisions[67] and regulations, cannot be directly enforced as between private litigant parties; this concept is known as 'horizontal direct effect'.[68] In this context, it would be fair to characterise Irish company law as being more permissive than other European jurisdictions and, in this respect is more similar to the neighbouring UK jurisdictions, in particular to the approach taken to company law regulation and theory in England and Wales.

II. National Sources

A. *Legislation*

1. The Constitution

52. All company law principles, whether derived from common law or from legislation, are subject to the provisions of the Irish Constitution, which includes provisions relating to separation of powers and guaranteeing fundamental rights and freedoms. All positive laws are subject to judicial review against these fundamental provisions in the same way that in the United States, Acts of Congress or of Government are subject to review by the courts. Accordingly, provisions of the Companies Acts have from time to time been challenged as being unconstitutional,[69] as have actions of the Government through its agencies in enforcing company law provisions. The constitutionality of provisions of company law is potentially difficult, particularly in the area of enforcement.[70]

2. Legislation

53. Increasingly in Ireland, as with other common law jurisdictions, the role of legislation has become significant in the area of company and commercial law. For many years, the 1963 Companies Act, was the principal piece of legislation, but as

---

65. *Francovich v. Italy* (Cases C-6 and C-9/90) [1991] ECR I-5357.
66. *Marleasing S.A. v. La Commercial International de Alimnetacion S.A.* (Case C-106/89) [1991] ECR I-4135.
67. *Defrenne v. Sabena* (No. 2) (Case C-43/75) [1976] ECR 455.
68. *Marshall v. Southampton and South-West Hampshire Area Health Authority* (Case 152/84) [1986] ECR 723.
69. For example, *Desmond v. Glackin* (No. 2) [1993] 3 IR 67 where the provision was successfully challenged; *O'Keeffe v. Ferris* where the challenge was unsuccessful. [1993] 3 IR 165.
70. For example, *Re Tralee Beef and Lamb Ltd (In Liquidation); Kavanagh v. Delaney* [2008] 3 IR 347.

explained above this and all other company legislation enacted up to 2013 was consolidated in a major statute, the Companies Act 2014.[71] In addition to this consolidation exercise, some reforms were made at that time, and additionally certain matters, for example, directors' duties were codified for the first time.[72] During the intervening period, this legislation has been amended on a number of occasions which will be mentioned where relevant in this text.

54. Since the late 1970s, a number of factors have contributed to significant growth in company legislation. The first of these is membership of the EU. The extent and scope of the influence of the European harmonisation project has been discussed earlier.[73] The second is the modernisation of the Irish economy, beginning with a period in the late 1980s when it became apparent that with an increase in economic activity, there were serious issues to be addressed in relation to awareness of, and compliance with, even the most basic of company law provisions. A third significant factor was the spectacular growth in the Irish economy during the 'Celtic Tiger' years (late 1990s–2005). This led to an increased awareness of the importance of ensuring adequate regulatory standards, but in addition, it also led to an awareness of the potential for company law and related areas of legislative activity to be enabling in some ways. This concept became particularly important in relation to the developing financial services industry, which along with biotechnology and information technology were, and continue to be, significant sectors in the continued economic performance of Ireland. Thus in relation to aspects of the financial services industry that interface with company law, we have seen the enactment of legislation that supports and regulates this kind of activity. This is particularly true of certain aspects of financial services activity such as the funds industry and the development of private equity investment vehicles.

55. As a result of the global financial crisis and the significance of the economic and banking crisis in Ireland, a 'bad bank' of sorts was created to take over the operation of a significant number of non-performing loans from a range of Irish banks. The National Asset Management Agency was created by the NAMA Act of 2009.[74] It was considered the best possible option available to address the collapse of the Irish property market and the consequent significance of this collapse for the domestic Irish banking sector which was heavily exposed to the construction and property sector. The purpose of the legislation was to provide a structure whereby 'bad' banking loans could be transferred from the banks to the National Agency together with all security rights and other rights and liabilities attaching to these loans. Its functions were described as follows:

---

71. *See* further Thomas Courtney, (gen. ed.), *Bloomsbury's Professional Guide to the Companies Act 2014* (Bloomsbury 2015).
72. Companies Act 2014, ss 227, 228.
73. *Supra.* Introduction, §2 III – *Development of European Company Law and Membership of the EU.*
74. *See* further Irene Lynch Fannon & Gerard N. Murphy, *Corporate Insolvency and Rescue* (2nd edn., Bloomsbury Professional 2012). Ch. 1.

56. "NAMA is, first and foremost, an asset management agency, established with the aim of transferring certain higher-risk property-related exposures from the balance sheets of the participating financial institutions in return for Government guaranteed securities." Further described by the Chief Executive of the Agency on its establishment the objective was that '[We] NAMA … will manage these loans with the aim of achieving the best possible return for the taxpayer over a seven to ten-year timeframe. Replacing these property-related loans with Government Guaranteed Securities will help remove uncertainty about the soundness of banks' balance sheets, provide the institutions with much-needed liquidity and should make it easier for the institutions over time to access capital (for some) and liquidity (for all) in the international capital markets.'[75]

57. Significant features of this legislation include very extensive powers provided to the State in relation to the operation and management of the loans taken over from the banks and the underlying securities. The powers therefore accorded to the relevant Minister, in this case, the Minister of Finance were commented on from the outset. For example, in the *McKillen* case,[76] the High Court described the 'general powers of NAMA' as being 'manifold'. The court stated that NAMA 'has all the powers necessary or expedient for, or incidental to, the achievement of its purposes and performances of its functions'. These powers included for example a right for the state agency to act as a receiver in relation to property with a broad range of powers. It is important to note therefore that in certain circumstances, company law is affected by provisions of the Act where one is dealing with assets and transactions arising from the operation of provisions of that Act.[77] Overall, as of 2023, NAMA has been regarded as a successful method of addressing a significant volume of non-performing bank loans. In its 2022 Annual Review NAMA stated in its 'Key Financial Updates' (www.nama.ie) that it had generated EUR 492 million in 2022 from its remaining portfolio and that it had generated EUR 47.4 billion in cash since its inception.

B. By-Laws and Articles

58. Corporate structures are governed by the Articles of Association and the Memorandum of Association. The 2014 Act maintained this structure for PLCs but for private limited companies, the standard-form set of Articles of Association were shortened and much of the governance structure of corporations is now governed by provisions of the legislation. Thus while the corporate structure of a PLC remains

---

75. As stated by Brendan McDonagh, Chief Executive of the Agency to the Committee of Public Accounts in November 2010. For a very complete treatment of the provisions of this legislation please refer to Hugh Byrne & Louis McEntaggart, *The National Asset Management Agency Act 2009: Annotations and Commentary* (Bloomsbury Professional 2010) and Maire Whelan, Mark Kennedy & Fintan O'Raghallaigh, *The National Asset Management Agency Act 2009* (Gill and MacMillan 2011).

76. *Dellway Investments and Ors v. NAMA and the Attorney General* [2011] IESC 364.

77. *See* further Irene Lynch Fannon & Gerard N. Murphy, *Corporate Insolvency and Rescue* (2nd edn., Bloomsbury Professional 2012) Ch. 1 for further discussion of the case law.

largely governed by Articles of Association in a standard form, for a private limited company the framework contained in the legislation, namely the Companies Act 2014, is even more important.

C. *Relationship Between By-Law and Articles*

59. Where the 1963 Act had provided a model for a standard-form set of Articles of Association for different types of companies, (essentially rules for the conduct of internal affairs that companies were required to create and that bound companies and their members), the 2014 Companies Act provides for the Constitution of a company. Many of the provisions which had hitherto been contained in the 'standard-form articles' are now statutory provisions, for example, the rule regarding the delegation of management powers from the shareholders to the board previously contained in Article 80 of the old Articles of Association is now provided for in section 158 of the 2014 Act.[78] These statutory provisions are either mandatory or optional and will be discussed in more detail in the text as they arise. However, the default principle is that the provisions of the legislation apply unless stated otherwise. In addition, the provisions of the legislation will prevail in some cases where a conflict arises, but in others, they may not. This depends on what is described as discretionary and what is not within the legislative framework. These matters will be addressed as they arise.

III. Hierarchy of the Law on Corporations and Partnerships

A. *The Constitution and Statute Law*

60. Any matters of company law or the law relating to partnerships will be subject to constitutional law. As described before, statute law will be subject to scrutiny through judicial review of any provisions which seem to be counter to the constitution.

61. That said as one would expect it is rare that provisions of company law are challenged as being unconstitutional. Some of these instances are described above.

62. Following the primacy of the constitution, the statutory framework, beginning with the Companies Act 2014 will prevail. Nevertheless, the relationship between statutory principles and case law is dynamic as in all common law systems, the courts will interpret statutory provisions and so the case law which pertains to the statutory provisions, if it exists, will also become part of the law and will have the effect of developing statute law.

78. *Infra* Part 1 Ch. 1, §4.

B. *Common Law Sources of Principle*

63. The influence of English company law principles (both statute and case law) and the approach of English courts and legislatures to company law matters is significant in relation to the development of Irish company law. This is a more accurate observation than might be made in relation to other areas of law that are of a more recent vintage, such as employment law or environmental law. Thus, the principles of Irish company law are still very similar to those of English company law and give expression to what could be described as an Anglo-American or common law approach to company law, as distinguished from the European approach taken in the civil law countries of Continental Europe. Irish company law is therefore first and foremost a common law system of company law and, as such, is in the first instance derived from a large body of case law. However, at this point in time, there is a significant statutory framework, some of which involves codifying case law. The passing of the Companies Act 2014 is a significant development in this context, representing both consolidation and some reform. Many of the cases setting out the principles followed in Irish company law were decided by English Chancery courts, sometimes stretching back to the Victorian period, relating to issues such as capital maintenance,[79] directors' duties'[80] and separate corporate personality.[81] Ireland achieved its independence in 1922, and the current legal system is based on the 1937 Constitution, *Bunreacht na hÉireann*. Since that time, the development of company law, as with any common law system, continues to rely to a great extent on the decisions of chancery courts. Since 1922, decisions of the English courts are of only persuasive authority before the Irish courts, in the same way as decisions of other common law jurisdictions, including the courts of Northern Ireland,[82] Australia[83] and New Zealand.[84] In addition to the persuasive authority of these cases, Irish courts follow doctrines of precedent in the same way as other common law jurisdictions, and so the hierarchy of the court system is also important.

C. *The Court System in Ireland*

64. The Constitution of 1937 under which the current system operates in Ireland follows the separation of powers model between the executive, legislative and judicial branches of government. The judicial branch consists of a Supreme Court, a Court of Appeal, a High Court, and lower courts of local and limited jurisdiction with rights of appeal.

---

79. Trevor v. Whitworth (1887) 12 App Cases. 407.
80. *Regal (Hastings) v. Gulliver* [1942] All ER 378; *IDC Ltd v. Cooley* [1972] 2 All ER 162.
81. *Salomon v. Salomon & Co. Ltd* [1897] AC 22.
82. In *Re Armagh Shoes Ltd* [1982] NI 59 (cited in, for example, *Re Keenan Brothers Ltd* [1985] IR 401).
83. *Kinsley v. Russell Kinsela Pty Ltd* (1986) 10 ACLR 395; *Walker v. Wimbourne* (1976) CLR 1 (cited in *Re Frederick Inns Ltd* [1991] ILRM 582).
84. *Nicholson v. Permakraft (NZ) Ltd* (in liq) [1985] 1 NZLR 242 (cited in *Re Frederick Inns Ltd* [1991] ILRM 582).

65. The Constitution provides for a Supreme Court as a final Court of Appeal and it also describes courts of first instance, including the High Court, which has full jurisdiction in civil and criminal matters, as well as courts of limited and local jurisdiction, including the Circuit Court and the District Court. A relatively new Court of Appeal hearing appeals from the High Court was established in 2014 following a Constitutional referendum. The Constitution provides for the supremacy of the law of the EU and as such recognises the jurisdiction of the CJEU in relation to the legal framework and laws emanating from the institutions of the EU.

66. The High Court currently consists of a President and thirty-six ordinary judges. This court has full original jurisdiction to determine all matters of law and fact in civil and criminal matters. It also has jurisdiction to review the validity of laws and executive actions having regard to the provisions of the Constitution. It has an appellate jurisdiction from decisions of the Circuit Court and various tribunals and may give rulings on questions of law from the District Court. Matters of company law are usually heard in the High Court,[85] from which an appeal could, in the past be brought to the Supreme Court. The appeal structure has now changed to incorporate the Court of Appeal. Additionally, there are some exceptions to the original jurisdiction of the High Court in company law matters, including an attempt in 2013 to facilitate the rescue of more SMEs by giving jurisdiction over certain kinds of examinerships to the Circuit Court.[86] The primary motivation for this change was to reduce the costs of rescue. Overall, there has not been a significant effect arising from this change. Accordingly, all references to 'the Court' in this text, insofar as court hearings refer to companies, should be interpreted as referring to the High Court unless otherwise stated. In 2004, the Rules of the Superior Courts[87] were amended to provide for the transfer of certain kinds of High Court proceedings to a dedicated Commercial List, with a view to expedited resolution of such matters as are admitted to that List. This is particularly important for company and commercial law matters. Applications for transfer to the High Court Commercial List may be made in respect of proceedings instituted on or after 12 January 2004 in accordance with the Practice Directions emanating from the High Court and the revised Order 63A of the Rules of the Superior Courts.[88] The judge dealing with the List has discretion as to which cases may be admitted, but a minimum EUR 1 million value threshold must be met.

---

85. Companies Act 12014, s. 2. The definition of court is more involved in this new Act. In particular the prosecution of offences under the Companies Act 2014 may under this definition be pursued in the District Court.
86. This change was originally contained in the Companies Act 2013 but has now been reconsolidated in Part 10 of the Companies Act 2014.
87. Order 63A of the Rules of the Superior Courts (S.I. No. 2 of 2004).
88. Order 63A provides for a definition of commercial proceedings to enable facilitation of the removal of certain kinds of cases from the High Court list to the High Court Commercial List. Interestingly, the rules do not refer specifically to matters arising under the Companies Acts 1963–2006, but refer to matters arising in relation to the operation of stock, share or other investment markets and also gives discretion to the Judge of the High Court Commercial List to approve other cases for entry to the list (Order 63A(b)).

67. Finally, a significant change was made in late 2014 with the establishment of a Court of Appeal.[89] This court occupies an appellate jurisdiction between the High Court and the Supreme Court. The Court of Appeal is composed of a President and nine ordinary judges. This is designed to reserve cases concerning important points of law to the Supreme Court and to allow ordinary appeals from the High Court which would hitherto have been heard by the Supreme Court to be heard in the Court of Appeal. Exceptions are those cases in which the Supreme Court has permitted an appeal to it on being satisfied that the appeal meets the threshold set out in Article 34.5.4 of the Constitution. The Chief Justice and the President of the High Court are ex officio judges of the Court of Appeal. The Court may sit in divisions of three judges. Some interlocutory and procedural applications may be heard by the President alone or by another judge nominated by the President. The Court has full jurisdiction including jurisdiction to hear appeals from the High Court on Constitutional law matters. Under the Court of Appeal Act 2014, the Court of Appeal was given the appellate jurisdiction previously exercised by the Court of Criminal Appeal. Appeals by the Director of Public Prosecutions against an acquittal or against a decision not to order a retrial also lie to the Court of Appeal. The decision of the Court of Appeal is final unless the Supreme Court permits an appeal under Article 34.5.3 of the Constitution. Questions of law which could previously be referred by the Circuit Court to the Supreme Court for determination (a 'case stated') are now determinable by the Court of Appeal.

§5. International Private Law (Conflict of Laws)

I. The General Rules

68. A person, whether artificial (as a company is) or real, can be sued in Ireland if, in the case of a natural person, he or she is present, as the common law rules determining jurisdiction depend on the idea of service on a person. For companies, the place of registration is taken as a location that represents the company for the purpose of service. Suing the partnership in the firm name is now possible, and this represents a change in the law in which each partner had to be named individually.

II. Choice of Forum

A. EC Regulation 44/2001

69. Regulation (EU) 1215/2012 on jurisdiction and the recognition and enforcement of judgments in civil and commercial matters (recast) ('the Recast Brussels

89. The Court of Appeal was established on 28 Oct. 2014 under the Court of Appeal Act 2014 which was passed following a referendum approving the 33rd amendment to the 1937 Constitution which provided for the creation of this court. Following the establishment of the Court of Appeal specified appeals pending in the Supreme Court which had been initiated before the establishment day and had not been fully or partly heard by that court were directed by the Chief Justice to be heard and determined by the Court of Appeal.

Regulation') came into effect in Ireland on 10 January 2015. The Recast Regulation replaced Regulation 44/2001 ('the Brussels Regulation').

70. Both Regulation 44/2001[90] and, in turn, the second iteration of this framework, the Recast Regulation 1215/2012 replaced the Brussels Convention on jurisdiction and the enforcement of judgments in civil and commercial law matters. The Regulation applies to all proceedings commenced after the date of commencement of the Regulation. Under the Regulations, the general rule is that persons shall be sued in the courts of the Member State in which they are domiciled. In those circumstances, therefore, the preliminary issue will be where the company is domiciled. Under Irish law, as with English law, the domicile of a corporation is determined by its place of incorporation as neither Irish nor English law applies the concept of 'real seat'. Irish-registered companies are considered to be domiciled in Ireland under Irish law, regardless of the scope and extent of their activities overseas. In the case of partnerships, the domicile of the principal partner or partners is the relevant criteria. More detailed provisions regarding the enforcement of contracts are provided for in the Regulation. Thus the Regulation provides that the relevant forum in matters relating to a contract is the courts of the place of performance of the obligation in question; and goes on to clarify that:

> 'for the purpose of this provision and unless otherwise agreed, the place of performance of the obligation in question shall be:'
>
> – in the case of the sale of goods, the place in a Member State where, under the contract, the goods were delivered, or should have been delivered;
> – in the case of the provision of services, the place in a Member State where, under the contract, the services were provided or should have been provided.

Article 5(1) of the Brussels Convention contained a similar provision, and the interpretation of this provision has been the subject of much litigation before the CJEU. The Convention provision was amended by the addition of paragraph 1(b) of Article 5, quoted above.

B. Council Regulation 848/2015

71. The Council Regulation on insolvency proceedings is of real importance in the corporate law context. As stated above, under Irish law, the jurisdiction issue (as it relates to companies) will generally begin by reference to the place of incorporation of the company. Council Regulation 1346/2000 on Insolvency Proceedings

90. Council Regulation (EC) No. 44/2001 on jurisdiction and the recognition and enforcement of judgments in civil and commercial matters (O.J. L012/1 16 Jan. 2001).

which was updated and replaced by Council Regulation 848/2015 refers to the 'centre of main interest' as being the determinant of jurisdiction in relation to a corporation or individual involved in insolvency proceedings. In turn the 'centre of main interests' is determined by reference to the place of incorporation of the debtor company, but, as with the previous Regulation, this presumption in favour of the place of incorporation as the determinative factor can be displaced by reference to an enquiry as to where the debtor 'conducts the administration of its interests on a regular basis and is therefore ascertainable by third parties'. The Insolvency Regulation and the 2015 Recast continue to provide a compromise between the 'place of incorporation' theory regarding corporate domicile and the 'real seat' theory more prevalent in continental European jurisdictions.[91] The recent regulation applies to all insolvency proceedings, including proceedings which concern restructuring of corporate entities. However, the Regulation does not apply to restructuring processes which are derived from company law. The latter will include English Schemes of Arrangements and similar provisions in Irish company law, now re-enacted in Chapter 1 of Part 9 of the Companies Act 2014.[92]

III. Choice of Law

72. In Ireland, as in England, the place of registration of companies is deemed to be paramount in determining the domicile of companies and accordingly, the jurisdictional law that applies to their affairs. This is very different from the position applicable in most European countries and therefore allows for the registration of companies in Ireland and England that may operate in other jurisdictions of the EU. Decisions of the CJEU holding that restraints on the activities of nationals of other Member States incorporating businesses in Ireland or England are in breach of the right to freedom of establishment, gives rise to a 'Delaware effect' where certain EU states have become popular locations for corporations as with Delaware in the United States. The possibilities of this competition for corporate business were finally brought into immediate focus in the significant decisions of the CJEU in the *Centros*,[93] *Uberseering*[94] and *Inspire Art*[95] cases. In these cases, the CJEU held that

---

91. *See* further Gabriel Moss, Ian Fletcher & Stuart Isaacs, *The EC Regulation on Insolvency Proceedings: A Commentary and Annotated Guide* (2nd edn., OUP 2002, 2009). *See* further the considerable commentary and treatment of this Regulation in the context of the much more recent Preventive Restructuring Directive 1023/2019 from the JCOERE project where the Reports are available HERE). *See also* Irene Lynch Fannon & Gerard N. Murphy, *Corporate Insolvency and Rescue* (2nd edn., Bloomsbury Professional 2012) Ch. 1. And finally see a consideration of this Regulation as it relates to corporate rescue in particular in Irene Lynch Fannon, Jenniferr LL Gant and Aoife Finnerty, *Corporate Recovery in an Integrated Europe: Harmonisation, Coordination, and Judicial Cooperation* (Edgar, 2022).
92. Discussed *infra*. Part 1, Chapter 1, §6.
93. *Centros Ltd v. Erhvervs -Og Selskabstyrelsen* (Case C-212/97) [1999] ECR 1459.
94. *Uberseering BV v. Nordic Construction Company Baumanagement GmbH* (Case C-208/00) [2002] ECR 9919.
95. *Kamer van Koophandel en Fabrieken voor Amsterdam v. Inspire Art Ltd* (Case C-167/01) [2003] ECR 10155. *See* further A. Looijestijn-Clearie, *Have the Dikes Collapsed? Inspire Art a Further Breakthrough in the Freedom of Establishment of Companies?*, 5 Eur. Bus. Org. L. Rev. 389 (2004).

no prima facie restrictions could be placed on the ability of individuals who were nationals of EU Member States to incorporate companies in other jurisdictions in the Union. There are a number of different aspects to the establishment of freedom to incorporate throughout the EU, but the dismantling of barriers relates primarily to the sidelining of the 'real seat' theory that prevails in a number of EU jurisdictions and to the dismantling of additional restrictions placed on foreign-registered companies before being permitted to operate in a particular jurisdiction. The 'real seat' theory, which is certainly alien to the common law countries of Ireland and the UK, prevents the incorporation of a company in the relevant jurisdiction, such as France, when its main activities are to take place outside France; it also provides that when a French company moves its main operations outside France, it will be wound up or liquidated. (Interestingly, *Centros* concerned a Danish couple wishing to avoid the minimum capital requirements imposed in Denmark described above by incorporating in the UK and setting up a branch of the company in Denmark while never engaging in any trading activity in the UK). These decisions have given rise to considerable debate about the desirability of the Delaware effect. While the debate has raged, some States – notably the UK, Ireland and, it would seem, the Netherlands – have continued to benefit from this phenomenon.[96] As the globalisation of economic activity continues to occur, it is possible that courts, other than Irish courts, may choose to apply Irish law. In the United States, it is common for courts to consider detailed arguments on two distinct questions, the first pertaining to the choice of forum and the second to the choice of law. In *Tomran Inc. v. William M. Passano, Jr et al.*, for example, Matricciani J. accepted jurisdiction in relation to certain matters involving an Irish banking corporation but also decided that the applicable law was Irish company law and proceeded to decide the case on that basis.[97]

IV. Overseas Companies

73. Companies from outside Ireland wishing to trade in Ireland may set up a subsidiary, and the subsidiary will be treated as an Irish company arising from its registration in Ireland. It is also possible for the overseas company to establish a branch, which will not be considered to be a separate entity. Under the Companies Act 2014, Part 21 deals with External Companies. Here a distinction is made between a 'branch' of an external company and a 'place of business' of an external company. This distinction determines the registration and filing obligations of the related enterprise, so that only a branch of a foreign-registered company must be registered in Ireland under sections 1300–1302 of the Companies Act 2014. Recent figures from the CRO for the presence of external companies in Ireland indicate that around 4,000 such companies are registered in Ireland.

96. *See* further Irene Lynch Fannon, *The Luck of the Irish or Just Plain Old Tax and Regulatory Planning? The Success of Venture Capitalism in Ireland*, 2 Entrep. Bus. L.J., 1–35 (2006).
97. Baltimore City Circuit Case N: 24–C–02–002561.

§6. The Labour Law Connection: Co-determination and Corporate Structure

74. *De minimis* classification of corporate governance systems would identify two categories of governance structures which underpin some differences between companies established in common law countries as compared with civil law companies. The 'arms length financial model' or 'outsider' model of corporate governance emphasises the role of shareholders and focuses on the shareholder-management relationship and on the market as a monitoring device.[98] This is the US model, sometimes referred to as the Anglo-American model. In contrast, the 'relational finance' model relies on close internally constructed relationships between the corporation and the providers of capital, including both shareholders and bankers or other financial institutions. This model is also described as an 'insider' model as it gives internal recognition through, for example, representative board membership for stakeholders in addition to shareholders. Such stakeholders include creditors (financiers) and employees. This type of model is exemplified both by the Japanese experience and in Continental Europe.[99] Whereas many corporate governance scholars regard the 'arms length financial model' as being Anglo-American in character with the common law being identified as its legal progenitor, this classification ignores the significant shift in the understanding of the appropriate corporate response to employees as stakeholders that have taken place in the United Kingdom and Ireland since the beginning of the last century and accelerated as a result of membership of the EU since 1972.[100] Furthermore, it underestimates significant local variations even in apparently similar corporate law rules governing, for example, the rights of minority shareholders.[101] Similarly, within the broad category of relational finance models, there are also significant local variations of these governance systems. This is true of continental European countries where differences are found as between Member States of the EU in relation to the recognition of workers' interests and rights, in relation to the recognition of minority shareholder rights,[102] and in relation to the recognition of the rights of creditors.[103] Under European Social Policy, which applies obviously throughout the entire EU, the corporation is seen as the appropriate subject of State regulation, where the object of

98. Armen A. Alchian & Harold Demsetz, *Production, Information, Costs and Economic Organisations*, 62 Am. Econ. Rev. 777–783 (1972) for a consideration of agency problems and costs in this kind of organisation. *See* further Eugene F. Fama, *Agency Problems and the Theory of the Firm*, 88 J. Pol. Economy, 288 (1988) and *Efficient Capital Markets*, 46 J. of Fin., 1575 (1991) for a description of how capital markets address some of these agency problems (in theory, at least).

99. Ronald J. Gilson & Mark J. Roe, *Understanding the Japanese Keiretsu: Overlaps Between Corporate Governance and Industrial Organisation*, 102 Yale L. J. 871 (1993); Rafael La Porta et al., *Legal Determinants of External Finance*, 52 J. Fin. 1131 (1997); *Law and Finance*, 106 J. Pol. Economy, 1113 (1998); *Corporate Ownership Around the World*, 54 J. Fin., 471 (1999).

100. Hans Kraakman et al., *The Anatomy of Corporate Law* (2nd edn., OUP 2009). Irene Lynch Fannon, *Employees as Corporate Stakeholders: Theory and Reality in a Transatlantic Context*, 27 J. Corp. L. Stud., 155 (2004).

101. Irene Lynch Fannon, *A Transatlantic Case: The Derivative Action as a Corporate Governance Tool*, 27 Dublin U. L. J. 1 (2005); Richard Nolan, *Indirect Investors: A Greater Say in the Company?*, 3 J. Corp. L. Stud. 73 (2003).

102. COM (2003) 284/final; MARKT/13.05.2005.

103. COM (2003) 284 final.

this regulation is to achieve broad-based social, employment or economic policies as distinct from simply delivering an acceptable level of corporate behaviour. Such policies and subsequent legislation can include legislation designed to facilitate investment in job creation and growth; legislation designed to assist in the elimination of social exclusion or poverty, such as legislation facilitating and supporting part-time workers to increase labour market participation;[104] initiatives to support a better work-life balance for employees;[105] or legislation ensuring environmental protection and sustainable development. From the European perspective, the corporation is seen as one of a number of social partners, all of whom have a role to play in contributing to the planning of both macroeconomic and social outcomes. In addition, the European approach considers it appropriate not only to regulate external corporate relationships with stakeholders such as employees or the community (environment) but also to regulate governance structures within the corporation. The aim of this regulation is to reinforce recognition of stakeholders' rights, specifically through mandated representation of stakeholders, creditors and/or employees on Boards of management.[106] The latter is a feature of a number of continental European corporate governance structures. In contrast, in the United States, this level of managed planning is not present. In addition, the 'free market' ideal militates against regarding the corporation as some sort of tool of state or government planning. Furthermore, the broader European concept of 'social partnership' inclusive of business and trade unions and other social groups is completely lacking. In theoretical terms, this has been described in earlier research by this author as a contrasting view from both sides of the Atlantic of the corporation as a public or private actor, and some examination of the significant philosophical and political theories underlying these particularly different approaches has been carried out.[107] Thus, the corporate governance systems of both Ireland and the UK provide an interesting bridge between these two models of governance, particularly concerning the labour law dimension.

104. Directives 97/81/EC O.J. (L 14) and 98/23/EC O.J. (L 131) on Part-Time and Fixed Term Workers.

105. Directives 92/85/EC O.J. (L 348) on Maternity Leave; Directive 96/34/EC O.J. (L 145) on Parental Leave; and Directive 93/104/EC, the Organization of Working Time Directive.

106. *See* Directive 2001/86/EC on worker representation on the board of the European company provided for under Council Regulation 2157/2001: The Statute for the European Company.

107. Irene Lynch Fannon, *Working within Two Kinds of Capitalism* (Hart Publications 2003). *See also* Marc T. Moore, *Corporate Governance in the Shadow of the State* (Hart Publications, 2013).

Part I. Corporations/Companies

Chapter 1. The Public Company

§1. CHARACTERISTICS

75. The different kinds of companies available under Irish law have been described in the General Introduction. By far the most popular type of incorporation format is that of the company limited by shares. Furthermore, within the limited liability company category, where this is a company limited by shares, the distinction between a public limited liability company and a private limited liability company is the most significant, with the private company limited by shares predominating as the corporate form most frequently registered in Ireland. The main distinguishing feature is that in a public company, shares can normally be traded on a public market. Much of the regulation of limited liability companies in Ireland is now statute-based under the provisions of the Companies Acts 2014 (as amended).[108] Nevertheless, a considerable body of case law sets out fundamental principles of company law and offers interpretation by the judiciary of this legislation. Many of the modern decisions are available on the website of the Irish Courts Service[109] or alternatively on the BAILII website.[110] Despite the prevalence of the private limited liability company, orthodox analysis of company law in Ireland, as with English jurisprudence, assumes that the rules apply to both private and public companies, with variations being highlighted where appropriate. Indeed the structure of this work reflects that traditional emphasis on the public company as being centre stage with the first chapter of Part 1 describing the provisions as they apply to public companies, and the second chapter of Part 1 describing the law as it relates to private companies. The Irish Companies Act 2014 reverses this emphasis, however, and focuses, in the first instance, on the private company limited by shares. The first fourteen parts of the legislation set out the rules relating to the private company limited by shares. Part 16 deals with Designated Activity Companies, (DACs) as a variation of this type of company. Part 17 then sets out the provisions which apply to public limited companies. Section 1002 provides a table which shows which provisions do not apply to PLCs. In keeping with the approach taken by the

108. All currently in force legislation applicable to Irish companies, and indeed Irish partnerships, is available on the official website www.irishstatutebook.ie. As stated the main consolidated piece of legislation for companies is the Companies Act 2014 which has been amended a number of times. All amendments are annotated against the Companies Act 2014 on this website.

109. www.courts.ie.

110. www.baillii.org.

publishers of this series, this monograph will take the approach adopted in the first edition, outlining company law as it applies to both public and private companies and highlighting variations for the private company limited by shares in Chapter 2. It should be noted, however, that the structure of the Irish legislation adopts the latter company as the default business organisation with the PLC being treated in one distinct part of the legislation.

§2. Formation of a PLC

I. Formal Requirements

76. The Companies Act 2014 (the '2014 Act') has altered the previous position whereby it was necessary to register a memorandum and Articles of Association. The 2014 Act has different requirements for different types of companies. For a private company limited by shares, the memorandum and articles have now been replaced by a single document, known simply as the 'constitution' of the company.[111] Whereas previously the model articles of Table A were the basis for extensive Articles of Association, the substance of the former Table A has been incorporated into the 2014 Act and therefore there is no real need to have extensive Articles of Association in a private company limited by shares. A PLC shall continue to have a memorandum and Articles of Association, which shall together be referred to as a 'constitution'.[112] The Articles of Association of a public company will be governed by the legislative provisions but may add additional matters and items. The Memorandum of Association of a PLC must comply with the requirements set out in section 1006 of the 2014 Act.[113]

77. Registration of a limited liability company in Ireland is simple and inexpensive. The CRO www.cro.ie is the central repository for Irish companies and provides extensive guidance to users on this website. All registrations and filings can be conducted online with very minimal cost. PLCs must file a form requesting to commence business with the CRO. The purpose of this form is primarily to confirm that the PLC has complied with the minimum capital requirements established for this business form.[114] The minimum capital requirement for a PLC in Ireland is currently set at EUR 25,000, of which one-quarter (25%) must be paid up before the company commences business,[115] and this must be stated in the memorandum.[116] A PLC may not reduce its company capital below the authorised minimum.[117]

111. Companies Act 2014, s. 21. The constitution shall comply with certain requirements set out in s. 19 of the 2014 Act.
112. Companies Act 2014, s. 1006.
113. In respect of a company which predated 1 Jun. 2015, the relevant provision is s. 1007 of the 2014 Act.
114. Companies Registration Office (Form A4/70).
115. Companies Act 2014, s. 1010.
116. Companies Act 2014, s. 1006.
117. Companies Act 2014, s. 1084.

II. Notification, Registration, Incorporation and Publicity

A. Registration and Notification

78. Registration requires the lodging of the 'constitution' of the company (which, for a PLC, will continue to include a Memorandum of Association and Articles, drawn up with reference to the provisions of the Companies Act 2014) together with the relevant CRO forms (Form A1 and A70). Details of a registered address to which all formal documents can be sent must be provided. It has been possible for a single-member private company to be formed in Ireland for some time and now under section 128 of the Companies Act 2014, it is possible for companies to have only one director. However, this provision is disapplied under section 1002 to PLCs. At least one of the directors of a company must be resident in an EEA State,[118] although it is possible for the company to be exempt from this provision if a bond is lodged to the value of EUR 25,000, which becomes payable to a person nominated by the Registrar of Companies or the Revenue Commissioners, as the case may be, for the purpose of discharging any fine imposed on the company.[119] There are statutory rules for assessing whether a director is a resident of an EEA State to comply with this requirement.[120] A person shall not, at a particular time, be a director of more than twenty-five private companies limited by shares, or twenty-five companies, one or more of which is a private company limited by shares and one or more of which is another type of company capable of being wound up under the 2014 Act.[121] PLCs are not counted for this purpose.[122] In addition, there is a requirement that an Irish-registered company must carry on an activity in the State,

118. Companies Act 2014, s. 137(1).
119. Companies Act 2014, s. 137(2). The bond provides that, in the event of a failure by the company to pay the whole or part of a fine imposed in respect of an offence under the Companies Acts 1963–2005 or the Taxes Consolidation Act 1997, or a penalty under the latter legislation, an amount of money up to the value of the bond will be paid by the guarantor in discharge of the company's liability. In addition, note that the provision whereby at least one director must be a resident of an EEA State does not apply where the Registrar of Companies grants a certificate under s. 140 of the 2014 Act, which is a certificate stating that the company has a real and continuous link with one or more economic activities in the State. Section 140(9) of the 2014 Act provides that such a 'real and continuous link' is established if one of the following conditions is satisfied:

    (a) the affairs of the company are managed by one or more persons from a place of business established in the State and that person or those persons is or are authorised by the company to act on its behalf;
    (b) the company carries on a trade in the State;
    (c) the company is a subsidiary or a holding company of a company or other body corporate that satisfies either or both of the conditions specified in paragraphs (a) and (b);
    (d) the company is a subsidiary of a company, another subsidiary of which satisfies either or both of the conditions specified in paragraphs (a) and (b).

120. Companies Act 2014, s. 44(8), (9) and (10).
121. Companies Act 2014, s. 142(1).
122. Companies Act 2014, s. 142(3).

but 'activity' for this purpose includes the holding or acquisition of property of any kind, thus reducing the efficacy of this legislation.[123]

79. The company must also have a company secretary. The Registrar must be informed of the first person to hold this position and of any subsequent changes (*see* §4, V, *infra*).

80. The memorandum of a PLC must state the name of the company,[124] and the Registrar may reject the registration if the company name is deemed to be 'undesirable'.[125] It is for the Registrar to identify what is undesirable for this purpose; the CRO website provides guidance in this regard. For example, a name might be refused if it is identical or similar to a name already on the register, if the name is offensive, or if it includes terms such as 'Ireland' that might suggest State sponsorship. Certain other terms cannot be used without the permission of relevant bodies. The words 'bank', 'banking' and (the Irish language equivalent 'banc') may only be used with permission from the Central Bank, and the word 'university' may not be used without permission from the Department of Education. An appeal lies to the High Court against a refusal by the Registrar to register a company name on the ground that the name is undesirable. A change in the company's name may only be effected by special resolution and with the consent of the Registrar.[126]

81. A company trading under a name other than its corporate name must register such trading name as well, but inclusion of the abbreviation 'Ltd' for 'Limited' or 'PLC' (or an equivalent in the Irish language) shall not of itself render such registration necessary.

82. The issuing of any prospectus is governed principally by Chapter 1 of Part 23 of the 2014 Act (*see* §2, IX, *infra*).

B. Publicity

83. Enforcement of company law, the effective governance of corporations and the adequate protection of various stakeholders, including in particular shareholders and creditors of all types, depend on effective corporate disclosure rules. The publication of company documents such as the Memorandum and Articles of Association (now referred to as the 'constitution' under the Companies Act 2014), various shareholder resolutions, and various other items pertaining to the financial situation of the company such as accounts and borrowing and the creation of charges on corporate property are all essential elements in an effective disclosure system and the

123. For a PLC, see Companies Act 2014, s. 1005; and as regards a private company limited by shares, *see* s. 18 of the 2014 Act.
124. Companies Act 2014, s. 1006. As regards a private company, *see* s. 19 of the 2014 Act.
125. Companies Act 2014, s. 26(5).
126. Companies Act 2014, s. 26(4) and s. 1008(4).

corporate governance structures built on these elements. The Registrar of Companies is charged with maintaining a file on each registered company. The CRO website[127] provides detailed guidance on what sort of documents need to be filed, and the CRO maintains company files that can be accessed online or in person through a company search on the payment of a fee.

84. In addition to the actual disclosure and filing obligations, there is also a notification of filing and receipt procedure instituted in 1973 following the enactment of the First Company Law Directive (68/15/EEC) through the European Communities (Companies) Regulations 1973. These matters are now to be published electronically since the European Communities (Companies) Regulations 2004.[128] Under this system, the filing of specified documents must be notified through *Iris Oifigiúil* (the name given in Irish to the Official Gazette). Other notices pertaining to the activities of the company must also be notified, such as resolutions that have been passed to liquidate a company; such notification must include the terms of the resolution. A further example includes the obligation to notify the names of those individuals who no longer have the authority to bind the company.[129] These must be notified to the Registrar of Companies, including any changes made from time to time, and such information must also be notified to the general public through publication in *Iris Oifigiúil.*

85. The operation of this filing and notification procedure also triggers the operation of the doctrine of notice, so that individuals who are dealing with a company may be deemed to have notice of certain kinds of information that have been so publicised. This is not quite the same as the operation of the doctrine of constructive notice, but it can potentially have the similarly harsh effect of individuals being imputed with certain kinds of knowledge they do not actually possess.

III. Contracts Made on Behalf of a Company

86. Because of the artificial nature of a body corporate, a conceptual difficulty arises as to whether a company can be bound by a contract that was entered into on behalf of the company or in relation to the business of that company before the company was formed. It is impossible for a company to enter into a contract before it is formed. The question raised is whether it is possible for a company to subsequently ratify such a contract – that is, a contract entered into on its behalf – once it is incorporated. At common law, this was considered to be impossible,[130] but legislation has altered that position. Thus, under the 1963 Act, and now, under the Companies Act 2014, any contract or transaction 'purporting to be entered into by a company prior to its formation or by any person on behalf of the company prior

127. www.cro.ie.
128. Companies (Forms No. 2) Order 2004 (S.I. 829 of 2004). These provisions are now contained in ss 39–40 of the Companies Act 2014.
129. Companies Act 2014, s. 39.
130. *Natal Land Co. v. Pauline Syndicate* [1904] AC 120 (P.C.) (holding that instead a new contract had to be entered into on the terms of the old one, after the company is incorporated).

to its formation may be ratified by the company after its formation … ', and, where such ratification takes place, the company is bound by the contract or transaction as if the company had been in existence on the date of the contract or transaction.[131] Absent such ratification, however, 'the person or persons who purported to act in the name or on behalf of the company shall in the absence of express agreement to the contrary be personally bound by the contract or other transaction and entitled to the benefit thereof'.[132] Thus, where contracts are being concluded between a company that has yet to be formed and, for example, a promoter of that company or indeed conversely by the promoter on behalf of the company with other parties, it is important to address this question of potential personal liability or the possibility of excluding such liability.

IV. Number of Subscribers

87. A public company may be incorporated with only one member,[133] as may a private company limited by shares.[134]

V. Initial Share Capital

88. Under Irish law, as with English law, a private limited company has no minimum capital requirement. As discussed above, the minimum capital requirement for PLCs is EUR 25,000, of which one-quarter (25%) must be paid up under the provisions of the 2014 Act.[135]

89. When a company is deciding on its capital structure, it can opt for any range of variations. For example, a company may decide to have one class of shares, normally referred to as 'ordinary shares'; there can be different classes of shares, such as Ordinary 'A' and Ordinary 'B' shares, often entitled to elect 'A' and 'B' Directors respectively; or the share capital can be divided into ordinary and preference shares, with preference shares being given to promoters or original subscribers and ordinary shares being given to other investors. Other structures can be adopted and in all cases usually described in the Articles of Association. Redeemable shares are governed primarily by section 105 of the 2014 Act.[136] In the context of shareholders' rights and minority rights, some specific rights attaching to shareholders,

131. Companies Act 2014, s. 45(1)–(2).
132. Companies Act 2014, s. 45(3).
133. Companies Act 2014, s. 1004.
134. Companies Act 2014, s. 17. Note that under s. 17 a private company limited shares shall have no more than 149 members, albeit that s. 17 provides that employees and former employees are not counted for this purpose, and it is also provided that where two or more persons hold one or more shares in a company jointly, they shall, for the purposes of s. 17, be treated as a single member.
135. Companies Act 2014, s. 1010.
136. Such shares can be cancelled or held as 'treasury shares'. *See infra*, Part I, Ch. 1, §4, III and IV.

including pre-emption rights, protection against the variation of shareholders' rights, voting rights[137] and notice provisions, generally, are considered in a later section.[138]

90. To raise capital, a company may issue and allot shares at the outset or issue and allot shares as the business grows. A company may start out with a particular authorised share capital but may need to increase this authorised share capital and issue and allot some of these shares with a view to raising more equity capital. The decision of the Board of Directors to issue shares will be considered under the heading of abuse of directors' powers when we consider directors' duties, where some of these actions have been challenged in the courts (the major reason being that a new issue and allotment can have a significant impact on the control structure in a company).[139] A number of legal principles will be considered both under directors' duties and under capital maintenance later in the text.

VI. Contributions in Kind

91. Limited liability is defined in section 655 of the Companies Act 2014, which deals with the issue of who is liable to contribute to the payment of a company's debts on winding up. Section 25(2) of the 2014 Act states that the subscribers and other members of the company will collectively become a 'body corporate' with the liability of the members to contribute to the assets in the event of winding up to be described in the Act. Section 655(1) addresses the liability of past and present members of a range of different kinds of companies, including those limited by guarantee or companies that are unlimited. The section goes on, in subsection 655(1)(d), to state that 'in the case of a company limited by shares, no contribution shall be required from any member exceeding the amount, if any, unpaid on the shares in respect of which he is liable as a present or past member'. In a PLC, this amount is set as described above, but in most cases concerning private companies, there is no amount unpaid on the shares, the issued share capital being usually minimal and the amount paid up at the formation of the company. In relation to the shares in a public company, these must be tradeable on a public market. Limited liability is complemented in its effect by the doctrine of corporate personality, which was first considered in England in the case of *Salomon v. Salomon & Co. Ltd.*[140] The decision in that case, and the jurisprudence following from it, form part of Irish company law (*see* §3 *infra*).

92. Various provisions of Irish company law seek to protect the capitalisation value of companies by ensuring that certain standards are complied with when shares are being issued and allotted. Accordingly, the following statutory provisions have a significant role in protecting such valuations, particularly in relation to PLCs.

---

137. The EU has previously considered proposals introducing some mandatory provisions regarding voting rights for shareholders (such as the European Policy Forum 2006), but these have not been pursued.
138. *See* Part I, Ch. 1, §4, III and IV.
139. *See* generally Part I, Ch. 1, §5, II, B and C (the abuse of power doctrine under directors' duties).
140. *Salomon v. Salomon & Co. Ltd* [1897] AC 22 (reversing *Broderip v. Salomon* [1985] 2 Ch. 232).

For the most part, these provisions do not apply to private companies. The predominant piece of legislation in this context was formerly the Companies Act 1983, which enacted modern provisions on the establishment of PLCs, the capitalisation of same, rules regarding the issuing and allotment of share capital, and the valuation of consideration. This Act has now been consolidated into the Companies Act 2014.[141] These provisions are described below at §4 VI.

93. In private companies, even though from a creditor's point of view the issues may be even more crucial, these rules do not apply.[142]

VII. Other Material Formation Requirements

A. *Incorporation Documents: An Introduction*

94. Incorporation requires the submission as described of various documents. Under the Companies Act 2014, 'the constitution' is the term used to describe the Memorandum of Association and the Articles of Association in the case of a PLC (For private companies, the term constitution is intended to replace these documents).[143] In either case, these documents form a contract between the members and the company under the provisions of section 31 of the 2014 Act.[144]

95. The Memorandum of Association of a PLC shall state: (a) its name, (b) that it is a PLC registered under Part 17 of the 2014 Act, (c) its objects, (d) that the liability of its members is limited, and (e) its authorised share capital, being the amount of share capital with which the PLC proposes to be registered which shall not be less than the authorised minimum, and the division thereof into shares of a fixed amount.[145] The constitution of a PLC shall also state the number of shares (which shall not be less than one) taken by each subscriber to the constitution.[146] In addition, the constitution shall be in accordance with the form set out in Schedule 9 of the 2014 Act or as near thereto as circumstances permit, the constitution shall be printed in an entire format, which is to say the memorandum and articles shall be contained in one document; and the constitution shall be signed by each subscriber in the presence of at least one witness who shall attest the signature and the constitution shall be authenticated in the manner set out in section 888 of the 2014 Act.

96. The purpose of stating the objects of a company in the memorandum was to provide an indication of the business of the company. The objects clause has

---

141. *See* generally *infra* Part 1, Ch. 1, §3.
142. *Infra*, Part I, Ch. 2, para. 333.
143. *See infra* Part 1, Ch. 2.
144. This section has been restrictively interpreted as applying only to liabilities and obligations imposed on a member *qua* member and not in any other capacity. *See Hickman v. Kent or Romney Marsh Sheepbreeders' Association* [1915] 1 Ch. 881.
145. Companies Act 2014, s. 1006(2).
146. Companies Act 2014, s. 1006(3).

become much less significant in Irish law for all types of companies. This is discussed below. (See §3 Essential Elements of the Legal Person).

97. The Memorandum and the Articles of Association provide the basic constitutional documents of the PLC. As described, these are now referred to as the Constitution under the Companies Act 2014.

98. It has already been noted above that much of what was contained in the standard-form articles is now contained in the body of the 2014 Act and applies by default. It can now be expected that Articles of Association should accordingly in future be more concise, but will nevertheless involve statements as to whether the provisions of the Companies Act 2014 apply in the particular case or not.

99. The articles may only be amended by special resolution, i.e., a resolution with the support of more than three-quarters (75%) of the members present in person or by proxy.[147] Any alteration or addition to the articles will, subject to the provisions of the Companies Act, be as valid as if originally contained in the Articles and can be subsequently changed.[148] The same rule (i.e., amendment by special resolution only) applies to an alteration of a provision of the memorandum which could have been contained in the articles.[149]

100. Generally, the Articles of Association (now the constitution) describe many of the rights of shareholders, in particular the classes of shares and their rights, which include voting rights, rights to dividends, rights to elect directors and so forth. In addition, the articles contained rules, which were again subject to the Companies Acts, on the operation of meetings. Now, under the Companies Act 2014, these rules are, for the most part, contained in the legislation. For example, the articles would previously have had a significant role in describing the relative positions of the Directors and the Board. Whereas, regulation 80 of Table A had previously provided that the business of the company shall be managed by the directors, subject to any of the other articles and the provisions of the 1963 Act, and subject also to such directions being not inconsistent with the directors' power of management as may be given by the members in general meeting, this statement is now contained in section 158(1) of the 2014 Act. Section 158(2) repeats the other important provision of regulation 80, namely that no such direction given by the members in a general meeting shall invalidate any prior act of the directors which would have been valid if that direction had not been given. Similarly, whereas regulation 79 of Table A, which had allowed the directors to exercise all powers of the company to borrow money, section 158(3) of the 2014 Act now contains this provision. All of the powers of directors and rules regarding the proceedings of directors which are set out in sections 158–165 of the 2014 Act are expressed to apply save where the constitution of the company provides otherwise.[150]

147. Companies Act 2014, s. 1015(1).
148. Companies Act 2014, s. 1015(2).
149. Companies Act 2014, s. 1016.
150. Companies Act 2014, s. 157.

§3. Essential Elements of the Legal Person

I. Seat

101. Under Irish law, the place of registration is considered the seat of the company. The 'real seat' doctrine has no place in general corporate law jurisprudence with the exception of where it may be considered under the application of principles derived from EU law. For example, the EIR Recast 848/2015 allows for the displacement of the presumption of the place of registration being the centre of main interests for the purpose of that legislation, where the principles of that regulation apply. This has been applied in Irish hearings.

II. Objects Clause

102. Given the traditional application of the *ultra vires* rule, which limited the company's legal capacity,[151] objects clauses tended to describe multiple facets of the company's businesses or potential business directions, in addition to listing various kinds of activities the company might pursue. As a result, these clauses tended to run into several pages. If the company went beyond its stated objects, its actions were *ultra vires* the company and therefore void.

This caused considerable problems in practical terms. While a statement of the company's objects was intended theoretically to serve a double purpose: (1) to afford protection to investors in the company, and (2) to enable outsiders who deal with the company to ascertain the extent of the company's powers,[152] the general consensus for some time is that this rationale has outlived its usefulness. Furthermore, the consequent lack of capacity, in addition to the doctrine of constructive notice applicable generally to documents of public record (*see* publicity requirements *supra*), was interpreted so that those dealing with a company acting in an *ultra vires* fashion were deemed to know of the lack of capacity. This led to some extremely harsh outcomes in the past.[153]

In Ireland, this legal position has now been significantly altered by the Companies Act 2014. A private company limited by shares shall now have *full and unlimited capacity* to carry on and undertake any business or activity, to do any act or enter into any transaction and for those purposes, it shall have full rights, powers and privileges.[154] The Act provides that this rule does not permit a company to deviate from the general law in any way.[155] In this sense, the legal personality or capacity of a private limited company has been extended. In the case of a PLC, the

151. *Ashbury Railway Carriage Co. Ltd v. Riche* (1875) LR 7 HL 653.
152. *Cotman v. Brougham* (1918) AC 514 *per* Lord Parker of Waddington.
153. *See*, for example, *Re Jon Beauforte Ltd* [1953] Ch. 131; *Parke v. Daily News Ltd* [1962] Ch. 297; *Re Introductions Ltd* [1970] 1 Ch. 199; in Ireland, *see Northern Bank Finance Corporation v. Quinn and Achates Investment Co.* [1979] ILRM 221; *Re Frederick Inns Ltd* [1994] 1 ILRM 387 an example of mischief.
154. Companies Act 2014, s. 38(1).
155. Companies Act 2014, s. 38(2).

Memorandum of Association must continue to list the objects of the company. However, the 2014 Act provides that the validity of an act done by a PLC shall not be called into question on the grounds of lack of capacity by reason of anything contained in the PLC's objects.[156] The purpose of an objects clause in terms of protecting investors from unexpected diversification continues to be protected by the following provisions. First, a member of a PLC may bring proceedings to restrain the doing of an act which, but for section 1012(1) of the 2014 Act, would be beyond the PLC's capacity. However, the act provides that no such proceedings shall lie in respect of any act to be done in fulfilment of a legal obligation arising from a previous act of the PLC. In addition, the 2014 Act provides that it remains the duty of the directors to observe any limitations on their powers flowing from the PLC's objects and actions by the directors which, but for section 1012(1), would be beyond the PLC's capacity and may only be ratified by the company by special resolution.[157] The balance between the expectations of investors and the interests of those dealing with a PLC is struck in favour of a bona fide external party. The act provides that a party to a transaction with a PLC is not bound to enquire as to whether it is permitted by the PLC's objects.[158] Therefore, the doctrine of *ultra vires* (which affected the validity of acts done by a company outside its objects clause) is effectively abolished as regards private and public companies limited by shares. As regards public companies in Ireland, the approach taken in the new legislation is similar to the approach taken under the UK Companies Act 2006.

However, it is possible to form a private company limited by shares as a DAC's, where business activities are stated in advance.[159] Where activities are described, section 966 of the Companies Act 2014 mirrors the provisions applicable to PLCs under section 1012, namely that the statement of activities serves to restrain the actions of the company. Effectively, in both cases, as with the UK provisions, the statement of objects or activities serves as a rule of *internal discipline* and does not affect the validity of actions done on behalf of a company insofar as bona fide third parties are concerned.[160]

An issue that has sometimes arisen in tandem with the *ultra vires* problem is the issue of whether a particular individual had the authority to bind the company that he or she claimed to have. This issue of the authority of agents is considered (*infra* §5 II B).

III. Corporate Personality: Judicial Doctrine and Judicially Defined Exceptions to the Principle

103. The doctrine of corporate personality applies in Irish law by virtue of the English House of Lords decision in *Salomon v. Salomon & Co. Ltd.*[161] This decision and the doctrine as set out by the House of Lords is a foundational part of common

156. Companies Act 2014, s. 1012(1).
157. Companies Act 2014, s. 1012(3).
158. Companies Act 2014, s. 1012(5).
159. Companies Act 2014, Part 16.
160. *See* further *infra* Part 1, Ch. 2.
161. *Salomon v. Salomon & Co. Ltd* [1897] AC 22 (reversing *Broderip v. Salomon* [1985] 2 Ch. 232).

law company law and, despite somewhat different understandings of the principle in other EU countries, continues to be applied in a strict manner in common law courts across the world. Irish courts are no exception. Briefly, the essential question in the case was whether the unsecured creditors of Salomon & Co. Ltd were entitled to have recourse to the assets of Salomon, who had originally traded as a sole trader but who had taken advantage of incorporation as provided for in the relatively new legislation enacted in England at the time. In the Court of first instance, Vaughan Williams J. held that the company, Salomon & Co. Ltd, was an *agent* of Salomon, the individual businessman, who was therefore obliged to indemnify the company for all its debts. The case was appealed to the Court of Appeal where arguments were unsuccessfully made against the finding of a per se agency relationship, *inter alia*. The primary focus of the judgments of the Court of Appeal was on the intention of the legislature. Lindley L.J. was clear that Salomon had made 'an attempt ... to use the machinery of the Companies Act, 1862 for a purpose for which it was never intended'. Lopes L. J. stated that if Salomon's 'scheme' were to be condoned by the courts, it would be tantamount to authorising a 'perversion of the Joint Stock Companies Acts' and giving vitality to 'a myth and a fiction'. 'It was never intended that the company to be constituted should consist of one substantial persona and six mere dummies, the nominees of that person, without any real interest in the company.' The case was finally appealed to the House of Lords, which unanimously took a very different view and established the doctrine which applies to this day. Lord Halsbury reprimanded the lower court judges for not allowing in their own minds:

> the proposition that the company has a real existence. They have been struck by what they have considered the inexpediency of permitting one man to be in influence and authority over the whole company, and assuming that such a thing could not have been intended by the legislature they have sought various grounds upon which they might insert into the Act some prohibitions of such a result.

In addition, the House of Lords rejected the notion of a per se agency relationship – that is, the notion that Salomon or any other promoter, director or shareholder of a company could be liable for its debts simply because of the relationships within the company. The court also addressed the position of the creditors of the company, both secured (debenture holders in this case) and unsecured creditors. Lord MacNaghten observed that the creditors had 'only themselves to blame' as they knew they were dealing with a limited liability company and were no longer dealing with an individual while observing that 'each creditor is entitled to get and to hold whatever security he can get'.

104. Since that time, the courts in Ireland have been careful to ensure that the doctrine of corporate personality serves its primary function – that is, to support limited liability – and will not in general support any invasion into the personal assets or even identity of anyone involved in a business run through the vehicle of a company. In other words, the veil between the company and the individuals behind the company and its business will not be removed to impose liability on those individuals in normal circumstances. 'Normal circumstances' as a rule of thumb involve everything short of fraud. However, there are some cases, usually described as exceptional circumstances in which the courts will lift the corporate veil or set aside the doctrine of corporate personality to establish circumstances surrounding certain activities or transactions. In fact, the exceptions were adumbrated by the House of Lords in *Salomon* and include fraud and avoidance of a legal duty by creating a corporate entity which is a 'sham', 'device', 'myth', or 'fiction'. Agency is a further possible exception,[162] but this was not argued successfully in *Salomon*, where it was clarified that no per se agency existed. There are also some statutory exceptions in which the courts disregard the corporate personality to identify directors and others who may then be liable for debts of the company. Primarily these exceptions arise in relation to fraudulent and reckless trading under Irish law. In Irish law (as in the law of New Zealand, but not significantly in English law), there is also a statutory exception for the imposition of liability for debts in relation to groups. With the emergence of two new EU Directives in the area of corporate sustainability, there may be further inroads within this statutory framework to the doctrine.[163]

105. The exceptions to the doctrine of corporate personality are described very clearly in the judgment of the High Court (affirmed in the Supreme Court) in *Fyffes PLC v. DCC PLC and Ors.*[164] These are briefly outlined below and remain the principal legal interpretation of this matter to date.

106. The courts may lift the veil when incorporation is being used to avoid a legal duty. In *Gilford Motor Co. Ltd v. Horne*,[165] the defendant had agreed to a restraint of trade clause in his original contract of employment with the plaintiffs but on leaving his employment set up a company, J. M. Horne Ltd, in which his wife and son were shareholders but he had no formal involvement. Nevertheless, customers and employees identified him as being in charge of the business. The company ran a business that competed directly with the plaintiff, and it was argued that the Court should disregard the separate corporate entity to establish that the defendant had used a corporate entity to facilitate the breach of the restraint of trade covenant. The Court acceded to this request. In contrast, however, in the Irish case of *Roundabout Ltd v. Beirne*,[166] it was held that the plaintiff had employed a legitimate

162. Once an agency relationship is established, this does not in fact form a real exception to the doctrine.
163. Directive Directive (EU) 2022/2464 of the European Parliament and of the Council of 14 December 2022 amending Regulation (EU) No. 537/2014, Directive 2004/109/EC, Directive 2006/43/EC and Directive 2013/34/EU, as regards corporate sustainability reporting. This Directive was passed in January 2023 and is due for transposition in 2025. A second proposed Directive on Corporate Sustainability Due Diligence will impose liability on parent companies and their management for failure to exercise due diligence regarding the activities of subsidiaries, further changes the common law landscape. Proposed Directive 2022/0051 amending Directive (EU) 2019/1937 COM(2022) 71 final Brussels, 23.2.2022
164. [2005] IEHC 477. Appealed, but not on this issue to the Supreme Court, *Fyffes plc v. DCC plc and Ors.* [2007] IESC 36.
165. [1933] Ch. 935.
166. [1933] IR 425.

legal subterfuge by incorporating and arranging to have the lease of the pub. The Roundabout transferred to the corporation with a view to avoiding the consequences of trade disputes that had been protected under the 1906 Trade Disputes Act. As Dixon J. stated, the use of the corporate form in this case was 'a subterfuge' but a legitimate one, wherein the second company is a legal entity distinct from the first company, the original owner, despite the fact that the same individuals were involved in both entities. The distinction between the two cases is clear: In the first, the defendant was using the corporate entity as a myth, fiction or sham to avoid legal obligations, whereas in the latter case, there is no legal obligation to continue a particular relationship with undesirable consequences.

107. Also adumbrated in the judgments in *Salomon* were the issues surrounding agency. In the House of Lords, it was held that there was no per se agency between an individual shareholder and his or her company by virtue of that relationship alone. Similarly, where there is a parent/subsidiary relationship or related company structure, there is no per se agency relationship. As in *Salomon* itself, this is particularly important regarding attempts to impose liability as between any of these parties or to identify the acts of the company as being the acts of any of the individuals. Therefore, if an agency relationship is to be established, this must be done in accordance with the ordinary rules of agency law. This question will be revisited in relation to groups of companies (*see* §8, *infra*).

108. In the *Fyffes* litigation,[167] the court held that certain companies, namely DCC and its Lotus Green could be regarded as a single economic entity 'for the purpose of preventing the avoidance of the availability of an effective remedy under s. 109 … [of what was then the Companies Act 1990 on insider trading] … and thus preventing an injustice to parties with a remedy under s. 109 if DCC is liable to account.' This could only occur, however, if:

(a) An evidential basis exists for finding that, as regards the holding and disposal of the shares, to borrow the terminology used by Murphy J in *Lac Minerals Ltd v. Chevron Mineral,*[168] there was a factual identification of the acts of Lotus Green and DCC.
(b) Not to so treat the companies [as a single entity] would allow the DCC Group to evade its obligations under 'Part V. of 1990 Act' (now re-enacted in the 2014 Act).

109. There have been some very strong decisions in recent times from the courts regarding the use of corporate personality by individuals who then seek to avoid the effect of the doctrine for their own ends. In *Prest v. Petrodel Resources Ltd.*,[169] a wife sought ownership following a divorce settlement of certain properties owned by companies controlled indirectly by her husband. It must be emphasised that the husband was not a shareholder or director of these companies. It was argued that

---

167. *Fyffes plc v. DCC plc and Ors.* [2007] IESC 36.
168. [1995] 1 ILRM 161.
169. [2013] UKSC 2013.

the corporate personality of this corporate group, PRL should be disregarded to establish the husband was the true owner of the properties and these should be transferred to the benefit of the wife. The decision of the United Kingdom Supreme Court in *Prest v. Petrodel* provides a summary of the law in England regarding the strength of the doctrine of corporate personality with interesting results. The wife's claim to have the corporate veil disregarded failed. The decision of the United Kingdom Supreme Court also pronounced strongly against the practice which had emerged in the family courts whereby the corporate personality of companies and the property ownership structures involved in incorporation were disregarded for the purposes of awards being made in marital disputes. While acknowledging that it was common practice for wealthy individuals to avail of incorporation to facilitate property ownership for various reasons, and while acknowledging that one or more of the properties in corporate ownership were for all intents and purposes regarded by all parties as marital property, the court nevertheless held that the doctrine of corporate personality and the fact that the properties were owned by the corporation could not be completely disregarded at will in such cases and would not be disregarded in this case. As a consequence, the wife could not claim ownership of properties held by a corporation. However, the court held that the company in question held some of the properties on resulting trust for the wife based on the husband's interest in the corporations.

110. Similarly, in the Irish case of *O'Donnell and Ors v. Bank of Ireland &Ors.*,[170] a complicated structure for the ownership of Gorse Hill, a family home occupied by the appellants in this Supreme Court case, who were the children of Brian and Dr Mary Pat O'Donnell was at issue. Gorse Hill was owned by a company called Vico Ltd. which had defaulted on a range of obligations to Bank of Ireland concerning loans made to Mr and Dr O'Donnell to the tune of EUR 14 million. Here it was claimed that the appellants were the true owners of the property with a view to evading action of the bank to enforce loans made to the company. These arguments were considered and rejected by the Supreme Court which referred to the decision of the UK Supreme Court in *Prest v. Petrodel* and approved the approach taken in that decision to preserve the integrity of corporate ownership.

IV. Attribution of Human Characteristics: Criminal Liability

111. One of the most interesting aspects of the separate corporate personality doctrine is the way the law relates the corporate form to certain concepts traditionally associated only with natural persons, such as domicile and residency status, criminal intent, and human rights. This is particularly significant in relation to tax, where the concepts of domicile and residence of corporations are important. Furthermore, attempts to attribute the human characteristic of criminal intent to corporations have become of interest in recent times in common law countries, although this does not seem to be as problematic in other legal systems.

170. [2014] IESC 77.

112. By analogy with a natural person, the attributes of nationality, domicile and residence can be given to a company. In common law countries, a company is domiciled in, and a national of, the State in which it has its registered office.[171] Under Irish law, the place of a company's registered office must at all times be within the State. Therefore, a company registered in Ireland is of Irish nationality[172] and domicile. In the event that a statutory exception applies, the Court, in ascertaining a company's residence, inquires as to where its 'central management and control' is located.[173] Thus, in some cases, the Court will look behind the corporate personality to establish where the company 'keeps house and does business',[174] where such questions might be pertinent to identifying the actual residence of a company for tax purposes. Another tax concept, domicile, is usually determined by the corporation's place of registration. In *De Beers,* it was successfully established that the company was ordinarily resident in the UK, illustrating that it is possible for a company to be ordinarily resident in a jurisdiction distinct from its place of registration, in this case, South Africa. While acknowledging that a company could not eat or sleep, *De Beers* held that the question of where a company 'keeps house and does business' was 'a pure question of fact to be determined, not according to the construction of this or that regulation or by-law, but upon a scrutiny of the course of business and trading'.[175]

113. It is clear that companies in Ireland are subject to the criminal law. This is so at common law,[176] and since 2005, as a matter of statutory interpretation, the word 'person' is to be read as including bodies of corporate and unincorporated associations.[177]

114. A necessary pre-condition of criminal liability in many contexts in common law is a mental element, whether that be intentional, reckless or grossly negligent conduct. With the exception of what are described as strict liability offences, *mens rea* must coincide with *actus reus*. A good starting point is the English case of

171. *Janson v. Dreifontein Mines Ltd* [1902] AC 484; *Gasque v. Commissioners of Inland Revenue* [1940] 2 KB 80.
172. *Janson v. Dreifontein Mines Ltd* [1902] AC 484, 497 ('My Lords, I assume that the corporation, which was plaintiff in the action and is now respondent here, was to all intents and purposes in the position of a natural-born subject of the late South African Republic. I do not think it can be entitled to any exceptional favour or to any peculiar indulgence by reason of the fact, if it be a fact, that the bulk of its shareholders were of European nationality. If all its members had been subjects of the British Crown, the corporation itself would have been none the less a foreign corporation and none the less in regard to this country an alien.' *Per* Lord Macnaghten).
173. This test derives from the old case of *De Beers Consolidated Mines Ltd v. Howe* [1906] AC 455.
174. *De Beers Consolidated Mines Ltd v. Howe* [1906] AC 455, 458 per Lord Loreburn LC.
175. *Ibid.*; *see also Unit Construction Co. Ltd v. Bullock* [1959] 3 All ER 831, 835–836.
176. *D.P.P . v. Mutual Enterprises Ltd* (unreported, High Court, 29 Nov. 1985); *D.P.P . v. Trident Homes Ltd* (*The Irish Times*, 19 Jul. 1997); *People (D.P.P .) v. Roseberry Construction Ltd* (Court of Criminal Appeal, Hardiman J.; 6 Feb. 2003); *D.P.P . v. Kent and Sussex Contractors Ltd* [1944] KB 146; *Moore v. Bressler* [1944] 2 All ER 515; *Tesco Supermarkets Ltd v. Nattrass* [1972] AC 153; *Meridian Global Funds Management Asia* [1995] 2 AC 500; *R v. Rozeik* [1996] 1 BCLC 380; *Attorney General's Reference 2/1999 under Section 36 of the Criminal Justice Act 1972* [2000] QB 796.
177. Interpretation Act 2005, s. 18(c).

Tesco Supermarkets Ltd v. Nattrass,[178] which arose from the prosecution of a supermarket chain for the offence of selling goods above the advertised retail price, a statutory offence requiring intent. In not holding the company liable, the court held that, apart from the recklessness of the branch manager, all other individuals within the company had been blameless regarding compliance with the Act and had ensured a system of supervision that would avoid such offences in most cases. Lord Reid cited the following passage from an earlier judgment of Denning L.J.:

> A company may in many ways be likened to a human body. It has a brain and nerve centre which controls what it does. It also has hands which hold the tools and act in accordance with directions from the centre. Some of the people in the company are mere servants and agents who are nothing more than hands to do the work and cannot be said to represent the mind or will. Others are directors and managers who represent the directing mind and will of the company, and control what it does. The state of mind of these managers is the state of mind of the company and is treated by the law as such.[179]

Lord Reid held that this was a correct statement of the law, and added that: 'Normally the Board of Directors, the managing director and perhaps other superior officers of a company carry out functions of management and speak and act as the company. Their subordinates do not.'[180] Lord Reid went on to say, however, that a Board of Directors may delegate management functions and empower delegates to act independently of instructions from them, so that 'within the scope of the delegation he can act as the company'.[181]

115. The case of *R v. P and O Ferries (Dover) Ltd*[182] illustrates the difficulties inherent in this approach. Following the capsizing of The Herald of Free Enterprise, attempts to prosecute the corporation that ran the ferry collapsed because of a failure to identify someone representing the company who had the necessary criminal intent. Following an official inquiry into the tragedy, from which a report had issued, the apportionment of blame was equivocal although the report noted that the corporation was 'infected with the disease of sloppiness' and that the underlying fault for these actions lay 'higher up in the company'. At the subsequent criminal trial for corporate manslaughter, the evidence indicated that the assistant bosun and chief officer had been careless in the execution of their duties, but Turner J. held that there was 'no direct evidence that a reasonably prudent person occupying the positions of any of the five senior defendants would have perceived the risk was obvious or serious'. The risk entailed setting sail with the ferry doors open, which in turn caused

178. *Tesco Supermarkets Ltd v. Nattrass* [1972] AC 153.
179. *Ibid.*, 171 (quoting *H. L. Bolton Engineering Co. Ltd v. T. J. Graham & Sons Ltd* [1957] 1 QB 159, 172). This 'directing mind and will' test was accepted by the Irish Supreme Court in the context of an allegation of insurance fraud in *Superwood Holdings PLC v. Sun Alliance & London Alliance PLC* [1995] 3 IR 30. *See also* the discussion of J. McCarthy as regards the tort of conspiracy in *Taylor v. Smith* [1991] 1 IR 142, 166.
180. *Ibid.*, 171.
181. *Ibid.*
182. *R v. P and O Ferries (Dover) Ltd* (1990) 93 Cr. App. Rep. 72.

the ferry to capsize and resulted in the deaths of 192 people. Similar failures of prosecution followed the Hillsborough football stadium disaster, and more recently, more than fifteen years afterwards, similar issues arose in relation to the Hatfield train crash. In that case, although Network Rail was convicted of safety breaches, five executives were cleared of responsibility. These executives had originally been charged with manslaughter but the Court dismissed these charges during the trial. Similar charges against the company had not been brought to trial.

116. This difficult concept of attributing criminal liability to a corporation has been considered in depth by the Irish Law Reform Commission which has published extensive studies on the matter[183] but as yet Ireland has no statute on corporate manslaughter, unlike the UK, which has passed legislation in this area.[184]

V. Attribution of Human Characteristics: Do Corporations Have Human or Constitutionally Protected Rights?

117. Ireland has a written Constitution, unlike the UK jurisdictions, and so a further important question arises in relation to whether corporations are entitled to the protection of constitutionally guaranteed rights protected under the Irish Constitution or rights that may be protected by human rights treaties or conventions, such as the European Convention of Human Rights, which has been incorporated into Irish law.[185]

118. In the United States, where constitutional jurisprudence has been developed for over a century, corporations early on sought protection under the Fourteenth Amendment, which had been enacted following the Civil War to provide equal protection of the law for African Americans and now other minorities. However, corporations were not slow to assert the same protection, and this has been successfully obtained from the United States Supreme Court. In contrast, the Irish courts have been much more conservative on this question. In *Quinn's Supermarket v. Attorney General,*[186] the Supreme Court considered a challenge to the provisions of a Ministerial Order that exempted the proprietors of Kosher shops from a ban on evening opening. Kenny J. offered the following interpretation of the human personality phrase as a justification for his rejection of the plaintiff's claim challenging the exception:

> This guarantee, however, is one of equality before the law in so far as the characteristics inherent in the idea of human personality are involved: it does not

183. Law Reform Commission, Report on Corporate Killing (LRC 77-2005) (October 2005). *See* further Law Reform Commission Report on Regulatory Powers and Offences Volumes 1 and 2. Law Reform Commission 2018. *See* further www.lawreform.ie.
184. Corporate Manslaughter and Corporate Homicide Act 2007 (UK).
185. This question has received thorough and comprehensive treatment by Dr Ailbhe O'Neill in her work *The Constitutional Rights of Companies* (Thomson Round Hall 2007).
186. *Quinn's Supermarket v. Attorney General* [1972] IR 1.

> relate to trading activities or to the hours during which persons may carry on business for neither of these is connected with the essentials of the concept of human personality.[187]

Walsh J. likewise held that Article 40.1 'refers to human persons for what they are in themselves rather than to any lawful activities, trades or pursuits which they may engage in or follow'.[188] Thus, the guarantee applies only to discrimination relating to some inherent aspect of the 'human person', such as ethnic, racial, social or religious background[189] – that is, persons' 'essential attributes as persons, those features which make them human beings'.[190]

119. In the EU context, Article 43 of the EC Treaty, which prohibits discrimination on the basis of nationality in the context of freedom of establishment, applies to legal persons as well as to natural persons.[191] It also bears noting that the European Court of Human Rights has accepted that Article 14 of the ECHR may be invoked by companies.[192]

120. Similarly, the Irish courts have held that property rights guaranteed under Articles 40.3 and 43.1 of the Constitution of Ireland 'cannot be construed as conferring a constitutional right on a corporate body'.[193] Thus, for example, in *Chestvale Properties Ltd v. Glackin*,[194] in which sections of Part II of the 1990 Companies Act were challenged on constitutional grounds relating to property rights, Murphy J. held that 'the absence of an individual Irish citizen asserting his own constitutional rights is fatal to the argument based on the constitutionality of the 1990 legislation'. A discordant note was struck in *Iarnrod Éireann v. Ireland*, where Keane J. expressed the view that, notwithstanding the language of Articles 40.3 and 43.1, 'artificial legal entities must also be protected by the laws of the State against unjust attacks on their property rights'.[195] There is a lack of clarity around two distinct questions that have not been fully teased out in case law, namely: Is it open to an individual member or shareholder to assert a threat to (or violation of) his or her constitutionally protected rights arising from damage to the corporation? And if so, can a further distinction be maintained between the individual's property rights as a shareholder and the corporation's property rights? The second question,

187. *Ibid.*, 31.
188. *Ibid.*, 13–14.
189. *Ibid.*
190. *Murtagh Properties v. Cleary* [1972] IR 1, 335. Aibhe O'Neill, *The Constitutional Rights of Companies*, n. 266, 259–260, expresses the view that although it has not done so explicitly, the Supreme Court appears to have edged somewhat away from this approach, while the High Court appears not to have always strictly applied the above quotations to their logical conclusion.
191. Case C-140/03, *Commission v. Hellenic Republic*, Opinion of Advocate-General Ruiz-Jarabo Colomer delivered on 7 Dec. 2004 at para. 5.
192. *Pine Valley Developments Ltd v. Ireland* (1992) 14 EHRR 319; *National & Provincial Building Society v. UK* (1997) 25 EHRR 127.
193. *Private Motorists' Provident Society v. Attorney General* [1983] IR 339, 349.
194. *Chestvale Properties Ltd v. Glackin* [1993] 3 IR 35, 45.
195. *Iarnród Éireann v. Ireland* [1996] 3 IR 321, 345–346.

in effect, asks whether, if the corporation does not enjoy the constitutional protection of property rights, would the joining of an individual member or shareholder to the potential corporate claim regarding its constitutional rights resolve the issue? This concept is questionable for reasons springing from the fundamental concept of corporate personality and, in particular, the consequences of what would effectively be the identification of an individual shareholder's interests with those of the company.[196]

121. In Ireland Article 40.6(1)(i) of the Constitution, provides that the State 'guarantees liberty for the exercise, subject to public order and morality, of … The right of the citizens to freely express their convictions and opinions'. It goes on to say:

> The education of public opinion being, however, a matter of such grave import to the common good, the State shall endeavour to ensure that the organs of public opinion, … while preserving their rightful liberty of expression, including criticism of Government policy, shall not be used to undermine public order or morality or the authority of the State.

122. In *Attorney General for England and Wales v. Brandon Books Publishers Ltd*,[197] Carroll J. held that the company had a constitutionally protected right of free expression under Article 40.6(1)(i) to publish information. Recently, the European Court of Human Rights has held in relation to a competition matter that a company is entitled to certain rights under the ECHR.[198] On this issue, the US approach[199] is the most conceptually clear, but whether it is the most doctrinally desirable is another matter.

123. Recently the Irish Supreme Court considered the same issue, namely whether particular human rights protected under the Constitution were available to companies. Although not central to the outcome of the case, the Supreme Court expressed considerable reservations regarding doctrinal developments on unenumerated rights in the Irish Constitution and effectively demurred on the question of whether there was a right to a healthy environment. Moreover, whether such a right ensured to the corporate plaintiff was an additional issue. The core question was whether the plaintiff company, *Friends of the Irish Environment CLG* had a constitutionally protected right to a healthy environment derived from a 'right to life' or a right to 'bodily integrity'. While the constitutional law issues are beyond the scope

---

196. *See Kerry Co-operative Creameries Ltd v. An Bord Bainne* [1990] ILRM 664; *O'Neill v. Ryan* [1993] ILRM 664; Ailbhe O'Neill, *The Constitutional Rights of Companies* 135 (Thomson Round Hall 2007).
197. *Attorney General for England and Wales v. Brandon Books Publishers Ltd* [1986] IR 597.
198. *See*, for example, *Societas Colas Est SA v. France* 2002-III 421; (2004) 39 EHRR 17 (holding that the right to respect for one's home under Art. 8 extended to protection of a company's head office against a search conducted without a warrant). *See* further A. Grear, *Challenging Corporate 'Humanity': Legal Disembodiment, Embodiment and Human Rights*', 7 Hum. Rights L. Rev. 511–543 (2007).
199. *See*, for example, the decision of *Nike v. Kasky* 539 US 654.

of this text, the conceptual lack of clarity regarding a corporate entity having a right to life or indeed bodily integrity or a right to a healthy environment is alarming in its own terms.[200]

VI. Corporate Personality: Statutory Exceptions

124. In addition to the judicially developed exceptions to the doctrine of corporate personality, some statutory provisions allow the fact of incorporation to be ignored with a view to identifying directors and others who may, because of their actions, incur liability for the debts of the company. The provisions are both an exception to the doctrine of corporate personality and a removal of limited liability.

A. Fraudulent and Reckless Trading

125. Under the fraudulent and reckless trading provisions in the Irish Companies Acts 1963–2006, the courts had the discretion to impose personal liability in certain circumstances. These provisions have been re-enacted in section 610 of the Companies Act 2014. The criminal offence of fraudulent trading, that is, where 'any person was knowingly part to the carrying on of any business of the company with intent to defraud creditors of the company, or creditors of any other person or for any fraudulent purpose' has also been re-enacted in section 722 of the Companies Act 2014. The section applies to directors and others, including shadow directors, and even to outside parties – in effect, anyone who is party to carrying on the business of the company as described above.

126. Judicial interpretation of the 1963 Act, the later enactment of this provision in the 1990 and the 2014 Companies Acts, and similar English provisions provide guidance on what amounts to fraudulent trading. It is clear that there must be an intention to defraud; the respondent must be knowingly a party to the conduct. As stated by Maugham J. in *Re Patrick and Lyon Ltd*,[201] the provisions require evidence of 'actual dishonesty involving, according to current notions of fair trading among commercial men, real moral blame'.[202] The court can impose personal liability on the respondents for all or any of the debts of the company. In *Re Aluminium Fabricators Ltd*,[203] O'Hanlon J. imposed personal liability following evidence of diversion of company funds for personal use by the directors. In *Re Kelly's Carpetdrome Ltd*,[204] Costello J. imposed personal liability on individuals who were not described as directors of the company. In fact, no formalities whatsoever had been

200. *Friends of the Irish Enviroment v. Government of Ireland and Ors.* [2020] IESC 49.
201. *Re Patrick and Lyon Ltd* [1933] Ch. 786.
202. This statement is considered to be closer to what is required than the behaviour described in earlier statements by the same judge in *Re William C. Leitch* [1932] All ER 71, [1932] All ER 892.
203. *Re Aluminium Fabricators Ltd* [1984] ILRM 399. O'Hanlon J. imposed personal liability following evidence of diversion of company funds for personal use by the directors.
204. *Re Kelly's Carpetdrome Ltd* (unreported, High Court, Costello J., 1 Jul. 1983). See also *Monck Properties Ltd v. Gaynor and Tuffy* (unreported, High Court, O'Hanlon J., 13 Jul. 1984).

complied with, and there was evidence of destruction of records and other evidence of irregular behaviour. In *Re Hunting Lodges Ltd*,[205] the respondents were respectively a director, a nominal director (spouse) and an outsider who transacted with the company and assisted in non-disclosure of the full value of assets. All of them were found personally liable to varying degrees by the Court, which exercised its discretion in accordance with its view of the culpability of the individual.[206]

127. Where a criminal charge of fraudulent trading is prosecuted, section 722 of the Companies Act 2014 provides that this is a Category 1 offence. Such offences carry the following penalties under the provisions of the Companies Act 2014, section 871:

(a) on summary conviction, … a class A fine or imprisonment for a term not exceeding 12 months or both, or
(b) on conviction on indictment, … a fine not exceeding €500,000 or imprisonment for a term not exceeding 10 years or both.

128. Despite the fact that this provision for criminal liability has been on the statute books since 1963, there have been very few criminal convictions on charges of fraudulent trading. In the first case,[207] the defendant sought investors for an investment scheme, promising annual returns of up to 20%. The money received was never invested; instead, it was put into a bank account. The defendant was imprisoned for four years and disqualified from acting as a director. In the second case,[208] on a plea of guilty, a director of a company in liquidation was convicted of fraudulent trading for failing to keep proper books of account and failing to file annual returns; the director received two concurrent sentences of six months, suspended for twelve months, in respect of the charges of fraudulent trading and failing to keep proper books.

129. The reckless trading provisions were introduced in Irish law under section 137 of the 1990 Companies Act inserting a redrafted section 297 into the 1963 Act. This is now repeated in section 610(1)(a) of the Companies Act 2014. The provision was introduced following the UK Cork Committee Report on insolvency, which, *inter alia,* recommended such a reform in light of the inadequacy of the fraudulent trading provisions. In the UK Insolvency Act of 1986, this is reflected in the imposition of a somewhat similar liability for 'wrongful trading'.[209] Section 610(1)(a) provides for civil liability only; there is no provision for criminal liability in respect of reckless trading in Irish law. Section 610(3) provides that an officer of a company shall be deemed to have been knowingly a party to the carrying on of any business of the company in a reckless manner if:

---

205. *Re Hunting Lodges Ltd* [1985] ILRM 75. In contrast *see Re PSK Construction Ltd* [2009] IEHC 538 where the partner of the main director was treated quite leniently in comparison.
206. *See infra*, Part I, Ch. 1 §4 on liability of nominal directors etc., §3.II.
207. *D.P.P. v. Synott* (unreported, Circuit Court, 7 May 1996).
208. *Director of Corporate Enforcement v. Gannon* (Naas District Court, 18 Mar. 2004); *see The Irish Times*, 19 Mar. 2004.
209. Insolvency Act 1986, s. 214 (UK).

(a) he was a party to the carrying on of such business and, having regard to the general knowledge, skill and experience that may reasonably be expected of a person in his position, he ought to have known that his actions or those of the company would cause loss to the creditors of the company, or any of them; or

(b) he was a party to the contracting of a debt by the company and did not honestly believe on reasonable grounds that the company would be able to pay the debt when it fell due for payment as well as all its other debts (taking into account the contingent and prospective liabilities).[210]

130. Section 610(8) provides a defence to reckless trading '[w]here it appears to the Court that the person in respect of whom a declaration has been sought … has acted honestly and responsibly in relation to the conduct of the affairs of the company … the Court may, having regard to all the circumstances of the case … relieve him either wholly or in part, from personal liability on such terms as it may think fit'. This defence, based on subjective notions of honesty, seems to displace the original purpose of the legislation, which was to introduce an objective standard of directorial behaviour.

131. In *Re Hefferon Kearns Ltd.*[211] Lynch J. held the respondents were not liable and observed that a defendant must be shown to have had 'knowledge or imputed knowledge that the defendant's actions or those of the company would cause loss to creditors: it is not sufficient that there might be some worry or uncertainty as to the ability to pay all creditors'. Lynch J. held that he was not satisfied that the defendants did not honestly believe on reasonable grounds that the company would be able to pay the debt as it fell due.

132. Although there have been one or two subsequent decisions where personal liability has been imposed for reckless trading, there has been very little litigation in this area with an even smaller number of successful cases.[212]

---

210. Companies Act 1963, s. 297A(1), as inserted by Companies Act 1990, s. 137.

211. *Re Hefferon Kearns Ltd* [1992] IRLM 51; [1993] 3 IR 191. *See* generally, Irene Lynch Fannon & Gerard N. Murphy, *Corporate Insolvency and Rescue* (Bloomsbury Professional 2012) Ch. 10.

212. *Re PSK Construction Ltd* [2009] IEHC 538 where the respondent was held personally liable for debts totalling over EUR 1 million and was disqualified from being a director of a company. His partner who also worked in the company was not held liable for reckless trading with the court finding that she had relied on assurances from the main director, the liable respondent and was, it seems entitled to do so. She was however, disqualified from acting as a director. A second decision where liability was imposed is found in *Re Kelly Trucks Ltd.* [2019] IEHC 6 where the defendant directors seemed to have shifted assets out of reach of creditors in breach of particular sections of the Companies Act 2014, specifically s. 608. The court held that 'both the first and second-named respondents acted fraudulently and recklessly with a view to defrauding their creditors in relation to the business of Kelly Trucks Limited and should therefore be held personally liable without any limitation of liability for all of the creditors' debts of Kelly Trucks Limited. The court therefore consider[ed]it proper to exercise its power under s. 610 of the Companies Act 2014 to declare that James Kelly the first respondent and Anne Kelly the second respondent shall be personally responsible without any limitation of liability, for all of the debts of the company.'

133. In a more recent decision from the Court of Appeal in *Appleyard Motors*, Hogan J. found the appellants not liable for reckless trading for a number of reasons. In this case, the directors of a motor leasing company had no notice of the bank withdrawing credit when they entered into an agreement for the supply of cars to fulfil a leasing arrangement. Once such notice was received, they took steps to minimise loss and ceased trading. The directors had been found liable for reckless trading in the High Court and had appealed to the Court of Appeal. At this point, it was noted by the judge that only one director was in fact an appellant, the other having declared bankruptcy and the final director withdrawing his appeal. On interpretation of the particular legislation, the court observed that the relevant provision was a 'deeming provision' where two instances or examples of reckless trading are described as being deemed reckless trading. The use of what is regarded as a deeming provision required closer interpretative scrutiny. Accordingly, the Court held the court must be satisfied that the officer in question must have known that the actions *would* cause loss to creditors – it was not enough to prove that the officer must have known that their actions *might* cause loss. In other words, the loss must have been foreseeable with a great deal of certainty. The Supreme Court approved these observations.[213] Generally, there is a view that these provisions require attention from those involved in reforming the law as the lack of utilisation of the provisions is curious. This problem is the subject of a CLRG Report published in 2021 and some proposed changes are included in a Bill currently under consideration by the Oireachtas.[214]

B. Other Insolvency-Related Provisions

134. Sections 281–282 of the 2014 Act impose an obligation to keep adequate accounting records. Adequate accounting records are those that are sufficient to: (a) correctly record and explain the transactions of the company, (b) enable, at any time, the assets, liabilities, financial position and profit or loss of the company to be determined with reasonable accuracy, (c) enable the directors to ensure that any financial statements of the company and directors' report which are required under the Act are compliant with the Act and, where applicable, Article 4 of the IAS Regulation and (d) enable those financial statements of the company so prepared to be audited. Section 282 of the 2014 Act addresses in further detail what shall constitute adequate accounting records.

The Court may impose personal liability on officers of the company where there has been a failure to keep proper books and accounts and such failure has '(i) contributed to the company's inability to pay all of its debts, or (ii) resulted in substantial uncertainty as to the assets and liabilities of the company, or (iii) has

---

213. *Toomey Leasing v. Sedgewick [2017] IESC*; *See* further Roz Breen: 'Re Appleyard Motors Ltd; Toomey Leasing Group Ltd v. Sedgwick: Another Nail in the Coffin for Reckless Trading?' (2018) 25(9) CLP 204. *See also* Roz Breen, 'Fictions or Guidelines? The Deeming Provisions in Section 610 of the Companies Act 2014' (2019) 26(9) CLP 168.

214. www.clrg.org See further Employment (Collective Redundancies and Miscellaneous Provisions) and Companies (Amendment) Bill 2023.

substantially impeded the orderly winding up of the company'.[215] The Court shall not make such a declaration in respect of a person who it considers took 'all reasonable steps to secure compliance by the company' with the requirement to keep adequate accounting records, or who had reasonable grounds for believing that a competent and reliable person acting under the supervision of a director had been formally allocated responsibility for compliance and was in a position to discharge that duty.[216]

135. It is important to note in this regard that directors have a right to inspect the company's books and records, and this may be enforced by injunction.[217] The courts, in the case of *Re Mantruck Services Ltd, Mehigan v. Duignan*[218] and subsequent decisions, have identified the following elements as essential to an application to have officers of the company fixed with personal liability for the company's debts:

(1) The company is being wound up.
(2) The company is unable to pay debts.
(3) There is a contravention of the requirement to keep proper books and records (or 'adequate accounting records' under the 2014 Act).
(4) Such contravention has contributed to the company's inability to pay all of its debts or has resulted in substantial uncertainty as to the assets and liabilities of the company or has substantially impeded the orderly winding up of the company.
(5) The officer (or former officer) of the company knowingly and wilfully authorised or permitted the contravention by the company, or, the 'officer' is a person convicted in relation to a statement concerning the keeping of proper books of account (or adequate accounting records).
(6) The discretion to apportion personal liability to officers must be exercised in a responsible and constitutional manner. Save in exceptional circumstances, liability should not be imposed for contraventions not resulting in loss or for losses reasonably foreseeable as a consequence of the contravention.[219]

136. The final insolvency-type provision that can be described as an exception to the corporate personality doctrine is found under section 612 of the 2014 Act, which provides for misfeasance proceedings. The provision applies to promoters, officers, a liquidator, a receiver and an examiner. Potential applicants include a liquidator, creditor or contributory of a company. The Court can order restoration or contribution of funds as it thinks just. Costello J. held in the *Mount Clare Hotel* case

215. Companies Act 2014, s. 609(1).
216. Companies Act 2014, s. 609(8).
217. *Healy v. Healy Homes Ltd* [1973] IR 309.
218. *Re Mantruck Services Ltd; Mehigan v. Duignan* [1997] 1 IR 341.
219. *Ibid.*, 356–357. The sixth proposition listed is taken from the judgment of the Supreme Court in *Re Ashclad Ltd (in liquidation)* (unreported, Supreme Court, Keane C.J., *ex tempore*, 21 Jan. 2004). At first instance in that case – *Re Ashclad Ltd* [2000] IEHC 174; Geoghegan J. said he 'broadly accept[ed] the approach – adopted and the principles – applied' by Shanley J. in *Re Mantruck Services Ltd.*

that liability for misfeasance requires a showing of 'something more than mere carelessness', rising instead to 'gross negligence'.[220] There is some debate as to the nature of this provision among Irish commentators. Some view it as simply a remedy that must be accompanied by a distinct cause of action. However, others view it as a cause of action in and of itself.

137. Section 567 of the 2014 Act provides that a number of provisions of the 2014 Act, including sections 281, 282, 286, 599, 609, 610, 611 and 612, may be invoked where the company is insolvent but not wound up. However, it must be shown that the reason or the principal reason for its not being wound up is the insufficiency of its assets.

VII. Corporate Personality: Groups

A. *Introduction*

138. In relation to groups of companies, the doctrine of corporate personality usually underlines the separate and distinct nature of each company within a corporate group. However, in Ireland, as in England, a line of jurisprudence has been developed that has recognised some judicially created exceptions to this doctrine. This line of case law, together with the statutory provisions referred to *infra* will be considered further in the section on Holding Companies and Subsidiaries (*see* Part I, Chapter 1, §8).

B. *Pooling and Contribution Orders*

139. The final important statutory exception to the doctrine of corporate personality applies under sections 599 and 600 of the 2014 Act to the group situation. This legislation does not have an equivalent under English company law and is in fact similar to legislation in force in New Zealand.[221] These provisions are discussed further in relation to groups (*see infra*, Part I, Chapter 1, §8).

VIII. Conclusion

140. In conclusion of this section on corporate personality, two observations are apt. First, as we consider these cases, it is important to bear in mind that they are representatives of a class of exceptional cases; some arise in common law and some arise because of particular provisions of statutes, but all are exceptions to the general position in company law as enunciated in *Salomon*. As Davies observes, the list of these cases and instances is now 'impressively long', but he also notes that even though company lawyers (and students) have expended much effort and thought on

220. *Re Mount Clare Hotel; Jackson v. Mortell* (unreported, High Court, Costello J., 2 Dec. 1986).
221. *See Lewis Holdings Limited & Others v. Steel and Tube Holdings Limited* [2014] NZHC 3311.

these exceptions, no general explanation can be found nor indeed is there any clear unifying rule.[222] It is well to remember the orthodox starting point of *Salomon* as we get lost in this particular maze. Secondly, as far as principle is to be maintained, a statement of Richmond P. in the New Zealand case of *Re Securitibank Ltd* (*No.* 2)[223] is instructive: 'any suggested departure from the doctrine laid down in *Salomon v. A. Salomon and Co. Ltd* should be watched very carefully'. Finally, the decision of the United Kingdom Supreme Court in *Prest v. Petrodel Resources* referred to above and its approval in Ireland is of utmost importance. This is true across the common law world.

§4. Capital and Shares

I. Different Concepts of Capital

141. Parts 3 and 4 of the consolidated Companies Act 2014 govern matters pertaining to share capital. The structure of the capital provisions in this Act is the same as for other matters, namely that Parts 3 and 4 describe provisions which are applicable to private companies limited by shares, using this type of company as a default model, and then the Act disapplies certain provisions in relation to each different type of company. Of particular relevance in this part of this work is the Table provided for in section 1002 of the Companies Act 2014 which disapplies some of the private companies limited by shares provisions to PLCs. The following provisions are disapplied to PLCs:

- section 68 which limits offerings of securities to the public;
- section 69 and section 70 in relation to the authorisation for allotment of shares;
- the enabling provision relating to reduction of capital in section 84(2)(a);
- the enabling provision regarding variation of capital in section 88 is disapplied;
- the enabling provision regarding capital in reorganisations in section 91(4)(a) is disapplied.[224]

The structure of share capital in most Irish companies continues as described in the following paragraphs. There are some additional exemptions referred to above which do not apply to PLCs. These will be considered in more detail in Part 1, Chapter 11. A number of terms are commonly used in Irish corporate finance law which may not find an exact equivalence in other jurisdictions.

222. Paul L. Davies, *Introduction to Company Law: Clarendon Law Series* (Oxford University Press 2002), Ch. 3.
223. *Re Securitibank Ltd* (No. 2) [1978] 2 NZLR 136, 159.
224. Note that an amendment to s 91 of the 2014 Act was passed in s. 16 of the Companies (CEA) Act 2021 so that a transaction under the provision can proceed even if there is no reorganisation of the company's capital; and a transaction can proceed without regard to this section where the company has adequate distributable reserves.

A. *Nominal Capital*

142. Nominal or authorised capital (theoretically the maximum capital) is the face value given to a share. Shares must be given a value and this must be stated in the Memorandum of Association or Constitution.[225] There is no minimum value required for a share. The 2014 Act gives discretion to companies to increase the authorised share capital, if the Articles of Association or constitution of the company provides for this.[226]

B. *Issued Capital*

143. Issued or allotted capital is the amount of capital that has been sold or allotted by the company based on its nominal value plus any premium received on the first sale or issue.

C. *Paid Up*

144. Called-up or paid-up capital is the amount of capital which is paid and reserve capital, which is provided for under section 79 of the 2014 Act, is capital generated by issuing or allotting shares above nominal value.

D. *Authorised Capital*

145. The amount of capital which the company's constitution has authorised initially, meaning the number of shares which have been authorised as part of the company's capital structure.

II. Alteration of Capital Requirements

A. *Introduction*

146. The following sections on changes to capital requirements concern the rules relating to both the increase of share capital and the reduction of share capital, including redemption of shares. These provisions also concern obligations imposed on companies concerning the maintenance of capital (generally considered to be for the benefit of creditors in particular). In the new structure provided for in the Companies Act 2014, a number of changes were introduced including the following.

225. Companies Act 2014, s. 1006.
226. Companies Act 2014, s. 83.

147. Private companies limited by shares may opt to state the amount of authorised share capital from the outset or may opt not to state that amount, but to state that the share capital of the company shall be divided into shares of a fixed amount as stated in the constitution – section 19(1)(d) Companies Act 2014.

148. Where a company does have a capital structure (which will be the case in all PLCs but will occur in private companies also), company capital is now defined in section 64(1) to include the following:

(a) the aggregate value, expressed in currency, of the consideration received by a company in respect of the allotment of shares and
(b) that part of the company's 'undenominated' capital constituted by transfer of sums referred to in ss 106 (4) and 108(3).

The definition continues in a supplemental provision which includes in the definition the following:

(i) amounts standing in the share premium account where premiums on previous share sales have been lodged;
(ii) capital redemptions reserve funds; and
(iii) capital conversion reserve funds pre-existing the legislation.

149. However, it became apparent that there were a 'number of perceived anomalies and other issues which arose regarding share capital included in the reforms introduced in the 2014 Act'. The CLRG established a particular review committee to consider these and it issued a report on these matters in 2017.[227] Some of these recommendations are included in the Companies (Corporate Enforcement Authority) Act 2021.[228] Although it may seem strange that alterations to the rules on capital and shares are contained in an Act primarily related to corporate enforcement, this is simply a matter of expediency in terms of legislative time.

150. In keeping with these new definitions, terminology in the legislation has changed. For example, the capital maintenance rules discussed below now explicitly refer to the concept of company capital rather than to share capital as in the previous legislation. In addition, the new provisions regarding reduction of capital contained in section 84 refer to 'company capital' and not share capital as before. The new legislation attempts to clarify the application of these rules to various kinds of capital received as a result of equity sales.

227. The Recommendations of the CLRG relating to Shares and Share Capital in the Companies Act 2014. CLRG 2017. www.clrg.org.
228. The range of amendments are technical in nature and thus outside the scope of this monograph. *See* further the above Report and the Companies (Corporate Enforcement Authority) Act 2021.

B. Variation in Capital

151. The starting point regarding the variation of share capital is section 83 of the 2014 Act. The section provides that a company may, except to the extent that its constitution provides otherwise, do a number of things regarding its capital structure including consolidation or division of shares, subdividing shares, reducing or increasing nominal value and increasing or cancelling shares. This provision is not disapplied in Part 17 and so also applies to PLCs. These matters can be effected by ordinary resolution.

C. Increase in Share Capital

152. Section 83(1)(f) provides that a company may increase its share capital by 'new shares of such amount as it thinks expedient'. This can be done by ordinary resolution.[229]

153. Irish PLCs may offer equity securities and debt securities for sale to the public. Under the Companies Act 2014, a new distinction is now made between private companies limited by shares on the one hand (these companies are prohibited from offering any type of security on a public market) and on the other hand, designated activity companies (DACs) – these are private companies limited by shares with designated activities specified in their constitution. DACs are permitted to list debt securities on a public market. This facility is also available to companies limited by guarantee (CLGs), private unlimited companies (PUCs) and public unlimited companies (PULCs). There is a significant volume of trading on the Irish Stock Exchange of debt securities.[230]

III. Preferential Right of Subscription

154. In relation to the allotment of existing authorised share capital, the statutory provisions relating to a private company are found in section 69 of the 2014 Act. This provision, however, is disapplied to PLCs under the table in section 1002 and accordingly, section 1021 of the Act applies to allotment of shares in a PLC. Section 1021 provides that the allotment of securities must be pursuant to a general authority granted by ordinary resolution or the constitution of the company and further provides that this authority will provide for a maximum number of securities which can be allotted and that the authority must be specified for a time not exceeding five years. Initially, the allotment can only be within the authorised share capital provisions.[231] The decision to allot shares will be made by the Board of Directors on the basis of a general authority as described. The authority to allot may be limited to a period which is renewable under section 1021(4)(3).

229. Section 83(1).
230. The Irish Stock Exchange describes itself as the 'leading European debt listing venue'.
231. Companies Act 2014, s. 1021(2).

155. Where allotments of authorised share capital are made, statutory pre-emption rights will apply (preferential rights of subscription). This is the right which shareholders have to be offered new shares on a pro rata basis, relative to their existing holding when the company engages in a new issue and allotment of shares. Pre-emption rights are now enshrined in legislation as a default rule in section 1022 for PLCs and in section 69(6) for private limited companies subject to certain instances in which they do not apply in PLCs. This will include the normal rule allowing directors who have a general power to allot shares following a special resolution under section 1021 of the Act to disregard pre-emption rights as provided for in section 1023(3).

156. Litigation on this issue regarding the abolition or abrogation of pre-emption rights is still relevant. In the second hearing in *Greenhalgh*,[232] the plaintiff sought to set aside a special resolution rejecting the pre-emption rights of the shareholders prior to the sale of a controlling interest to an outsider. The plaintiff's argument was that the shareholders, in voting for the removal of pre-emption rights, had not acted 'bona fide for the benefit of the company as a whole'. The Court held that on any particular vote, a shareholder must proceed on the basis of what he honestly believes is for the benefit of the company as a whole and that the latter phrase ordinarily does not mean the company as a commercial entity as distinct from its corporators, but rather the corporators as a general body. The Court was satisfied that the resolution in this case had been passed *bona fide*. This reasoning would apply to the abrogation of pre-emption rights on a sale or allotment.

157. When different classes of shares are created and offered, further rules apply in relation to the protection of those existing shareholders. Shareholders must consent *by class* to the alteration of the Articles of Association, now the constitution of the company. Established case law provides a narrower interpretation of when shareholders' rights are altered than one might first imagine. Thus, in the English case of *Greenhalgh v. Arderne Cinemas*,[233] (a second hearing in the case is referred to in the preceding paragraph) the plaintiff held 40% of the pre-existing class of two shilling shares and argued that the proposed split by the company of each ten shilling share (hitherto in a separate class) into five two shilling shares was an alteration of his rights, thus requiring consent of the class of two shilling shares (which he would have been in a position to withhold, given his percentage). The court held that despite the effective swamping of the plaintiff's existing holding of 40% of the two shilling shares, there was no variation of his rights per se. The plaintiff's rights had not been varied, only the context in which they were exercised.

232. *Greenhalgh v. Arderne Cinemas Ltd.* [1951] Ch. 286. Note that the series of actions pre-date the introduction of the equivalent of a right of a shareholder to sue for oppression which is now part of English company law. Section 459 Companies Act 1985 and its re-enactment in s. 994 of the Companies Act 2006).

233. *Greenhalgh v. Arderne Cinemas* (No. 1) [1946] 1 All ER 512.

IV. Issues of Shares at a Premium and at a Discount

158. Under the 1983 Act, and now under the Companies Act 2014, considerable improvements were made to the maintenance of the capital fund provisions; in particular, significant clarity was provided in relation to the operation of these provisions. As a rule, the relevant provisions in the Companies Act 2014 apply primarily to public companies with exemptions provided for private companies.

A. *Issuing of Shares at a Discount*

159. The common law rule regarding the prohibition on issuing shares at a discount provided for in the House of Lords decision in *Ooregum Gold Mining Company of India v. Roper* is now provided for in section 71 of the 2014 Act. An exempting provision allows for the payment of a commission of not more than 10% to facilitate the underwriting of an issue of shares, but indications are that this would be strictly interpreted, following English case law. This rule will not prevent the issuing of bonus shares within the terms of Part 3 of the 2014 Act.

B. *The Share Premium Account*

160. Where shares are issued at a price above the nominal value of the shares, the difference between the nominal or par and the market value is referred to as the 'share premium'. Section 71(5) seeks to protect capital by providing that where a company issues shares at a price in excess of the share's nominal value, whether for cash or otherwise, a sum equal to the value of the excess capital will be included in the definition of the 'company capital' as described above. This is now described as being part of the 'undenominated capital'. As stated in the introductory paragraph, the 'company capital' will also include amounts standing in the share premium account where premiums on previous share sales have been lodged, and will also include capital redemption reserve funds and capital conversion reserve funds. This rule regarding the share premium account is subject to some specific provisions contained in sections 72, 73 and 75 regarding mergers, group restructurings and share swaps. So, for example, section 72(2) provides that 'if the equity shares in the issuing company allotted … in consideration for the acquisition or cancellation of shares in the other company … (ie a share swap or exchange) … are issued at a premium s. 71(5) does not apply … ' to those premiums. In this context, section 106(4) and section 108(3) provide for the different treatment of premiums raised during the acquisition or redemption of its own shares by a company.

C. *Payment for Shares in Non-Cash Consideration*

161. As stated, most of the Irish provisions on capital maintenance are now derived from EU Directives. Under the 1983 Act, the following provisions were enacted pursuant to the Second EC Company Law Directive regarding the issuing or distribution of shares for consideration, in particular for non-cash consideration. The 1983 Act has now been repealed and these provisions have been re-enacted in Part 3 of the Companies Act 2014. In providing that a share allotment may be paid for in non-cash consideration, section 71(1) recognises a common law principle of long-standing.

162. However, prohibitions apply to public limited companies (PLCs) as before, although these are now contained in separate provisions in Part 17 of the Act in keeping with the revised structure of the Irish legislation. Thus, section 1025(1) provides that:

> 'A PLC shall not accept at any time, in payment up of its shares or any premium on them, an undertaking given by any person that he or she or another should do work or perform services for the company or any other person.'

163. Regard should also be had to section 1027 of the 2014 Act, which provides as follows:

> (1) A PLC shall not allot shares as fully or partly paid up (as to their nominal value or any premium payable on them) otherwise than in cash if the consideration for the allotment is or includes an undertaking which is to be or may be performed more than five years after the date of the allotment.

164. Sections 1028 and 1029 and sections 1031 and 1033 of the 2014 Act provide certain controls regarding the independent valuation of non-cash consideration in all other cases and these are discussed in the section on Promoters. Effectively these sections are a re-enactment of the 1983 Act which, in turn, was derived from provisions of EU Directives. Accordingly, the provisions are enacted to take account of any developments since that time. In particular provisions of the Investment Funds, Companies and Miscellaneous Provisions Acts 2005 and 2006.

V. Public Issue Requirements, Prospectuses and Promoters

A. *Prospectus*

165. A prospectus is defined in section 2 of the 2014 Act as:

> a document or documents in such form and containing such information as may be required by or under Irish prospectus law or EU prospectus law (within the meaning of Chapter 1 of Part 23 [of the 2014 Act]), howsoever the document or documents are constituted, but does not include any advertisements in newspapers or journals derived from the foregoing.

A prospectus will be used by a company in an issue of new shares when the company is already quoted on the stock market. A prospectus will also be used in a 'flotation', sometimes now referred to as initial public offerings (IPOs), in which the company is being floated on the market for the first time, having been a private company. A third instance is when a company is 'privatized'– that is, when the shares were largely or entirely state-owned but are now being offered to the public through the stock market. Once a company issues a prospectus involving an offer of shares to the public, there are certain obligations attached to disclosure of information about the company's affairs to the public. These obligations, described initially in the Companies Act 1963 and later overhauled by Investment Funds, Companies and Miscellaneous Provisions Act 2005 (the '2005 Act'), Part 5 (as amended further by an Act of the same name in 2006) and the Prospectus Directive (2003/71/EC) Regulations 2005 (S.I. 324 of 2005), are now to be found in Part 23 of the 2014 Act.

166. Section 1349 of the 2014 Act provides that certain persons shall be liable 'to pay compensation to all persons who acquire any securities on the faith of a prospectus for the loss or damage they may have sustained by reason of – (a) any untrue statement included therein; or (b) any omission of information required by EU prospectus law to be contained in the prospectus'. The persons liable for any such misstatements or omissions are:

(i) the issuer who has issued the prospectus or on whose behalf the prospectus has been issued;
(ii) the offeror of securities to which the prospectus relates;
(iii) every person who has sought the admission of the securities to which the prospectus relates to trading on a regulated market;
(iv) the guarantor of the issue of securities to which the prospectus relates;
(v) every person who is a director of the issuer at the time of the issue of the prospectus;
(vi) every person who has authorised himself or herself to be named and is named in the prospectus as a director of the issuer or as having agreed to become such a director either immediately or after an interval of time;
(vii) every person who is a promoter of the issuer;
(viii) every person who has authorised the issue of the prospectus (not being the competent authority designated under Irish prospectus law).

Section 1348(6) of the 2014 Act excludes professional advisers (and underwriters and professional advisers to underwriters) from the definition of a 'promoter,' or person authorising the issue of a prospectus.

167. Defences available focus primarily on a defendant's state of knowledge or position in relation to the information provided in the prospectus. So a defence is available when there is a reasonable belief in the truth of statements in a prospectus under section 1350 of the 2014 Act. A defence is available for a director where consent to be a director is withdrawn. Similarly, a defence is available to any individual who withdraws consent to a prospectus or when a prospectus was issued without a person's knowledge or consent; or where without a person's knowledge or consent, a prospectus contained a false statement or omitted required material; or where untrue statements or omissions are based on expert advice and believed to be properly included or omitted. Section 1353 of the 2014 Act requires consent from any expert to statements made in a prospectus purporting to be made by such an expert. Special exceptions apply to a prospectus issued solely in respect of non-equity securities. In all cases, consent must be in writing and not withdrawn before the issue of the prospectus, and a statement to this effect must be in the prospectus.

168. Section 1357 of the 2014 Act provides for criminal liability and sanctions for persons authorising the issue of a prospectus that includes any untrue statement or omits any information required by EU prospectus law, unless he or she proves (i) as regards an untrue statement, that it was immaterial or he or she honestly believed it to be true, or (ii) as regards any information omitted, that it was immaterial or he or she did not know it, or (iii) that the making of the statement or omission ought reasonably be excused.

B. Promoters

169. In Irish company law, the term 'promoter' refers to an individual who forms and establishes a company and its business. In the PLC context, a promoter may well be someone who has been involved with the business of the company while it operated as a private company or may become involved in reforming the company as a PLC with a view to bringing the company to the market. A promoter may also be the person who establishes a company in which he or she transfers a business hitherto conducted on a sole trader basis. In common law, a promoter was defined as 'one who undertakes to form a company with reference to a given project and to set it going and who takes the necessary steps to accomplish that purpose'.

170. As a promoter, an individual owes a range of duties that can be divided into two broad categories: first, the duty which he or she owes to the company as fiduciary and, second, the duties which he or she may owe to investors on foot of prospectuses, where this arises. However, as we have seen in the above discussion on prospectuses, such obligations in relation to prospectuses are obviously not confined to promoters alone. In relation to the first category of duties, the promoter is identified as occupying a position of trust not dissimilar to that occupied by company directors. In this capacity, the promoter is fixed with a similar range of fiduciary obligations which the law attaches to directors and others who occupy similar positions of trust. These duties will be considered in considerable detail in the sections on directors, but in essence, fiduciaries are prohibited from placing themselves in a position where their interests conflict with those of the company. They are prohibited from making undisclosed profits at the expense of their companies and must disclose any profits they make by virtue of their positions of trust. As Sealy and Worthington note, 'The principles of fiduciary obligations are rules applied by the courts of equity to impose high standards of selfless conduct upon trustees and others, such as agents and solicitors, who undertake responsibility to look after their interests or handle the property of others. Company promoters and company directors are subject to these rules.'

171. Older cases involving a promoter who seeks to sell an asset to a newly formed company, with the money for the transaction being raised from a public flotation of the company's shares include *Re Darby*,[234] a case of outright fraud, and *Gluckstein v. Barnes*,[235] where the full benefit of a transaction accruing to the promoters was not disclosed. In both cases, the promoters were held to have breached their fiduciary duties to the company. Nowadays, cases of a two-stage transaction, in which an asset is sold to the company and the money to pay for it is raised from an unsuspecting investing public (as occurred in *Gluckstein* and *Re Darby*), are less likely to occur as the second stage of the transaction, the raising of money from the investing public through the issue of a prospectus, is now heavily regulated. Nevertheless, the first stage of the transaction, the selling of an asset either at an overvalue or without full disclosure of the promoter's interest is still governed by fiduciary principles. These cases are rare, but an Irish case illustrating the operation of these principles is the decision of the High Court in *Hopkins v. Shannon Transport Systems Ltd.*[236] Thus, although aspects of the older cases that involve making offers of shares to the public are rendered obsolete by modern-day regulation of the securities market, these principles remain relevant in relation to the obligations imposed on promoters regarding the acquisition and sale of property to their companies, whether these companies are public or private. It bears emphasising though that, as with the breach of directors' duties, disclosure and ratification by the shareholders may save the promoter from liability. As Phillimore J. stated in *Re Darby*, 'if disclosure had taken place the transaction might have stood'. Some discussion of what amounts to adequate disclosure has arisen in older cases such as *Erlanger v. New Sombrero Co.*[237] and *Lagunas Nitrate Co. v. Lagunas Syndicate*,[238] but perhaps decisions of the courts in relation to disclosure by directors might be more apt as they are generally more recent.

172. In cases regarding transactions between promoters and their companies, there are some modern statutory provisions that regulate these kinds of transactions. (*See supra*, Part I, Chapter 1, §4 III regarding the transfer and allotment of shares for a detailed discussion of these provisions.) These provisions – sections 71, 1027, 1028 and 1035 of the 2014 Act – do not specifically relate to the duties of promoters alone, but regulate the kind of transaction often entered into by a promoter when he or she seeks to transfer property into his or her newly formed company. The provisions only apply to PLCs and so would arise on the transfer of property to a newly floated PLC in return for consideration that involves shares or in return for other kinds of consideration. (These provisions would apply to the factual scenarios in the *Gluckstein* and *Darby* cases outlined *supra*.) Nowadays a more difficult problem is presented by the activities of a promoter that might involve the sale of shares in a company to the public, activities of a kind that were central to the frauds perpetrated in the *Darby* and *Gluckstein* cases.

---

234. *Re Darby, ex parte Brougham* [1911] 1 KB 95.
235. *Gluckstein v. Barnes; Re Olympia Ltd, Ex Parte Gluckstein* [1900] AC 240.
236. *Hopkins v. Shannon Transport Systems Ltd* (unreported, High Court, Pringle J. 10 Jul. 1972).
237. *Erlanger v. New Sombrero Co.* (1878) 3 App Cas 1218.
238. *Lagunas Nitrate Co. v. Lagunas Syndicate*, (1889) 2 Ch. 392.

VI. Stock Exchange Introduction Requirements

173. The section on Prospectuses §4 V A *supra* is relevant to this matter. Furthermore, sections 71, 1027, 1028 and 1034 of the 2014 Act deal with the allotment of shares to individuals at flotation point or where there may be second and third issues and allotment of shares during the course of the life of the company. These provisions seek to capture the worst sort of excesses sometimes seen in relation to the allotment or issue of shares for worthless or over-valued consideration. Section 71 of the 2014 Act provides that shares may be paid up in money or money's worth (including goodwill and expertise) but shares shall not be allotted at a discount on their nominal value. However, as described, this provision applies to private companies limited by shares. In contrast, the provisions regarding PLCs are much more strict. The following is a summary and recaps some information included above:

- Section 1027 of the 2014 Act prohibits the company from accepting as payment for shares any consideration that involves an undertaking to be performed outside five years from the date of allotment.
- Section 1028 of the 2014 Act provides that any non-cash consideration for shares, such as property, must be independently valued.
- Section 1034 of the 2014 Act provides that any transaction within two years of incorporation of a PLC where the original subscriber or member sells a non-cash asset for over one-tenth of the nominal value of the entire issued share capital to a company must be independently valued.

A. Additional Market Requirements

174. In addition to these provisions of statutory company law, listing or entry in the Irish stock exchange is also governed by rules set by the Stock Exchange itself. Currently, the Irish Stock Exchange is operated by Euronext and listing details and requirements for equities are available on the website under a section entitled IPO (Initial Public Offering) Journey https://www.euronext.com/en/raise-capital/how-go-public/ipo-journey. Although not centrally relevant to this monograph, the Irish Exchange is also a central listing site for debt or bond securities and the Euronext website describes itself as 'The world's leading bond listing venue.' Details for entry requirements are available here.

VII. Forbidden Reductions of Capital and Acquisition of Shares by the Corporation Itself

175. The phrase 'maintenance of capital' or 'capital maintenance' is used in common law to describe the practices mentioned in this heading. Irish company law contains a number of rules regarding the maintenance of capital. The sources of these rules are varied: some derive from principles originally set out in case law, some of which have been codified in statute, while others derive from more modern statutory provisions (including in particular, the enactment of EU Directives). In all cases, the statutory provisions are subject to judicial interpretation. The theoretical rationale for capital maintenance rules is primarily to protect creditors from dilution of the capital fund and to secure the integrity of the capital value of the company for all. This is particularly important in the context of creditors' remedies. The minimum capital requirement for a PLC in Ireland is currently set at EUR 25,000.[239] of which a quarter must be paid up before the company commences business, and this must be stated in the memorandum as part of the constitution of the company but in Ireland, as with the UK, there is no minimum capital requirement for private companies or indeed no requirement at all for a private limited company to state an authorised share capital under section 19 of the 2014 Act. Generally, these rules are driven by provisions of EC Directives.[240] Nevertheless, statutory provisions will apply even in this case or even where there are few creditors or shareholders.[241] Thus, in private companies, the rules are relevant even in companies with little or no issued capital. The capital maintenance rules generally have the following aims:

- Ensuring value is maintained in the company by ensuring that the company receives value for its shares. This objective is served by provisions such as those prohibiting the issuing of shares at a discount, provisions regarding the maintenance of the share premium account and provisions regarding the valuation of consideration paid for shares, in particular non-cash consideration.
- Ensuring that a stated capital structure is not changed without the consent or authorisation of shareholders and without the knowledge of creditors. Such provisions include provisions regarding redemption or purchase by a company of its own shares and provisions regarding the alteration or reduction of share capital.
- Protecting the company's working capital, which includes provisions regarding the payment of dividends by a company or other kinds of distribution of a company's profits.[242]
- Section 84 of the Companies Act 2014 states that the capital maintenance rules apply to the reduction of 'company capital' (defined above) and not 'share capital' as stated by the provisions of the 1963 Act.

A. *Acquisition by a Company of Its Own Shares*

176. The prohibitions regarding a company acquiring its own shares are now contained in Chapter 6 of Part 3 of the Companies Act 2014. A company cannot acquire its own shares unless the transaction is one of the transactions described therein. The original provision in Irish law (provided for in the 1963 Act) enacted the general prohibition provided for at common law in the House of Lords decision in *Trevor v. Whitworth*,[243] which held that the acquisition of its own shares by a

239. Section 1000(2).

240. *See* Ch. 2 on the Private Company and new provisions which provide more flexibility in this context for private limited companies.

241. *See* generally Keane, *Company Law* (4th edn., Tottel 2007), Ch. 15. *See* Courtney: The Law of Companies Courtney: Paras [10.001]–[10.010].

242. Part 3, Ch. 7 ss 117ff Companies Act 2014. Courtney: The Law of Companies (Bloomsbury Professional, 2012) paras [8.073]–[8.078] pp. 450–453 and [10.089]–[10.096]. pp. 601–604, 606.

243. (1887) 12 App. Cas. 409.

company was *ultra vires* and therefore void. The decision also held that this was the case regardless of whether, as in this case, it was authorised by the objects. The authorisation was invalid. As Lord Watson observed, creditors and others who deal with a company 'rely upon the fact that the company is dealing with a certain amount of capital already paid up, as well as the responsibility of its members for capital remaining at call; and they are entitled to assume that no part of the capital which has been paid into the coffers of the company has been subsequently paid out, except in the legitimate course of its business'.[244]

177. The development of the legislative rules in this context has now tended towards a liberalisation of the rule as traditionally set out in the case law. The liberalisation of the general prohibition outlined in *Trevor v. Whitworth* began with the recognition that a limited company could reduce its capital by special resolution if so authorised by its articles. Accordingly, section 102(1)[245] of the 2014 Act states somewhat more positively that: 'Subject to the provisions of this Chapter a company may acquire its own fully paid shares' and goes on to list when this can occur. These include:

(i) transfer or surrender otherwise than for valuable consideration;
(ii) cancellation following reduction of capital;
(iii) as a remedy for oppression under section 212;
(iv) redemption of shares;
(v) permissible purchase under section 105;
(vi) redemption of preference shares under section 108; or
(vii) pursuant to a merger or division under Chapters 3 and 4 of Part 9.

The provision goes on to state in subsection (2) that '… a company may not acquire any of its own shares otherwise than as described in the preceding subsection …'. Very importantly this provision also states (although already included above) that 'nothing in that subsection or any other provision of this section affects the lawfulness of a merger effected in accordance with Chapter 3 of Part 9 or a scheme of arrangement sanctioned under that Part'.[246]

178. The shift away from the stringency of the common law approach began in earnest in 1983 where following the Second EU Company Law Directive, the range of exemptions from the general rule against a company acquiring its shares expanded to the exemptions which are now included in section 102 of the Companies Act 2014 as described above.

244. *Ibid.*, pp. 423–424.
245. Section 1039 Adaptation of s. 102(1) and (2) in relation to a PLC. 'Section 102(1) and (2) shall apply in relation to a PLC as if references in them to Chapter 3 or 4 of Part 9 were references to *Chapter 16,* or as the case may be, *Chapter 17* of this part.' These Chapters of Part 17 relate to divisions and mergers.
246. *See* below s. 7 on Mergers and Acquisitions including Reconstructions.

179. Under Irish law, further facilitating provisions were enacted in Part XI of the Companies Act 1990 and these facilitating provisions are re-enacted in the Companies Act 2014. Section 102 provides the list of situations where this is permissible. The provisions relevant to capital concern the cancellation of shares following reduction of capital; redemption of shares and the purchase of shares under section 105.

180. Section 105 of the Act provides power to a company to acquire its shares by purchase. A company may also redeem or purchase its shares which were issued as redeemable shares. The provisions of section 105 relating to funds available to purchase such shares must be complied with. There is also a provision for the cancellation of these shares, or alternatively, there is provision for the holding of such shares as 'treasury shares' under section 106 of the Act. In addition to these provisions, supplemental provisions regarding PLCs are provided for in Part 17 Chapter 5. Section 1071 provides 'Additional (general) provisions relating to acquisition by PLCs of own shares.' Section 1072 makes a distinction between 'market' and 'off-market' purchase of shares and the provisions reflect that distinction. Section 1074 provides for the market purchase of its shares by a company, once authorised by the company by ordinary resolution in a general meeting. Section 1074(4) outlines the terms of the authorisation from the members, which can be quite general in nature, but which must specify the number of shares that can be acquired, the maximum and minimum price to be paid, and the period of the authorisation which shall not be longer than five years.[247]

181. Section 1075 mirrors the provisions of section 105 regarding the authorisation of 'off-market' purchases of shares, which will obviously be more pertinent to private companies. This requires authorisation by the shareholders in a general meeting through a special resolution. A significant feature of these provisions is the notification provision toward the end of the relevant part of the legislation. Section 112 provides for copies of the contracts regarding either kind of purchase (market or off-market) to be kept at the registered office of the company for a period of ten years and provides that these must be available for inspection by any member or, in the case of a public company, by any member of the public. In the same vein, section 116 provides for returns of such purchases to be made to the Registrar of Companies.

182. These obligations are amplified for PLCs under sections 1079, 1080 and 1081 where the latter section imposes obligations regarding the notification of the 'authorised market operator'. Non-compliance with the provisions attracts criminal liability as specified in the legislation. Failure to notify the Registrar is a Category 3 offence under section 116(3) and failure to notify the market operator is similarly a Category 3 offence under section 1081(4).

247. *See* s. 1074(4)(c). Readers are advised to consult Part 17 Ch. 5, generally, where specific detailed provisions are contained relating to PLC actions in this context.

B. Reduction of Share Capital

183. Although obviously involving a change in the capital structure of the company, provisions regarding the reduction of share capital are usually considered with the body of rules regarding capital maintenance. These matters are addressed in Part 3, Chapter 4 of the 2014 Act. Certain provisions are disapplied in relation to PLCs.

184. Section 84 of the 2014 Act deals with the reduction of share capital arising from a simple alteration of capital structure. Section 84(2) provides that such reduction can be effected either by the company:

(a) employing the Summary Approval Procedure (SAP); or
(b) passing a special resolution that is confirmed by the court.

185. However, the SAP is disapplied for PLCs. Where PLCs wish to reduce their capital, they must use the more formal procedure provided for in section 84(2)(b). Where shareholders in different classes are treated differently, the consent of each class is required, in addition to the approval of the general meeting.[248] These resolutions must then be confirmed by the Court. In considering an application to approve the reduction of share capital, the Court will consider: whether the reduction is fair and equitable and whether shareholders in the same class are treated similarly. The creditor protection element is strong here, and so the legislation provides that creditors must be notified and may object at the relevant court hearing where the proposed reduction of share capital involves either diminution of liability in respect of unpaid share capital or the payment to any shareholder of any paid-up share capital.[249] In other cases where no payments are being made to shareholders – that is, where the capital structure is being altered to reflect reality – the Court may direct that the provisions just noted as to creditors' entitlements to notification and to object shall not apply as regards any class or classes of creditors.[250]

186. If no such authorisation is to be found in the company's articles, a general meeting must pass separate special resolutions providing authorisation and approving the specific proposed purchase. Before the Court confirms a reduction of share capital, it must be satisfied that the resolution was passed bona fide and that the reduction is fair, equitable and reasonable as between the shareholders generally and as between any different classes of shareholders. A reduction will be regarded as fair and reasonable when the same order of priorities is followed as would be obtained in a winding up. Furthermore, following the order of priorities as would apply on a winding up means that the reduction does not constitute a variation of class rights, such as having to be approved by different classes of shareholders.[251]

248. *Re John Power and Sons Ltd* [1934] IR 412.
249. Companies Act 2014, s. 84. *See also* Companies Act 2014, s. 83.
250. *Ibid.*
251. Companies Act 2014, s. 85(4).

C. The Provision of Financial Assistance for the Purchase of Its Own Shares

187. Such transactions are generally prohibited under section 82 of the Companies Act 2014. Again, there is a blanket prohibition for PLCs, but an exemption is provided for private companies where the conditions as set out in the legislation are followed. These provisions have been included in the SAP. The blanket prohibition applicable to PLCs provides that a company cannot give financial assistance for the purchase of its own shares. Prohibited financial assistance includes loans, guarantees from the company to potential purchasers and security from its assets to secure loans entered into between a bank and the purchaser, for example, and any other securitised transactions. These provisions apply to any transaction that displays these characteristics.[252] For a PLC, there are some limited exceptions that address specific situations, covering such matters as payment of dividends, discharge of lawfully incurred debts and lending by financial institutions in the ordinary course of business, but generally, these transactions are prohibited.[253]

188. The consequences of the section being contravened are severe as the transaction is 'voidable', and thus unenforceable, 'at the instance of the company against any person (whether a party to the transaction or not) who had notice of the facts which constitute [the] breach'.[254] There has been considerable case law in relation to whether the party has notice of the transaction or not, the required notice must be actual and not constructive in any way. However, in more recent case law, such as the decision in *CH (Ireland) Inc. v. Credit Suisse Canada*,[255] the courts have been less sympathetic to parties who failed to appreciate the significance of various pieces of information available in the course of the transaction. As observed by McCracken J. in that case, there was a clear statement of a particular fact that directly informed CSC of the nature of the transaction, namely that the transaction amounted to a breach of company law. In these circumstances, the Court cannot protect parties who may not have appreciated the legal significance of the facts disclosed. In addition, where a company gives financial assistance in breach of section 82, there is a provision for criminal liability whereby 'every officer of the company who is in default' shall be liable to conviction of an offence. Following a particular transaction involving movements by Anglo-Irish Bank (prior to its collapse and ultimate liquidation post-financial crisis) to support its share price a number of individuals were prosecuted under this provision, other prosecutions were dismissed.[256]

189. The difficulty with this provision is that in certain circumstances, transactions that might be beneficial to the company will be prohibited, such as management buy-outs where some part of the finance is raised through securitisation of the

252. *Wallersteiner v. Moir* [1974] 3 All ER 217.
253. Companies Act 2014 s. 82.
254. *Ibid.*
255. *CH (Ireland) Inc. v. Credit Suisse Canada* [1999] 4 IR 542. *See Quinn and Ors v. Irish Bank Resolution Corporation Ltd. And Anor.* [2012] IEHC 36. *Re Cognotec Ltd.* [2010] IEHC 309 and *Eccles Hall Ltd. v. Bank of Nova Scotia* (Unreported, High Court, February, 1995, Murphy J.).
256. *See Quinn and Ors v. IBRC Ltd.* [2012] IEHC 36 for a discussion of the context of these transactions. *See* further *DPP v. Fitzpatrick, McAteer and Whelan* (Circuit Criminal Court, 2014).

company's assets, changes in share structure using corporate assets, or corporate restructuring where corporate assets are used by way of security or direct finance to fund the transaction. It is not universally agreed that all of these kinds of transactions will be detrimental to the company over time, and so some argue that a blanket prohibition does not necessarily serve the company or its stakeholders. This argument has been recognised in English law,[257] and was reflected in the views expressed by Murphy J. in an Irish decision in *Eccles Hall Ltd. v. Bank of Nova Scotia.*[258] In Ireland, the Companies Act 2014 added section 82(5) which provides that the section 'does not prohibit the giving of financial assistance in relation to the acquisition of shares in a company or in its holding company if the 'principal purpose' of the financial assistance transaction is not for the acquisition of shares and that the 'giving of the assistance for that purpose is only an incidental part of some larger purpose of the company'. The facts in *Eccles Hall Ltd.* are illustrative of what might be involved in such a case. Here the company had received a number of loans from two primary individuals in return for shareholding in the company. Eventually, due to disagreement between the parties, it was necessary to both redeem the loans from Mr L and to 'buy him out'. This was achieved by the company borrowing from a third-party bank, the respondent, and the money being used to both pay back the loan received from Mr L and to facilitate the purchase of his shares. In reality, the value of the shares provided to the court (50 pounds) bore no resemblance to the value of the loan from Mr L (350,000 pounds) which was redeemed. The court was satisfied having considered the details of the arrangement that the purchase of the shares was incidental to the main transaction which was to repay the loans and to facilitate a 'parting of the ways' of the respective parties. That said, the English decision of *Brady v. Brady*[259] in interpreting a similarly worded provision in English law has been met with some criticism in Ireland on the grounds that the interpretation of this exemption is too constrained.[260] The prohibition on financial assistance transactions in relation to private companies has been removed from English law since then. This is not the case in Ireland. *See* further Chapter 2 for a discussion of the decision in *Re Cognotec Ltd.*[261] which aptly illustrates the mischief and artificiality of some applications of this provision.

VIII. Classes of Shares

190. Any company may divide its shares into different classes of shares depending on its corporate finance requirements. Irish and English company law provides a great deal of flexibility to companies in this respect. As described above, §2, VIII, in private companies limited by shares, the Articles of Association of a company have been replaced by the constitution of a company which must contain a capital clause. In a PLC, there will be a capital clause contained in the Memorandum of

257. Companies Act 2006 (UK), ss 677–683.
258. (3 Feb. 1995, Murphy J).
259. [1989] AC 755.
260. *See* generally Courtney: *The Law of Companies* (Bloomsbury, 2016) pp. 627–628
261. [2010] IEHC 309.

Association as before. The rights of different classes of shareholders may be contained in the constitution of the company in a private company limited by shares if these rights vary from the Companies Act 2014 or, in the case of a PLC, in the Articles of Association. In both cases, these rights are subject to the provisions of the Companies Act 2014.

A. *Ordinary Shares*

191. Ordinary shares are the most common kind of shares adopted by companies of all different sizes and types. The ordinary share will generally carry the right to a vote, without any particular weighting attached to that vote. In addition, an ordinary shareholder will typically be entitled to participate in any surplus funds on a pro-rated basis, which may be left after all the creditors have been paid. They are thus described as being the residual claimants in a company. Although generally not carrying weighted voting rights, it is common to see ordinary shares in more sophisticated share structures being delineated into different classes of ordinary shares; for example, they may be denominated as Ordinary Shares Class A, Ordinary Shares Class B with rights to vote on the election of B directors or A directors or some such structure.

B. *Preferred Stock and Preference Shares*

192. Preference shares carry preferential rights, which generally are financial rights and relate to rights to dividend or capital. Preference shareholders' entitlements to dividends are generally expressed as a right to a percentage per annum of the nominal amount of the share. Such shares may be described as cumulative preference shares so that when the dividend is declared, the shareholder is entitled to a cumulative dividend and may have a preferential entitlement to the payment of this dividend in full before other shareholders are paid dividends. A share that is preferred as capital entitles the member to have his or her capital investment in the company repaid in full before the ordinary shareholders are returned their capital in a winding up. These rights are largely undetermined by any statutory provisions and are generally described as a matter of contract law.

C. *Deferred Rights and Voting Rights, Non-Voting, Multiple Voting*

193. As described, the Companies Act 2014 creates a different framework from that which had existed hitherto, particularly for private companies. There is no model set of internal regulations (i.e., no Table A) available in the Act. Instead, many of the rights and provisions which were contained in Table A are now presented as statutory 'default' provisions which may be disapplied by the company's constitution. Parts 1–14 of the Act concern the governance of the private company limited by shares and Part 17 of the Act deals with the PLC by way of modification or adaptation of these standard provisions. Section 1002 of the Act sets out the table of provisions which are disapplied or modified in relation to the PLC. Section 1006 of the Act provides that the Constitution of a PLC will comprise a Memorandum and Articles of Association (as before).[262]

194. The bundle of shareholders' rights will be contained in this Constitution. It is expected that as with current practice whereby a PLC's articles exclude Table A, the new format will involve an exclusion of all the statutory default provisions and that the PLC Constitution will be created on a bespoke basis.[263] That is not to say that the statutory default provisions will not be included in the Constitution of the PLC but that these will be included as a matter of choice. The bundle of shareholders' rights therefore will normally include voting rights, but not necessarily. It should be noted that normally the shareholder has a vote per share, but again shares may have weighted voting rights exercisable in some circumstances or on all occasions. In addition, the shareholder is entitled to dividends[264] once these are declared by the Board of Directors and not vetoed by the shareholders in the general meeting. However, there is no obligation on the directors to declare dividends out of distributable profits if there is a decision that such profits ought to be retained by the company. The entitlement to dividend (created once the dividend is declared) is also determined by the kind of share, whether this is an ordinary share, preference share, cumulative preference share and so on. As previously mentioned, the shareholder is also considered to have residual rights to a pro rata distribution of surplus funds on dissolution if surplus assets are available once the creditors have been paid. However, where a dividend has been declared, the shareholders' rights to payment of that dividend is a contractual right while the company is solvent, but these claims become deferred claims in insolvency. The shareholders' rights can also be deferred depending on the rights attached to the issue of the shares. The shareholders' rights are described in the company's Constitution and are also described in contracts referred to as 'shareholders' agreements', which are entered into in addition to the framework rules provided for in the 'constitution' of the company. All rights so described are subject to the overriding principles of common law and in particular to the principles enshrined in the Companies Acts 2014. These rights can be altered through an alteration of the company's Constitution.[265] In addition, section 1013 allows for the alteration of the provisions of the Memorandum of Association of a PLC. This section provides that any alteration of the objects which is made in accordance with this section 'shall be as valid as if originally contained therein, and be

262. Companies Act 2014, s. 1000(2).

263. T.B Courtney, *Changes in the Basics, Constitutions, Share Capital and Governance* (Bloomsbury Professional Seminar Series). *See also* Bloomsbury's Professional Guide to the Companies Act 2014. (Bloomsbury, 2015) Ch. 2.

264. Dividends are declared subject to rules contained in the Companies Act 2014, Part 3, Ch. 7.

265. The Articles of Association of a PLC can be altered in the manner described in the Companies Act 2014 s. 1015:

> (1) Subject to the provisions of this Act and to the conditions contained in its memorandum, a PLC may by special resolution alter or add to its articles.
>
> (2) Any alteration or addition so made in the articles shall, subject to the provisions of this Act, be as valid as if originally contained therein, and be subject in like manner to alteration by special resolution.

subject to alteration in like manner.' *See* further §5 for a full treatment of voting rights in governance structures, meetings, etc.

D. Other: Redeemable Shares

195. Redeemable shares are shares the company is entitled to redeem from its members. When shares are redeemed, the company generally cancels them. However, a treasury share is retained on redemption by the company and can subsequently be re-issued.

E. Other: Bonus Shares

196. Bonus shares are issued to the shareholders in proportion to their existing shareholdings. They are issued as having been fully paid up – that is, the shareholders are not required to pay for them. They are usually paid from accumulated profits that have been transferred to capital that is capitalised.

IX. Transfer of Shares

A. Introduction

197. The free transferability of shares is one of the elements of what has been described as 'the genius of company law', which supports the creation of one of the most flexible forms of business vehicles used today – namely, the limited liability company. In PLCs, the free transferability of shares is axiomatic to the working of capital markets. Chapter 5 of Part 3 of the Companies Act 2014 sets out the law in relation to the transfer of shares for all companies. These provisions codify provisions which hitherto would have appeared in the company's Articles of Association. As stated previously, the structure of the Act is such that the main provisions are stated and then disapplied in relation to particular types of companies, in this case, PLCs. However, none of the provisions of Chapter 5 of Part 3 are automatically disapplied for PLCs. Therefore, the restrictions on transfers of shares must be expressly disapplied by the particular PLC. In particular, the right of the Board of Directors to refuse to register certain transfers is now provided for in section 95(1)(a) for all companies *including* PLCs and so the Articles of Association will have to disapply this provision.

198. Pre-emption rights are provided for in section 1022 of the 2014 Companies Act in relation to the *allotment* of shares in PLCs and in section 69(6) of the 2014 Companies Act for private companies. Section 1022(1) provides that when a company issues equity securities, a pro rata offer of these securities must be made to the holders of 'relevant shares' or 'relevant employee shares'. Supplemental provisions are found in section 1023 which includes the statutory definition of 'equity securities' which excludes subscriber shares and bonus shares. The operation of the statutory provision does not apply to allotments of shares that are wholly or partly paid up, otherwise than in cash[266] or to allotments of shares that would be normally held under employees' share schemes.[267] The relevant period of the offer is stipulated at fourteen days under section 1022(9). During this time, the offer to existing shareholders must stand until it is refused.

199. Chapter 5 of Part 3 of the Companies Act 2014 governs the transfer of shares. Section 94(4) of the Companies Act 2014, provides that a transfer of shares cannot be registered unless a proper instrument of transfer has been delivered to the company. Under the Stock Transfer Act 1963, section 2, registered securities to which the Act and its provisions apply may be transferred 'by means of an instrument under hand in the form set out in the First Schedule to this Act (in this Act referred to as a stock transfer)'. Section 94(8) of the Companies Act 2014 states that section 94 is without prejudice to the Stock Transfer Act 1963 'save to the extent that a company's constitution regulates the execution of instruments by any particular company or other body corporate'.

B. Registration

200. Once a transfer has occurred, the registration of a shareholder is significant as the shareholder cannot exercise rights without being registered. Section 66(6) of the Companies Acts 2014 provides that:

> except as required by law, no person shall be recognized by a company as holding any share upon any trust and the company shall not be bound by or compelled in any way to recognize, (even when having notice of it) (a) any equitable, contingent, future or partial interest in any share or any interest in any fractual part of a share or (b) save only as this Act or other law otherwise provides, any other rights in respect of any share, except an absolute right to the entirety of it in the registered holder.

201. The practical implication of this provision is that the company is only bound to serve notice on and to be subject to the exercise of rights solely by those registered as shareholders.[268] Accordingly, in relation to the transfer of shares, there are essentially two stages in the process of acquiring rights exercisable by the shareholder, namely the completion of the transfer, at which point the shareholder will

266. Companies Act 2014 s. 1022(5).
267. Companies Act 2014 s. 1022(6).
268. This has become significant in relation to the creation of modern trust and shareholding arrangements. *See* further Irene Lynch Fannon, *A Transatlantic Case: The Derivative Action as a Corporate Governance Tool*, 27 Dublin U. L. J., 1 (2005) and Richard Nolan, *Indirect Investors: A Greater Say*, 3 Co. J. Corp. L. Stud., 73 (2003).

acquire an equitable interest in the shares,[269] and registration of the shareholder, without which the shareholder cannot exercise any of the rights normally attaching to the share. Therefore registration is of the utmost importance.

1. Directors' Decision to Accept or Refuse Registration

202. The absolute discretion to refuse to register a transfer of shares which had hitherto been given to directors of private companies in the standard-form Articles of Association is now enshrined in statute, in section 95 of the Companies Act 2014 which applies this discretion, 'save where the constitution of the company provides otherwise'.

203. The principles governing the exercise of this discretion are described in Part I Chapter 2, *infra*.

C. Transmission of Shares

204. When a shareholder dies, his or her shares, as with all other items of property, vest in a personal representative. Section 94(5) provides that nothing in subsection (4) of the section described above 'shall prejudice any power of the company to register a shareholder or debenture holder, any person to whom the right to any shares in or debentures of the company, has been transmitted by operation of law'. The personal representative (i.e., as a person to whom the rights to any shares or debentures have been transmitted by operation of law) can be registered as a member under section 96(4)(a) of the Companies Act 2014 Act), or may elect under section 96(4)(b) to have a nominee registered as the transferee, thus enabling the exercise of rights attaching to the shares. For many reasons, the personal representative may not wish to be registered as a member and can proceed to transfer the shares without such registration. This is facilitated by the operation of section 94(6) which provides that: 'A transfer of the share or other interest of a deceased member of a company made by his personal representative shall, although the personal representative is not himself a member of the company, be as valid as if he had been such a member at the time of the execution of the instrument of transfer.' Where shares are partly paid, the personal representative will become liable for any calls on the shares if he or she is registered under the decision in *Buchan's Case*,[270] whereas the liability ensures to the shareholder's estate if the personal representative is not registered.

---

269. *Wood Preservation Limited v. Prior* [1969] 1 WLR 1977; *Musselwhite v. Musselwhite* [1962] 1 Ch. 964.

270. *Buchan's Case* (1879) LR 4 App. Cas. 549.

D. Stock Exchange

205. The discretion directors have to refuse registration is not disapplied automatically in section 1002 to public companies so the Articles of Association of a PLC will have to disapply this provision. In relation to shares held on a stock exchange or indeed private mortgages of these shares can present some difficulties. Shares can form a significant part of an individual's asset base. Because of the effect of section 66(6) of the Companies Act 2014, legal mortgages of shares are not common, because the mortgagee rather than the mortgagor will be liable for calls[271] and other obligations relating to share ownership. In view of the impracticalities of this situation, equitable mortgages are more common; these are achieved by the deposit of the share certificate or indeed an equitable charge can be created by agreement, which is more relevant where share certificates are no longer issued.[272] Furthermore, shares can be held under a trust agreement, where usually the trustee will be registered as the shareholder to facilitate the exercise of the rights attaching to the share, which will be exercised in accordance with the terms of the trust deed.

206. In modern times, the use of trust deeds has facilitated the quotation of shares of companies on non-domestic stock exchanges, such as the NASDAQ and New York Stock Exchange in the case of Irish and British companies. The holding instruments are referred to as, American Depository Receipts or American Depository Securities (ADR or ADS). Again, because of the operation of section 66(6) of the Companies Act 2014 and its equivalent in English company law, such arrangements are not without their difficulties for those holding securities under such trust instruments.[273]

E. Protection of Shareholders in a Tender Offer

207. This matter is dealt with under Schemes of Arrangement and Reconstructions considered in §7 *infra.*

F. Insider Trading

208. Insider trading is prohibited under the Companies Act 2014 as it had been under the preceding Companies Act 1990. The significant decision of the Supreme Court in *Fyffes* litigation[274] still stands as one of the few litigated cases in Irish law. There were a number of matters regarding the interpretation of the legislation at issue in this case including the identification of the entire act of insider trading with

271. *Re Land Credit Company of Ireland; Weikersheim's Case* (1873) LR 8 Ch. App. 831.
272. *Swiss Bank Corporation v. Lloyds Bank* [1981] 1 WLR 893.
273. *See* Irene Lynch Fannon, *A Transatlantic Case: The Derivative Action as a Corporate Governance Tool*, 27 Dublin U. L. J., 1 (2005) and Richard Nolan, *Indirect Investors: A Greater Say*, 3 Co. J. Corp. L. Stud. 73 (2003): n. 76.
274. *Fyffes PLC v. DCC PLC* [2005] IEHC 477 ; [2007] IESC 36

a particular corporate entity in possession of insider information. This process of identification involved disregarding the corporate personality of related companies which the court did. (*See supra* §3 C).

209. This important decision included the interpretation of the statutory provisions on insider trading which remain relevant since the time of the decision. In addition, as with many stock exchanges, the Irish stock exchange, now trading as Euronext, has additional rules and policies surrounding insider trading and these are available on the relevant website.

G. Other

210. The use of shareholders' agreements by those forming companies, in particular, private limited companies or by those facilitating new investment agreements between family members or, between an existing company and new investors is very common. It is very difficult to identify the exact legal relationship between the shareholder agreement and the *ex ante* statutory framework. Clearly, the intention between signing parties is that the shareholders' agreement varies the existing governance structure of the company whether this is found in the Constitution of the company or in the statutory framework. A key shift from the use of constitutional documents (namely the Memorandum of Agreement and Articles of Association) in private companies to a statutory framework took place under the Companies Act 2014. For this reason, the legal effect of a shareholders' agreement is now intended to alter the provisions of a statute which is quite a different matter from altering the provisions of Articles of Association which was always regarded as being a type of contract between the company and its members. Whether there are legal consequences attaching to the alteration of a statute by shareholder agreement is as yet an untested legal question. There has, however, been litigation arising from shareholders' agreements in recent times. In *Hayes v. Kelleher and Ors.,*[275] the interpretation of a shareholders' agreement arose for consideration by the High Court. It should be noted that this arose in a context created by the parties prior to the 2014 Act. Here the plaintiff insisted on her right as a majority shareholder to control membership of the Board regardless of the terms of the Articles of Association of the company. The shareholders' agreement had given her a 51% majority shareholding voter rights and a specific power to appoint five of the nine directors. The court held that the rules of contract law were important and relevant when interpreting both Articles of Association and shareholders' agreements. Such rules and principles include rules of 'common sense' and the idea that 'business sense' should prevail.[276] This includes the idea that 'business people will be assumed to know what they are doing; that 'detailed semantic and syntactical analysis of words must yield to business common-sense' and finally that 'unambiguous language must however be applied, irrespective of the question of commercial sense'. Therefore here, the shareholders' agreement took precedence over the Articles of Association. This

275. *[2015] IEHC 509.*
276. *Ibid.*, paras 37–41.

would seem to be an acceptable principle when both are effectively contractual in nature. However, the fact that the normal rules on shareholders' rights in relation to Board composition are now contained in the statute, namely section 158 ff of the Companies Acts 2014 raises questions as to whether the statute can be varied by a private contract between parties. Of interest in this context is that the High Court observed in the Hayes case that 'It is not for the court … to import into an arrangement a meaning, which although available from the general context, is not deducible by the use of the interpretive rules described.' This may well be an appropriate statement as regards contract law, but is perhaps insufficient when it comes to the question of how and when a private contract supersedes a statutory provision.

H. Liens

211. A lien is an equitable charge, and it is possible for shares to become the subject matter of a lien, to provide security regarding non-payment of certain kinds of debts. Usually, a lien is created by an individual asserting rights of possession over the asset until whatever liability is due to him or her is met. Section 80 of the Companies Act 2014 governs the creation of liens over shares and provides a set of default provisions which a company may disapply by virtue of its constitution. Section 80(2) states that a company shall have a 'first and paramount lien on every share (not being a fully paid share) for all money (whether immediately payable or not) called, or payable at a fixed time, in respect of that share'. Section 80(2) provides that the directors may exempt some shares from this provision and section 80(3) states that the lien will extend to 'all dividends payable on it'. Additional provisions apply,[277] (*See* further, *infra*, Part I, Chapter 2.)

X. Debentures

A. Introduction: Equity and Loan Capital

212. Even though the issue of debentures can be considered under the general heading of raising capital, the nature of loan capital as distinct from equity capital, is very different. Whereas the provision of equity capital in the form of shares for cash is essentially a 'control for capital' transaction, the provision of loan capital is not understood in this way. In common law structures (unlike some continental European civil law systems), the essential differential in these systems is between what is called 'arms-length financing' and 'relational financing'. It is not the primary motive of the lender to achieve control of decision-making in the company but rather to lend capital with a view to making a profit through the charging of interest. In a generalised sense, the lender does not seek control over the company's activities. However, the lender will usually seek control over some assets, as we will see later. *See infra*, Part I, Chapter 1, §6 on Liquidations. In providing capital in this

277. *See* further Companies Act 2014, s. 80.

way, the lender is much more risk-averse than the provider of equity capital whose investment may return substantial profits over time but is at risk of returning no profit at all. The lender's investment, in contrast, will usually not involve the risk of a fluctuating return. Leaving aside issues of control and risk, equity capital is cheaper to obtain where possible from the company's point of view, whereas loan capital must be paid for through the payment of interest. Capital raised through lending is not considered 'capital' for most company law purposes and is not subject to the rules on capital maintenance, statements of capital and so forth described in previous paragraphs.

B. Issuing Debentures

213. A debenture document is the term used to describe the loan document issued by a company to the lender. The issuing of debentures is governed primarily by the Constitution of the company, which will give the directors the power to borrow and to secure borrowing on assets over which securities can be created. The loan document will typically describe a payment date, or dates where instalments are concerned, and will also describe the assets charged to secure repayment. The debenture document can be one document issued in relation to one loan, or it can be one of a series of documents or instruments issued to a number of lenders. The company can issue debentures to the public in identical terms but for different amounts, but it is more common now to see this as an issue of debenture stock to the public, much like a Government bond. The company will thus issue debenture stock to individuals or other entities, and this stock indicates their particular share in the loan fund. The holder of debenture stock is thus able to avail of free transferability of the debenture stock. Underlying the issue of debenture stock in this manner will be a trust deed executed between the company and trustees, who are appointed to look after the interests of the debenture stock holders. The company agrees under the trust agreement to repay the capital sum secured at a fixed date or in some other manner. Section 422 of the Companies Act 2014 provides that any provision in a trust agreement that exonerates or relieves trustees of liability for breach of their trust to debenture holders where there is a failure to show 'care and diligence' required of them will be void.

C. Charging the Assets

214. Any charges created to secure the lending described in the debenture document, which will also describe the terms and conditions of the lending, must be registered under section 409 of the Companies Act 2014. The registration process has been changed considerably under the 2014 Act by introducing a built-in option of registering the charge in a 'one stage procedure' – section 409(3) or in a 'two stage procedure' – section 409(4). Failure to register the charge in one or other of these ways will lead to the charge being void 'against the liquidator and any creditor of the company'. This provision and the issues that have been raised regarding the creation of charges will be discussed in Part I, Chapter 1, §6 on Liquidations.

D. Transferring Debentures

215. As with shares, debentures or debenture stock can be transferred. As described above under section 94(4) of the Companies Act 2014, a transfer of shares cannot be effected without a valid instrument of transfer that must be delivered to the company. Similarly, the same section provides that a company cannot register the transfer of a debenture, where this is applicable unless a proper instrument of transfer is delivered to the company, the same principle that applies to share transfers discussed *supra*. The company usually will keep a register of debenture holders, and if this is done, it must be done in the prescribed form. However, it is possible to issue bearer debentures, the transfer of which is effected in much the same way as share transfers. Bearer debentures are regarded in law as negotiable instruments.

E. Convertible Debentures

216. It is also possible for a company to issue debentures that can later be converted into shares, depending on the terms of the loan agreement of document. Such debentures are usually referred to as 'convertible debentures' and are designed to capture a certain degree of flexibility between the predictability of a loan investment and the less risk-averse advantages of an equity investment. The conversion rates and terms will be specified in the debenture document.

F. Remedies of a Debenture Holder

217. The debenture document is essentially a loan document, and so the document will describe remedies available to the debenture holder in the event of the company defaulting on the loan or on any of its repayment terms. The remedies included will usually include the right to appoint a receiver, which is a significant feature of Irish insolvency law discussed in Part I, Chapter 1, §6. Alternative remedies are to commence a winding up and in certain circumstances, where it might seem advantageous to the lender to do so, to appoint an examiner. These processes and remedies are described *infra* in §5. The realisation of any charges securing the loan will be an integral part of the debenture holder's remedies. If a debenture stock trust deed has been created underlying, as has been described, the issuing of debenture stock, the trustee normally exercises the rights relating to the remedies.

§5. Shareholders, Management and Control

I. Shareholder Control Mechanisms

218. The following is a description of the powers and responsibilities within the corporate structure of most companies. In recent times, the study of corporate governance has become a lively area of enquiry. Corporate governance is particularly concerned with issues of accountability of management to shareholders in the first instance and to what are called 'other stakeholders' in the second instance. In addition, corporate governance is significant beyond corporate law because of the impact the governance movement has had on institutions generally.

219. Under the organic theory of company law, the organs of the company are those bodies that can act on behalf of the company. These include the shareholders in a general meeting, the Board of Directors, the Managing Director, the Company Secretary in relation to specific functions, and similarly the Auditor in relation to other functions. The theory recognises the shareholders in a general meeting as residual owners of the company who delegate their authority to the Board, which in turn delegates to the Managing Director, the Company Secretary and the Auditor. Prior to the enactment of the Companies Act 2014, these particular relationships were recognised and governed by the standard-form Articles of Association, the companies' legislation and judicial interpretations of both decided in case law. The Articles of Association have now been displaced by provisions of the new Companies Act 2014. Accordingly, PLCs will have specific 'bespoke' Articles of Association drafted with reference to, and subject to these provisions and it is expected that private limited companies will largely be governed by the provisions of the Companies Act 2014 without reliance on Articles of Association. There are, of course, other possibilities for specific delegation of duties, such as from the Board to a particular individual or employee, but these delegations will be conducted primarily through contract law and are not regulated under company law in a general way. Section A of this part concerns shareholders' meetings. Section B deals with shareholders' rights, as between majority and minority interests. Section C deals with Annual Accounts and Reports.

A. *Shareholders' Meetings (Kinds, Convening, Proxies, Powers)*

220. The law relating to shareholders' meetings is now codified, in the Companies Act 2014. Generally, the rules relating to shareholders' meetings are contained in sections 177–195 of the 2014 Act. The principal source of law and regulation relating to the conduct of meetings is the 2014 Act. During the COVID pandemic and following intensive consultations with stakeholders, including engagement of the CLRG, the Companies (Miscellaneous Provisions) (COVID-19) Act 2020 was passed to provide for virtual meetings of shareholders and creditors respectively. These provisions have been extended to December 2023 by Ministerial order and it is expected that these might be continued, despite reservations expressed by the International Corporate Governance Network. Much of what was previously contained in the standard-form Articles of Association has now been adopted into the 2014 Act which replaces the former 'Table A' as the default regulation of company meetings. The shareholders in general meetings are considered to be capable of acting on behalf of the company and making decisions on behalf of the company. The theory is that as residual owners, the shareholders' meeting is often described as the repository of all residual un-delegated powers.

1. Annual General Meeting (AGM)

221. Four types of meetings are described in the Companies Act 2014. First, there is the AGM, which normally must be held on an annual basis. Despite its nomenclature, however, the requirement to hold an AGM does not correspond exactly to a calendar year. The AGM must be held within each calendar year but does not necessarily have to be held within twelve months of the preceding AGM. There is a limit on the intervening period of fifteen months. On first formation, this period of time between formation and the holding of the AGM can be up to eighteen months. However, the obligation to hold an AGM can be dispensed with for LTDs under section 175 of the Companies Act 2014. This exemption had applied to single-member private companies since 1994 but the 2014 Act extends this to LTDs. Section 175(3) states that AGMs can be dispensed with where all the members sign a written resolution acknowledging receipt of the financial statements which are usually presented at the AGM and the resolution also resolves all matters which would have been resolved at the AGM. The same exemption is not extended to multi-member DACS[278] or to PLCs.[279] A member of the company can apply to the Director of Corporate Enforcement to call or direct the convening of an AGM when one is overdue.[280]

2. Extraordinary General Meeting (EGM)

222. An EGM will be held where extraordinary matters of business arise. Effectively an EGM is conducted as an AGM would be, except that the function of the meeting is to consider matters of business beyond the normal items of business conducted at the AGM. The Companies Act 2014 states that 'all general meetings of a company, other than AGMs, shall be known, and in this Act are referred to, as "extraordinary general meetings"'.[281]

223. EGMs are normally called by directors when an item of business out of the ordinary must be considered, such as a certain transaction for which the approval of the members is required under the Companies Acts 2014. The directors of a company may, whenever they think fit, convene an extraordinary general meeting (EGM).[282] If, at any time, there are not sufficient directors capable of acting to form a quorum, any director of the company or any member of it may convene an EGM in the same manner as that in which meetings may be convened by the directors.[283] Reduction of capital and removal of pre-emption rights are just two examples of transactions that cannot be accomplished without the approval of the shareholders in a general meeting. The directors are also obliged to convene an EGM in certain

278. Companies Act 2014, s. 988.
279. Companies Act 2014, s. 1089.
280. Companies Act 2014, s. 175(5).
281. Companies Act 2014, s. 177(1).
282. Companies act 2014, s. 177(2).
283. Companies Act 2014, s. 177(3).

other circumstances specified under the Companies Acts, for example where the company's net assets (i.e., total assets less total liabilities) have fallen to 50% or less of its called-up share capital.

3. Meetings of Particular Classes of Shareholders

224. Where there are different classes of shares, such shareholders may have separate meetings of the particular class, depending on the authority and decision-making capacity reserved for them in the articles. There are also particular times when the Acts require a separate meeting of different classes of shareholders, such as in relation to a proposed scheme of arrangement that would affect different classes differently.

4. Court-Conducted Meetings

225. Finally, and exceptionally, the 2014 Act provides for the convening of meetings of the shareholders by the High Court where it otherwise proves impossible for a meeting to be convened in any other way. The Court may order an EGM to be held on the application to it of a director, a member or the personal representative or assignee in bankruptcy of a member, or the Court may call a meeting of its own motion:[284]

> The Court shall not require a meeting to be held unless it is satisfied that for any reason it is impracticable or otherwise undesirable – (a) for any person to call a general meeting of the company in any manner in which meetings of that company may be called; or (b) to conduct a general meeting of the company in any manner provided by this Act or the company's constitution.[285]
>
> The Court may attach any conditions or give directions as to the conduct of the meeting as it thinks fit.[286] These sort of situations typically involve some kind of deadlock either due to the deterioration in relationships within the company or because technical difficulties have arisen regarding procedural aspects of holding the meeting such as providing a quorum. The Court may direct that one member of the company, or the personal representative of a deceased member of the company or the assignee in bankruptcy of a bankrupt member of it, present in person or by proxy, is a quorum.[287]

B. Shareholders' Power to Requisition a Meeting

226. A meeting of the shareholders may be requisitioned in a number of ways:

---

284. Companies Act 2014, s. 179(1) and 179(3).
285. Companies Act 2014, s. 179(2).
286. Companies Act 2014, s. 179(4).
287. Companies Act 2014, s. 179(5).

(i) One or more members of a company holding, or together holding, at any time not less than 50% (or such other percentage as may be specified in the constitution) of the paid-up share capital of the company as carries voting rights may convene an EGM.[288] This rule is subject to amendment by the constitution of the company.[289]

(ii) The directors of a company must convene an EGM on the requisition of one or more members holding, or together holding, not less than 10% of the paid-up share capital as carries voting rights.[290]

(iii) If the directors do not, within twenty-one days of the requisition, call an EGM for a date within two months, the requisitionists (or 50% or more of them) may convene an EGM themselves.[291]

C. Procedure at Meetings: Quorum

227. The default rule concerning quorums at meetings is that no business shall be transacted at any general meeting of a company unless a quorum of members is present at the time when the meeting proceeds to business.[292] Save to the extent that the Constitution provides otherwise, two members shall constitute a quorum.[293] Obviously, this will not apply to single-member companies.

In the case of a single-member company, one member of the company present in person or by proxy at a general meeting shall be a quorum.[294]

The general rules under the 2014 Act regarding the absence of a quorum (subject to amendment by the Constitution of the company) are that if, within fifteen minutes after the time appointed for the holding of a general meeting, a quorum is not present: (a) where the meeting has been convened upon the requisition of members, the meeting shall be dissolved; or (b) in any other case: (i) the meeting shall stand adjourned to the same day in the next week, at the same time and place or to such other day and at such other time and place as the directors may determine; and (ii) if at the adjourned meeting, a quorum is not present within half an hour after the time appointed for the meeting, the members present shall be a quorum.[295]

D. Procedure: Notice of Meetings

228. Save where the constitution of the company makes provision for the giving of greater notice, a meeting of a company, other than an adjourned meeting, shall

288. Companies Act 2014, s. 178(2).
289. *Ibid.*
290. Companies Act 2014, s. 178(3).
291. Companies Act 2014, s. 178(5).
292. Companies Act 2014, s. 182(1).
293. Companies Act 2014, s. 182(2).
294. Companies Act 2014, s. 182(3).
295. Companies Act 2014, s. 182(5). Note that during the COVID pandemic special procedures were introduced under the Companies (Miscellaneous Provisions) (COVID-19) Act 2020 providing for online meetings. These provisions have been extended until December 2023 by Ministerial order.

be called – (a) in the case of the AGM or an EGM for the passing of a special resolution, by not less than twenty-one days' notice; (b) in the case of any other EGM, by not less than seven days' notice.[296] A meeting of a company shall, notwithstanding that it is called by shorter notice than that just outlined, be deemed to have been duly called if it is so agreed by – (a) all the members entitled to attend and vote at the meeting; and (b) unless no statutory auditors of the company stand appointed in consequence of the company availing itself of the audit exemption under the 2014 Act, the statutory auditors of the company.[297] In the case of a PLC which is classified as a 'trading PLC' the possibility of a seven-day notice period for the holding of an EGM and the possibility that the members and statutory auditors may agree to waive the necessary notice period (whether twenty-one days or seven days) does not apply, save to the extent that the constitution of the company shall provide otherwise.[298] However, the 2014 Act further provides that a general meeting of a traded PLC (other than an AGM or an EGM for the passing of a special resolution) may be called with not less than fourteen days' notice, if: (a) the members are provided with a facility to vote by electronic means; and (b) a special resolution reducing the necessary notice period to fourteen days was passed at the immediately preceding AGM or at a general meeting held since that meeting.[299]

Where notice of a meeting is delivered by post, it shall be deemed to have been effected on the expiration of twenty-four hours following posting[300] and in determining whether the correct period of notice has been given by a notice of a meeting, neither the day on which the notice is served nor the day of the meeting for which it is given shall be counted.[301]

The company shall be given twenty-eight days' notice of intention to move a resolution to remove a director or appoint someone else in place of a director so removed at the meeting at which he is removed except when the directors of the company have resolved to submit it; and on receiving such notice, the company shall give the members not less than twenty-one days' notice of the holding of the meeting.[302] Any resolution which does not comply with the foregoing provisions shall not be effective, except that if, after notice of the intention to move such a resolution has been given to the company, a meeting is called for a date twenty-eight days or less after the notice has been given, the notice, though not given within the time required (i.e., twenty-one days), shall be deemed to have been properly given.[303] It has been commented that the intention behind the latter rule was to prevent a company from frustrating a member's resolution for the removal of a director by deliberately calling a meeting at insufficient notice, in order to have the meeting rendered ineffective.[304]

---

296. Companies Act 2014, s. 181(1).
297. Companies Act 2014, s. 181(2).
298. Companies Act 2014, s. 1102(1).
299. Companies Act 2014, s. 1102(2).
300. Companies Act 2014, s. 181(3).
301. Companies Act 2014, s. 181(4).
302. Companies Act 2014, s. 146(3).
303. Companies Act 2014, s. 146(4)–(5).
304. Lyndon MacCann & Thomas Courtney, *The Companies Acts 1963–2009* 143 (Bloomsbury Professional 2010).

Extended notice of twenty-eight days shall also be given for certain types of resolutions regarding a company's statutory auditors, namely the following: (a) a resolution at an AGM of a company appointing as statutory auditors any persons other than the incumbent statutory auditors or providing expressly that the incumbent statutory auditors shall not be re-appointed; (b) a resolution at a general meeting of a company removing statutory auditors from office; and (c) a resolution at a general meeting of a company filling a casual vacancy in the office of statutory auditor.[305]

E. Procedure: Voting and Proxy Voting

1. Polls

229. Save to the extent that the company's constitution provides otherwise, the following rules apply to proceedings at general meetings of the company. Every resolution shall be decided by a show of hands unless a poll is demanded.[306] Unless a poll is demanded, a declaration by the Chairman that a resolution has been carried or lost on a show of hands will be conclusive evidence of the proceedings.[307] Where there is an equality of votes, whether on a show of hands or on a poll, the chairperson of the meeting at which the show of hands takes place or at which the poll is demanded, shall be entitled to a second or casting vote.[308]

A poll (vote) may be demanded as follows: by the Chairman of the meeting; by at least three members voting in person or by proxy; by any member or members present in person or by proxy and representing not less than one-tenth of the total voting rights of all the members having a right to vote at the meeting; or by a member or members holding shares conferring voting rights, being shares on which an aggregate sum has been paid up equal to at least 10% of the total amount paid up on all voting shares.[309] The right to demand a poll is a statutory right.

2. Proxies

230. Any member of the company who is entitled to vote at a general meeting of the company can appoint a 'proxy'.[310] A proxy is a person nominated by the member to attend the meeting and to exercise the member's vote on his or her behalf. A proxy is also entitled to speak at the meeting on behalf of the member. Unless the company's constitution otherwise provides, a member of a company shall not be entitled to appoint more than one proxy to attend on the same occasion.[311]

305. Companies Act 2014, s. 396.
306. Companies Act 2014, s. 187(7).
307. *Ibid.*
308. Companies Act 2014, s. 187(8).
309. Companies Act 2014, s. 189(2).
310. Companies Act 2014, s. 181(1).
311. Companies Act 2014, s. 183(3).

The instrument appointing a proxy (the 'instrument of proxy') shall be in writing (a) under the hand of the appointer or of his or her attorney duly authorised in writing; or (b) if the appointer is a body corporate, either under the seal of the body corporate or under the hand of an officer or attorney of it duly authorised in writing.[312]

The instrument of proxy shall be deposited at the registered office of the company not later than forty-eight hours (or such lesser period as the company's constitution may provide) before the time for holding the meeting or adjourned meeting at which the person named in the instrument proposes to vote.[313]

A vote given in accordance with the terms of an instrument of proxy shall be valid notwithstanding the previous death or insanity of the appointer or revocation of the proxy or of the authority under which the proxy was executed or the transfer of the share in respect of which the proxy is given, except if notice in writing of such death, insanity, revocation or transfer is received by the company concerned at its registered office before the commencement of the meeting or adjourned meeting at which the proxy is used.[314]

F. Majority Rule Including Legal and Statutory Protection of Minority and Majority

231. In relation to shareholders' meetings, there are five types of resolutions by which the shareholders in general meetings make their decisions:

(i) The first type of resolution is an ordinary resolution, which requires a majority of 50% plus one vote, or a simple majority, on a show of hands. A meeting at which an ordinary resolution is passed must be preceded by seven days' notice to shareholders.[315]

(ii) The second type of resolution is a special resolution, which requires a 75% majority or three-quarters of the votes on a show of hands. These resolutions require a twenty-one-day notice period for the holding of the meeting. The terms of any proposed special resolution must also be provided in the notice.

(iii) Third is a hybrid resolution, which in effect, is a simple resolution to which particular notice requirements are attached because of the nature of the subject matter. In effect, these resolutions require the same simple majority as a normal ordinary resolution but require a longer notice period of twenty-eight days for the meeting at which the resolution will be considered. The Companies Act specifies what kind of resolution is required; thus, in the case of these hybrid resolutions, section 146 of the 2014 Act refers to the ability of shareholders to remove directors from the Board. This requires a vote by ordinary resolution but requires a longer notice period of twenty-eight days. Where it is proposed to pass a resolution to do so, this can be done by an ordinary resolution of the shareholders, but a longer notice period of twenty-eight

312. Companies Act 2014, s. 183(4).
313. Companies Act 2014, s. 183(6).
314. Companies Act, s. 183(9)–(10).
315. Companies Act 2014, s. 1919(1).

days must be provided. Similarly, section 396 of the 2014 Act states that a resolution to replace an auditor or a resolution to remove an auditor before the expiration of his or her term of office can be passed but requires longer notice.

(iv) Unanimous written resolutions are now provided for in section 193 of the Companies Act 2014. These kinds of resolutions were originally permitted in common law. In *Buchanan v. McVey*,[316] it was held that evidence of unanimous informal agreement can bind any company in the absence of dishonesty or some provision in the Memo or Arts to the contrary. This case is considered in *Re Greendale Developments Ltd.*[317] [in the context of *ultra vires*]. The principle in *Buchanan v. McVey* was originally given statutory effect in section 141(8) of the Companies Act 1963. The 2014 Act provides that, notwithstanding anything else contained in the Act, a written resolution of all of the members who would be entitled to attend and vote at a general meeting shall be as valid and effective for all purposes as if the resolution had been passed at a general meeting of the company duly convened and held. Such a resolution shall be deemed to have been passed at a meeting held on the date on which it was signed by the last member to sign.

(v) The Companies Act 2014 also provides for majority written resolutions which will be considered to be valid where the requisite majority signs the relevant resolution. This is provided for under section 194 and applies to both ordinary resolutions under section 194(1) and special resolutions under section 194(2). It will not apply where there is a resolution to remove a director under section 195 of that Act.

232. It is important to note that many of these requirements in relation to the requirement of physical attendance or where the requirement relies on physical presence have been altered under the Companies (Miscellaneous Provisions) (COVID-19) Act of 2020 to deal with obvious difficulties caused by quarantine during the pandemic. Most of these provisions have been extended until December 2023 by Ministerial order and are therefore in operation at the time of writing (2023).

233. As regards the rights described in the preceding paragraphs, shareholders have remedies in relation to the specific enforcement of each of the rights described. It is common in the provisions of the Companies Act 2014, which describe such rights to provide for a method by which specific rights can be enforced. It is also common that particular enabling sections are provided for a minority shareholder remedy. For example, section 1013 of the 2014 Act which provides for the alteration by special resolution of the objects clause of the Memorandum of Association of a PLC, permits a minority of 15% to petition the court to object to the changes proposed. In addition to specific remedies regarding each enabling provision, the

316. [1954] IR 89.
317. [1998] IR 8.

shareholder has a specific remedy provided for under section 212 of the 2014 Act, which is somewhat equivalent to the 'unfair prejudice' remedy under English company law.

234. Section 212 of the 2014 Act provides that a member of a company who complains that 'the affairs of the company are being conducted or that the powers of the directors of the company are being exercised in a manner oppressive to him or any of the members (including himself), or in disregard of his or their interests as members' may petition the High Court for relief. Members of the company, as well as personal representatives of deceased members, may apply for relief under what is now section 212 but which was section 205 under the Companies Act 1963. Persons whose names remain on the register despite having disposed of their shares do not have standing, however.[318] 'Member' has the meaning given to it by section 168 of the 2014 Act.[319] Under section 168(2), a person to whom shares have been transferred but whose name has not been entered on the register is not a member of the company,[320] and cannot petition under section 212. English cases holding that ex-shareholders[321] and employees[322] also lack standing to petition under the English equivalent legislation, will similarly apply in Ireland. Perhaps more controversially, the High Court (Gannon J.) has held that the definition of 'member' in section 168 (as it is now) is exhaustive for the purposes of section 212 (as it is now), and that accordingly where shares are held on trust, the beneficial owners do not have standing.[323] This restrictive provision has been reiterated in modern case law by the Irish High Court in *Kevin Devlin and John O'Driscoll v. SGC Global Advanced Technologies Ltd.*[324] However, the negative effect of this restrictive principle on shareholders' rights and remedies has not been adverted to in argument in any of the recent cases. Where investors invest in Irish companies listed on foreign stock exchanges through trust vehicles such as American Deposit Receipts or equivalent instruments, the fact that investors are simply beneficial owners of shares bars them from taking action.[325]

---

318. *See Re Via Net Works* [2002] IESC 24 (unreported, Supreme Court, 23 Apr. 2002) (shareholder-petitioner held not to have standing, even though he retained his shares, because he had contractually bound himself to divest himself of all shares in the company).
319. Section 168 of the 2014 Act provides: '(1) The subscribers to the constitution of a company shall be deemed to have agreed to become members of the company, and, on its registration, shall be entered as members in its register of members. (2) Every other person who agrees to become a member of a company, and whose name is entered in its register of members, shall be a member of the company.'
320. As noted by Carroll J. in *Ramathan Arulchelvan v. Wright* (unreported, High Court, Carroll J, 7 Feb. 1996).
321. *Re Baltic Real Estate Ltd* (No. 1) [1993] BCLC 498.
322. *Jaber v. Science and Information Technology Ltd* [1992] BCLC 764.
323. *Re Allied Metropole Hotel Ltd; O'Tuama v. Allied Metropole Hotel Ltd* (unreported, High Court, Gannon J, *ex tempore*, 19 Dec. 1988).
324. *Devlin v. O'Driscoll and SGC Global Advanced Technologies Ltd [2020] IEHC 630 which followed a clear statement of this principle by Laffoy J in Re Charles Kelly Ltd. [2010] IEHC 38.*
325. *See* generally Irene Lynch Fannon, *A Transatlantic Case: The Derivative Action as a Corporate Governance Tool* 27 DULJ (2005) 1–27.

235. Must a petitioning member be a *minority* shareholder? There is no doubt that a 50% shareholder may apply, at least in the case of a company made up of equal 50–50 shareholders.[326] In *Re Westwinds Holding Company Ltd*, Kenny J. said '[t]he word "minority" does not appear in any part of the section and the heading is merely a convenient way of describing the majority of cases in which the section will apply'. Thus it appears that, in theory at least, a majority member could apply for relief under section 212. The point has not been conclusively decided, although in one English case, a motion to strike out a petition, on the ground that the petitioner was a majority shareholder, failed.[327]

236. A final point to note regarding standing is that the second limb of section 212 refers to conduct 'in disregard of his or their interests *as members*', a qualification that is absent from the preceding 'oppression' limb. The courts have accordingly held that a shareholder who is also a director, employee or creditor of the company may apply to the court on foot of conduct alleged to be *oppressive* of him or her in one of those other capacities, rather than strictly *qua* shareholder. For example, an injunction may be granted under section 212 restraining the company in general meeting from exercising its power under section 146 to remove a director, pending the hearing of a section 212 petition.[328] Likewise, in *Re Murph's Restaurants Ltd*,[329] McWilliam J. at the interlocutory stage was of the view that section 205 applied 'only to members of a company as members'. But in the later full hearing, Gannon J. (though ultimately ordering that the company be wound up) did not doubt that the Court would have had jurisdiction to make an order under section 205 on foot of complaints by the petitioner that he was excluded as a director.[330]

237. The concept of oppression has been held to refer to conduct of the company's affairs (or exercise of directors' powers) 'in a manner burdensome, harsh and wrongful'.[331] In *Re Irish Visiting Motorists' Bureau Ltd*,[332] Kenny J. held that the affairs of a company may be conducted oppressively, even though those in charge are acting honestly and in good faith. It is not an answer that those conducting the company's affairs or exercising the powers of directors *believe* they are within their rights. The question rather is whether conduct, 'judged by objective standards', is oppressive.[333] Nothing in the statute requires a deliberate scheme or intent.

238. The phrase 'disregard of his or their interests as members' in the second limb of section 212 encompasses more than a petitioner's strictly defined legal

326. *Irish Press PLC v. Ingersoll Irish Publications* (unreported, High Court, 16 Dec. 1993).
327. *Re Baltic Real Estate Ltd* (No. 1) [1993] BCLC 498.
328. *Gilligan v. O'Grady* [1999] 1 IR 46, [1999] 1 ILRM 303 (disapproving of *Feighery v. Feighery* [1999] 1 IR 321).
329. *Re Murph's Restaurants Ltd* [1979] ILRM 141.
330. *Ibid.*, J. Gannon said 'the purported exclusion of [the petitioner] by the [respondents] in an irregular and arrogant manner is undoubtedly oppressive'. (*Re Murph's Restaurants Ltd* [1979] ILRM 141, 152).
331. *Re Greenore Trading Company Ltd* [1980] ILRM 94, 100–101 (citing *Scottish Co-operative Wholesale Society Ltd v. Meyer* [1959] AC 324, 342 per Viscount Simonds).
332. *Re Irish Visiting Motorists' Bureau Ltd* (unreported, High Court, 7 Feb. 1972).
333. *Ibid.*, 33.

rights. A petitioner must point to an identifiable interest related to, and prejudiced by, the conduct of the affairs of the company or exercise of the directors' powers.[334] A single act or transaction, if sufficiently prejudicial, may be sufficient for the court to invoke the jurisdiction of section 212,[335] and the contrary view (that there is some rule or presumption that an isolated act cannot amount to oppression) cannot be regarded as correct, being an unnecessary gloss on the wording of the statute.[336]

239. The court has wide discretion to make 'such order as it thinks fit', and in doing so, section 212 permits it to cancel or vary any transaction, order the purchase of shares of any member's shares by other members or by the company (with the consequent capital reduction), or make an order regulating the company's future affairs. The section provides that the remedy ordered by the court must be made 'with a view to bringing to an end the matters complained of'. Prior to the coming into operation of the 2014 Act, the Supreme Court had held that this remedial discretion does not extend to awarding compensatory damages,[337] where such an award adds nothing to the ending of the matters complained of, but that when an order is made that a petitioner's shares be purchased, determination of a fair price might validly include 'an incidental element of compensation'.[338] Section 212(3) of the 2014 Act now provides that among the types of order which the Court may make on a section 212 petition is an order 'for the payment of compensation'. However, this order must be made with a view to bringing an end to the matters complained of, so that it is still possible that an argument could be made against a substantial award of compensatory damages on this ground.

240. All of these elements in this remedy point to a great deal of flexibility. The section 212 remedy has proved popular with shareholder litigants and is particularly useful in addressing particular issues that arise in private companies. *See* further *infra*, Part I, Chapter 2.

G. Annual Account and Report, Profits and Dividends

241. The business of the AGM shall include certain items which are set out in statute:[339]

(a) the consideration of the company's statutory financial statements and the report of the directors and, the report of the statutory auditors on those statements and that report;

---

334. *Re Leeds United Holding PLC* [1996] 2 BCLC 545 (sale of a member's shares cannot amount to conduct of the 'affairs of the company').
335. *Re Westwinds Holding Company Ltd* (unreported, High Court, 21 May 1974), 17 (sale of lands was 'fraudulent and oppressive to the petitioner and was in total disregard of his interest as a member of the company'); *Re Williams Group Tullamore Ltd* [1985] IR 613.
336. *Re Greenore Trading Company Ltd* [1980] ILRM 94.
337. *Irish Press PLC v. Ingersoll Irish Publications Ltd* (No. 4) [1995] 2 IR 175.
338. *Ibid.*, 190. *See also Horgan v. Murray* [1997] 3 IR 23.
339. Companies Act 2014, s. 186.

(b) the review by the members of the company's affairs;
(c) save where the company's constitution provides otherwise – (i) the declaration of a dividend (if any) of an amount not exceeding the amount recommended by the directors; and (ii) the authorisation of the directors to approve the remuneration of the statutory auditors (if any);
(d) where the company's constitution so provides, the election and re-election of directors;
(e) the appointment or re-appointment of statutory auditors; and
(f) where the company's constitution so provides, the remuneration of the directors.

242. Irish company law distinguishes between the *ordinary* and *special* business of a general meeting.

The AGM may also deal with any other business, which could include, for example, the amendment of the company's Memorandum or Articles of Association. It must be noted, however, that this business can only be conducted by vote through a special resolution; thus, this kind of business is indicated as being a special business. Special business must be set out in at least general terms in the notice convening the meeting; otherwise, the notice will be invalid.

H. Dividends

243. In general, under Irish company law, the shareholders have no entitlement or right to a dividend.

244. The rules set out below apply, save to the extent that the company's constitution provides otherwise.[340] A company may, by ordinary resolution, declare dividends but no dividend shall exceed the amount recommended by the directors of the company.[341]

The directors of a company may from time to time – (a) pay to the members such interim dividends as appear to the directors to be justified by the profits of the company, subject to section 117; (b) before recommending any dividend, set aside out of the profits of the company such sums as they think proper as a reserve or reserves which shall, at the discretion of the directors, be applicable for any purpose to which the profits of the company may be properly applied, and pending such application may, at the like discretion either be employed in the business of the company or be invested in such investments as the directors may lawfully determine; (c) without placing the profits of the company to reserve, carry forward any profits which they may think prudent not to distribute.[342]

340. Companies Act 2014, s. 124(1).
341. Companies Act 2014, s. 124(2).
342. Companies Act 2014, s. 124(3).

The principal rule is that dividends can only be declared where the company has realised a profit net of all losses and liabilities. These are now calculated in accordance with rules derived from EU Directives enacted in the Companies Act 2014. As observed by Clarke J in *Re Irish Life and Permanent PLC,*[343] '... profits for the purposes of considering whether distribution under s. 45 can take place, must mean profits calculated in accordance with the relevant applicable accountancy standards. It follows, therefore, that it is movements in the assets of the company by reference to such standards that need to be considered in the context of determining whether profits within the meaning of the Act, can be said to have occurred.' However, even where such a profit is realised in any given year, there is no obligation on the directors to declare a dividend. Doing so is entirely a matter at the discretion of the board. Once the dividend is declared, this must be presented to the shareholders to approve. The shareholders retain what is essentially a right to veto the declaration of the dividend, but they are not entitled to recommend a particular amount or take the initiative in declaring the dividend. It may be that in extreme situations, the shareholders may force the payment of a dividend where there has been persistent non-declaration of a dividend over a number of profitable years. This occurred in the famous US case of *Dodge v. Ford Motor Company*, but a perhaps more relevant and compelling authority in Irish law is the English case of *Re Sam Weller & Sons Ltd.*[344] Finally, it should be noted that where a company is solvent upon liquidation, the shareholders are entitled to a pro rata distribution of surplus funds as residual owners of the company's assets.

II. 'Administrative' or Management Body

A. *Directors and 'Administrative Board': General Structure of Management as Provided for in Statute*

245. As described in earlier sections, what were hitherto the Articles of Association have been largely codified into statutory form under the Companies Act 2014. To recap, the Memo and Articles of Association of a private company limited by shares have been replaced with a Constitution, a much shorter document. For PLCs, the Constitution of the company is a term used to collectively describe the Memorandum and Articles of Association. The statute provides the default provisions in the case of PLCs and it will be a matter of opting out of these default provisions for a PLC. Generally, this structure will govern the composition of the Board of Directors and to some extent, the management of a company. It should be noted that the term 'administrative board' is not used in common law company law codes.

343. *Re Irish Life and Permanent plc* [2009] IEHC 567.
344. *Re Sam Weller & Sons Ltd* [1990] Ch. 682, [1990] BCLC 80; *Dodge v. Ford Motor Company* 170 N.W. 668 (1919).

1. Board of Directors

246. Section 158 of the Companies Act 2014 and the following provisions create the structure for the operation of the Board of Directors in Irish company law. Generally, the term Administrative Board or Administration is not part of common law terminology.

2. Directors and Administrative Board: Appointment, Remuneration and Dismissal

247. In governance terms, shareholders in any company are considered to be the residual owners of the company with residual ownership of the company's power to act. Previously, the standard-form Articles of Association provided for the appointment of the Board of Directors and then a general delegation of these powers to the Board and from the Board on to the Managing Director. However, the Companies Act 2014 now provides for appointment and delegation by statute. Accordingly, the provisions of what was Article 80 of the standard-form Articles of Association in Table A of the 1963 Act are now included as provisions of the Companies Act, 2014. Section 158 states that:

> (1) The business of the company shall be managed by its directors … who may exercise all such powers of the company as are not, by this Act or by the constitution, required to be exercised by the company in general meeting, but subject to any regulations contained in the constitution; the provisions of this Act; and such directions, not being inconsistent with the foregoing regulations or provisions, as the company in general meeting may (by special resolution) give … .

248. Similarly, the authority of the Managing Director which used to be provided for in standard-form Articles of Association (Articles 110–112 inclusive described the position of the Managing Director) is now described in section 159 of the Companies Act 2014 which states that:

> The directors of a company may from time to time appoint one or more of themselves to the office of managing director (by whatever name called) for such period and on such terms as to remuneration and otherwise as they see fit, and, subject to the terms of any agreement entered into in any particular case, may revoke such appointment … .

249. Section 160(8) of the Companies Act now replaces the old Article 104 of the Articles of Association. It provides that:

> The directors may elect a chairperson of their meetings and determine the period for which he or she is to hold office, but if no such chairperson is elected, or, if at any meeting the chairperson is not present within 15 minutes

after the time appointed for holding it, the directors present may choose one of their number to be chairperson of the meeting.

3. Removal

250. Under sections 146 and 147 of the 2014 Act, the shareholders in general meetings may remove any director on foot of an ordinary resolution. This right on the part of the shareholders is an important element in the balance of power between the shareholders in a general meeting and the Board of Directors. This power to remove directors is without prejudice to any rights under contract the directors might have. In addition, some authority in Ireland indicates that the directors may have constitutional rights in relation to procedure. This shall not, in the case of a private company, authorise the removal of a director holding office for life. Irish company law still allows for directors to be appointed for life in private companies, but this is not permissible in public companies where directors must retire from office after a period of years.

B. Powers of Management and Representation

251. Before the enactment of the Companies Act 2014, the standard-form Articles of Association envisaged a general delegation of management functions to the Board of Directors, which in turn delegates to a managing director. Section 158 of the Companies Act 2014 repeats this delegation in statutory form. Established principles of company law indicate that the effect of this provision (hitherto contained in the Articles of Association) is to render void and inoperative a shareholder resolution passed in a general meeting purporting to instruct the board to carry out its management functions in a particular manner. This principle also applies most importantly to the decision to initiate litigation. The Companies Act 2014, section 158(3) also specifically refers to borrowing powers to be exercised by the directors on behalf of the company. Any limitations on the authority of a director to act on behalf of the company are now dealt with under section 40 of the Companies Act 2014. This provision states that the 'board of directors of the company; and b) any registered persons' shall be deemed to have authority to exercise any power of the company and to authorise others to do so. It goes on to provide that any person who is authorised by the Board to bind the company must be registered. (This provision is similar to that which has pertained under the European Companies Regulation 1973 and complies with EU Regulations). So for example, a director who has been elected as a Managing Director usually has power to bind the company. This person should be registered under section 40 for clarity and certainty.

1. Representation

252. Any outsider is entitled to rely on the authority of an individual registered with the authority to bind the company.

2. The Managing Director

253. Section 159 goes on to elaborate the powers of a Managing Director as described above and section 159 simply states in subsection (4) ' Without prejudice to section 40, the directors may confer upon a managing director any of the powers exercisable by them upon such terms and conditions and with such restrictions as they may think fit.'

3. The Chairman of the Board

254. In accordance with the statutory scheme described above, section 160 places the old Article 104 of the standard-form Articles of Association and now describes the role of the Chairman of the Board.

4. Board Meetings

255. As with shareholders' meetings, the rules regarding the conduct of Board meetings are now statutory default rules and must be specifically excluded by the company's constitution if they are not to apply. Section 161(1) provides that a resolution in writing signed by all the directors of a company shall be valid as if it has been passed at a meeting of the directors. But note that section 166 concerning minutes cannot be excluded.

256. The delegation of the power of shareholders to the Board and from the Board to the Managing Director will always be subject to the Companies Act 2014. The Companies Act will therefore explicitly reserve to the shareholders, in general meeting, a number of important powers.

257. Section 40 of the Companies Act 2014 provides that '(a) the board of directors of the company; and (b) any registered persons' shall be deemed to have authority to exercise any power of the company and to authorise others to do so. Any person who is authorised by the Board to bind the company must be registered. When all is done appropriately, this statement is not problematic. However, where individuals act without actual authority, these provisions must be considered in the light of the existing case law.

258. Several cases[345] form the basic framework for resolving issues surrounding the authority of a company's agents. Specifically, this problem normally arises in relation to either a director or a managing director purporting to act on behalf of the company where he or she lacks authority. Authority is usually described as being

345. *Holdsworth and Co. Ltd v. Caddies* [1955] 1 WLR 352; *Freeman and Lockyear v. Buckhurst Park Properties Ltd* [1964] 2 QB 480; *Hely -Hutchinson v. Brayhead Ltd* [1968] 1 QB 549; *Allied Irish Banks v. Ardmore Studios International Ltd* (No. 2) (unreported, High Court, Finlay J., 30 May 1973); *Ulster Investment Bank v. Euro Estates Ltd* [1982] ILRM 57.

actual or implied. Where there is actual authority, there is usually no difficulty as the acts of the director or others are agreed to by the company. However, where a company seeks to deny the actions of the director, difficulties arise. Where the director or other officer has actual authority, the company is bound:

> Actual authority can be expressly conferred on a company's board of directors or it can be expressly conferred by the board of directors on an agent or it can impliedly be conferred by them on an agent. Thus, when a board of directors appoints a 'managing director' or a 'secretary' it impliedly confers on the person so appointed the powers usually associated with holders of such offices.[346]

259. Where there is no actual authority, the authority may be implied or ostensible. The different kinds of authority are described by Henchy J. for the Supreme Court in *Kett v. Shannon and English*[347] (following the analysis of English case law in the decision of Diplock L.J. in *Freeman and Lockyear v. Buckhurst Park Properties Ltd*):[348]

> Actual authority exists when it is based on an actual agreement between the principal and the agent. … Ostensible authority, on the other hand, derives not from any consensual arrangement between the principal and the agent, but is founded on a representation made by the principal to the third party which is intended to convey, and does convey, to the third party that the arrangement entered into under the apparent authority of the agent will be binding on the principal.

These principles have been applied consistently over time in both the English and Irish courts. In *Ulster Factors Ltd v. Entonglen Ltd and Maloney*,[349] the court held that the plaintiffs were entitled to rely on the ostensible authority of the agent in question as the company had made a tacit representation of his authority upon which the plaintiff had relied, and the authority had not been explicitly rebutted by any action of the company.

260. In this context, the doctrine of constructive notice is important in terms of imputing knowledge to the third party of the authority or otherwise of the alleged agent. Although the common law assumes that persons dealing with ostensible agents have read the company's publicly available constitutional documents (i.e., the Memorandum and Articles of Association which form the constitution of the company), the rule in *Royal British Bank v. Turquand*,[350] also known as the 'indoor management rule', ameliorates the position by allowing any third party or outsider

346. *Thomas Williamson Ltd v. Bailieborough Co-Operative Agricultural Society Ltd* (unreported, High Court, Costello J., 31 Jul. 1986).
347. *Kett v. Shannon & English* [1987] ILRM 364. *See also EES -Food ES v. Crown Shipping (Ireland) Ltd* [1991] ILRM 97.
348. *Freeman and Lockyer v. Buckhurst Park Properties (Mangal) Ltd* [1964] 2 QB 480.
349. *Ulster Factors Ltd v. Entonglen Ltd and Maloney* (unreported, High Court, Laffoy J., 21 Feb. 1997).
350. *Royal British Bank v. Turquand* (1856) 6 E & B 327; [1843–60] All ER 435.

dealing with the company to proceed on the basis that any matter that is properly regarded as an internal management matter has been properly effected with no irregularities. This reflects the fact that such matters are not matters of public record and cannot be verified by an outsider dealing with the company.[351] Thus, for example, when an ordinary resolution or board resolution is required to effect a particular transaction, the outsider is entitled to rely on representations that such resolutions have been passed. However, the rule now provided for in section 40(9) of the 2014 Act which states that where a question of ostensible authority arises, no 'reference shall be made to the company's constitution' may disadvantage an outsider in certain circumstances. In effect this provision does not allow for the corporate documents to be used to 'build' up the authority of an ostensible agent. Section 40(11) states that the entire section is 'in addition to, and not in substitution for, the Rule in *Royal British Bank v. Turquand*' otherwise known as the 'indoor management rule.' This changes the position of the outsider when they are dealing with unregistered persons as an individual's authority is more directly linked to provisions in the Companies Act 2014 as they pertain to the office of director or managing director, coupled with the question of whether the individual is registered or not. If an individual is not registered, or where the individual is not registrable in that this individual has only been given limited authority, the effectiveness of the registration system contained in section 40 is limited and the case law will apply where there are issues around ostensible or 'held out' authority.

261. In summary:

The following changes from the previous position have been made pursuant to the Companies Act 2014:

(i) The registration of particular individuals with the authority to bind the company is much more important under Irish law.

(ii) Where representations are made or transactions entered into by an individual without authority, any such representations made by an unregistered person present the third party with a slightly different proposition from before as now there is a formal system of registration. An individual acting in good faith would be obliged to enquire as to why the person is not registered.

(iii) Following on from this section 40 of the Companies Act 2014 now provides that the constitution of a company cannot be relied upon to build up authority. (This is slightly different from the position under previous case law).

(iv) Finally, section 40 states that the rule in *Turquand's* case still applies. In *Re Motor Racing Circuits Ltd* Blayney J. stated: '… Turquand's case says that where a matter appears to be regular then the party dealing with the company is not affected if in fact by reason of some error in the internal management of the company there is an irregularity.'

351. *Ulster Investment Bank Ltd v. Euro Estates Ltd* [1982] ILRM 57; *Cox v. Dublin Distillery Co.* (No. 2) [1915] IR 345; *Montreal and St Laurence Light and Power Co. v. Robert* [1906] AC 196.

However, this applies only to internal errors, and not where the irregularity is of public record.

C. Duties of Directors

262. The duties that directors owe are primarily fiduciary in character and are in part derived from principles of equity. They are inclusive of a duty of loyalty and inclusive of a duty to exercise powers of the company which are delegated to them in good faith and for the benefit of the company. The duty of skill and care is generally not considered to be of the same fiduciary provenance. It is regarded as being derived from common law principles but is significant and becomes increasingly so with the advent of new legislative standards discussed *infra*. These duties are now codified in sections 224, 224A, 227 and 228 of the Companies Act 2014.

1. To Whom Are the Duties Owed?

263. Section 227(1) of the Companies Act 2014 states that 'Without prejudice to the provisions of any enactment (including this Act), a director of a company shall owe the duties set out in section 228 (the "relevant duties") to the company (and the company alone).' This reiterates the position under the existing case law – namely that directors' duties are owed to the company itself as a separate entity and are not, as a matter of course, enforceable by individual shareholders.[352] The company is therefore the proper plaintiff in all cases enforcing these duties. Where the company is in insolvency, the liquidator will have this cause of action against directors. In certain narrow circumstances, the rule that the company is the proper plaintiff in enforcing directors' duties does not hold. It is sometimes possible that a director may owe a duty to particular shareholders enforceable by them, such as by virtue of a representation or undertaking made by a director.[353] As to when directors' duties to the company may be enforced by shareholders on behalf of the company, *see* paragraphs 245 ff., *infra*. In regard to other 'corporate stakeholders', section 228(1)(h) of the Companies Act 2014 states that directors owe a duty to take into account the interests of members of the company in addition to the statement in section 224 that directors must have regard to the interests of employees. These provisions reflect the statement previously contained in the 1990 Act which stated that '[t]he matters to which the directors of a company are to have regard in the performance of their functions shall include the interests of the company's employees in general, as well as the interests of members'.[354] The relevant section goes on to provide that 'the duty imposed by this section on the directors shall be owed by them to the company (and the company alone) and shall be enforceable in the same way

352. *Percival v. Wright* [1902] 2 Ch. 421.
353. *Crindle Investments v. Wymes* [1998] 2 ILRM 275; *Coleman v. Myers* [1977] 2 NZLR 225; *Re Chez Nico (Restaurants) Ltd* [1992] BCLC 192; *Peskin v. Anderson* [2000] 2 BCLC 1.
354. Companies Act 1990, s. 52(1).

as any other fiduciary duty owed to a company by its directors'.[355] As a company nears or enters insolvency, it appears that directors owe duties (albeit of uncertain scope) to creditors. This duty is now codified following the enactment of the European Union (Preventive Restructuring) Regulations 2022 which enacts Article 19 of the Preventive Restructuring Directive (EU) 2019/1023. Directors owe duties where they are aware of insolvency under the amended section 228(1)(i) (where sub section (1)(i) has been added by the Regulations, and where they know or ought to have known of probable insolvency under section 224A.[356] Section 227 of the Companies Act 2014 clarifies the position regarding the codification of all of these duties as follows: 'The relevant duties (other than those set out in section 228 (1)(b) and (h)) are based on certain common law rules and equitable principles as they apply in relation to the directors of companies and shall have effect in place of those rules and principles as regards the duties owed to a company by a director' However, even though the above statutory language states that the codified rules shall have effect in place of case law section 228(5) goes on to state that:

> The relevant duties (other than those set out in section 228 (1)(b) and (h)) shall be interpreted, and the provisions concerned … shall be applied, in the same way as common law rules or equitable principles; regard shall be had to the corresponding common law rules and equitable principles in interpreting those duties and applying those provisions.[357]

264. The following text provides a synopsis of the case law on these duties and the relationship between the case law and the statutory provisions.

2. No Secret Profits

265. Duties that are fiduciary in character include a no-conflict principle, which prohibits a director from placing himself or herself in a position of conflict of interest. A fiduciary may not 'enter into engagements in which he has, or can have, a personal interest conflicting, or which may possibly conflict, with the interests of those whom he is bound to protect'.[358] A subset of this is the rule that a director cannot use his or her position to make a secret profit. If this occurs, the director will be liable to account for the monies so made. In *Regal (Hastings) v. Gulliver*,[359] the directors made a somewhat incidental profit in relation to the transfer of the shares

355. Companies Act 2014, s. 224(2).
356. *Re Frederick Inns Ltd* [1994] 1 ILRM 387; *Jones v. Gunn* [1997] 2 ILRM 245; *Parkes v. Hong Kong & Shanghai Bank Corp.* [1990] ILRM 341. It should be noted that the CLRG in its Report on the Protection of Employees and Unsecured Creditors 2017 that this duty ought to be codified in s. 224A of the Companies Act 2014. This duty came under review for a second time in 2020–2021 by the CLRG and again it was recommended this would be codified. It is now codified following the transposition of the European Preventive Restructuring Directive (EU) 2019/1023.
357. The duties set out in s. 228(1)(b) and s. 228(1)(h) are the duties to act honestly and responsibly and the duty to members, respectively.
358. *Aberdeen Railway Co. v. Blaikie* (1854) 1 Macq HL 461, 471 *per* Lord Cranworth LC.
359. *Regal (Hastings) v. Gulliver* [1942] All ER 378; cf. *see also Aberdeen Railway Co. v. Blaikie* (1854) 1 Macq HL 461 and *Bray v. Ford* [1896] AC 44.

in Regal Hastings, which was part of a restructuring plan. The directors had originally invested in shares of Regal to assist in financing the company. Despite the fact that this agreement was entered into in good faith and partly for the benefit of the company, this matter was held to be irrelevant. The House of Lords held that:

> The rule of equity which insists on those who by use of a fiduciary position make a profit, being liable to account for that profit, in no way depends on fraud, or absence of bona fides; or upon questions or considerations as whether the property would or should otherwise have gone to the plaintiff, or whether he took a risk or acted as he did for the benefit of the plaintiff, or whether the plaintiff has in fact been damaged or benefited by his action.[360]

The House indicated that if the profit had been disclosed and ratified by the shareholders, the directors would have been exonerated from liability. Essentially disclosure is key to absolution of directors. Certain kinds of transactions are not capable of ratification though, and the dividing line in that regard is uncertain. Finally, in Regal, this liability to account only applied to the investors who were directors. The company's solicitor, Garton, was not liable as he was not in a fiduciary position to the company. Nor, indeed, was Gulliver, who, although a director, had not invested himself but had simply sought investment from the directors. This authority has been expressly followed by the Irish courts in a decision in *AIB and Ors. v. Diamond and Ors.*[361]

D. Corporate Opportunity Doctrine

266. A second aspect commonly played out in the case law on directors' fiduciary duties is the rule against directors taking corporate opportunities. This rule prohibits a director from taking for themselves or 'direct[ing] to another person or company with whom or which he is associated'[362] a business opportunity properly belonging to the company. In *IDC Ltd v. Cooley*,[363] the defendant undertook to secure contracts for the plaintiff with the Eastern Gas Board in England, but in the course of negotiations, he was given an indication that the Gas Board would be interested in contracting with him personally rather than with the plaintiff company. The defendant resigned and took up this opportunity. Subsequently, the company successfully sued the defendant to account for all profits made under this contract. These duties are regarded as almost similar to strict liability claims, in that once a breach is found, the director is liable to account for all profits, regardless of the loss his or her actions actually caused and regardless of the probability of the company receiving the benefit, as is aptly illustrated by *IDC Ltd v. Cooley*. Furthermore, the issue of good faith or bad faith is not centrally relevant to the liability being

360. *Ibid.*, 386 *per* Lord Russell of Killowen.
361. [2011] IEHC 505
362. *Canaero v. O'Malley and Ors.* [1974] S.C.R. 592, 606–607.
363. *IDC Ltd v. Cooley* [1972] 2 All ER 162.

imposed. In *Canaero Ltd v. O'Malley*,[364] Laskin J. found against the defendants and imposed on them the liability to account for all profits to the company. The resignation of the defendants was held to be immaterial as the opportunity had come to their attention prior to their resignation while they were still directors.

267. These lines of authority are now encapsulated in the following provisions of the Companies Act 2014:

> '228. (1) A director of a company shall – … .
> (d) not use the company's property, information or opportunities for his or her own or anyone else's benefit unless –
> (i) this is expressly permitted by the company's constitution; or
> (ii) the use has been approved by a resolution of the company in general meeting;'
>
> And
>
> '228. (1) A director of a company shall – … .
> (f) avoid any conflict between the director's duties to the company and the director's other (including personal) interests unless the director is released from his or her duty to the company in relation to the matter concerned, whether in accordance with provisions of the company's constitution in that behalf or by a resolution of it in general meeting.'

268. There are some possible defences to be made out on the facts. For example, it is possible for the defendant director to argue that the opportunity which the plaintiff company seeks to reclaim is not a corporate opportunity, either because the company had already rejected the particular opportunity, as occurred in *Peso Silver Mines Ltd v. Cropper*,[365] or because the particular contract can be separated from the pattern of trading in which the company was engaged and regarded as a separate opportunity. In *Peso*, apart from the fact that the company had rejected the opportunity offered to it, it was also considered to be significant that the defendant had come across the information regarding the licence agreement separately and outside of this position on the Board. In *Island Export Finance Ltd v. Ummuna*,[366] the information at issue related, it was argued, to a separate, albeit similar, contract. The defendant argued that even where previous contracts he had negotiated with the third party on behalf of the plaintiff were subject to the full range of fiduciary duties, the contracts at issue were not. The Court found as a fact that the defendant had resigned out of dissatisfaction with the plaintiff company rather than out of a desire to appropriate its business and that at that time, the plaintiff was not actively seeking repeat or further orders of that type. In effect, the defendant had left the company and pursued similar opportunities but not the same opportunities that had been pursued when he was a director of the plaintiff. The court accepted this argument.

364. *Canaero v. O'Malley and Ors* [1974] S.C.R. 592.
365. *Peso Silver Mines Ltd v. Cropper* [1966] S.C.R. 673.
366. *Island Export Finance Ltd v. Ummuna* [1986] BCLC 460.

269. *Bhullar v. Bhullar*[367] involved a family company owned and run by two brothers and their families. Relations between the two families broke down, and it was agreed in principle that the company should not acquire any further properties. Two member-directors, who together with their father held 50% of the shares and a 3:2 board majority, purchased a property adjacent to an investment property owned by the company in the name of a separate company controlled by them. The other 50% of shareholders – in effect, the other family – issued a petition under section 459 of the Companies Act 1985 (UK),[368] (the equivalent provision to the Irish s. 212) seeking that the respondents be ordered to sell their shares and/or an order that the purchase was a breach of fiduciary duty. The Court granted the latter relief, and that ruling was upheld by the Court of Appeal. It was sufficient for liability that the respondents did not disclose an opportunity that would have been advantageous to the company. 'Whether the company could or would have taken the opportunity, had it been made aware of it,' said Jonathan Parker L.J., was 'not the point'. The appellants' query to their solicitor as to whether there may be a conflict of interest was 'eloquent of the existence of a possible conflict of duty and interest,'[369] It is arguable that, if the petitioners in *Bhullar* wished to allege breaches of fiduciary duties, the correct course would have been to proceed by way of derivative action. That latter remedy is considered further *supra* (*see* paragraphs 243 ff.).

E. Involvement with a Competitor

270. A further subset of this area of law is whether a director is permitted to be involved in a competing company while a director of the first company. In *Bell v. Lever Bros Ltd*,[370] the Courts held that there is no absolute bar to this kind of activity, but nevertheless, the courts are wary of such arrangements. For example, in the older Irish case of *Moore v. McGlynn*,[371] the Court advised a trustee of a trust who was involved in an arrangement that potentially placed him in a conflict situation with the trust that he ought to resign as trustee as a precautionary measure. However, in the commercial world, such a recommendation is not always practicable, and so the courts have provided some leeway. Nevertheless, in *Spring Grove Services Ltd*,[372] the court expressed the view, albeit on a motion for discovery, that a director's fiduciary duties 'include a duty not to compete with the company', in the context of an allegation that a director had used confidential information obtained as director otherwise than for the benefit of the company.

271. Section 231(1) of the Companies Act 2014 states that:

---

367. *Bhullar v. Bhullar* [2003] 2 BCLC 241.
368. The Irish equivalent cause of action under Companies Act 2014, is provided in s. 212 discussed *supra*.
369. *Bhullar v. Bhullar* [2003] 2 BCLC 241, 256.
370. *Bell v. Lever Bros* [1932] AC 161.
371. *Moore v. McGlynn* [1894] 1 IR 74.
372. *Spring Grove Services (Ireland) Ltd v. O'Callaghan* (unreported, High Court, 31 Jul. 2000).

> It shall be the duty of a director of a company who is in any way, whether directly or indirectly, interested in a contract or proposed contract with the company, to declare the nature of his or her interest at a meeting of the directors of the company.
>
> (2) Subsection (1) does not apply in relation to an interest that cannot reasonably be regarded as likely to give rise to a conflict of interest.

F. Abuse of Power Doctrine

272. The abuse of power doctrine imposes an obligation on directors to exercise powers delegated to them by the shareholders in a general meeting for proper purpose, in good faith and for the benefit of the company. In surveying the litigation, the sorts of powers that are usually at issue are the powers to issue shares, the power to borrow and the power of giving guarantees and making payments or donations. In other jurisdictions, most notably the US (in particular, the state of Delaware), where the incidence of corporate litigation is higher, the cases have also focused on decisions directors and boards have made regarding takeover bids and executive remuneration. *Smith (Howard) Ltd v. Ampol Petroleum Ltd*[373] is illustrative of this category of case. In this case, the actions of the directors in issuing shares to a 'white knight' takeover bidder in defending a takeover bid from a competing and hostile shareholder interest were challenged. It was held that, in considering the purpose for which a particular power has been exercised, courts should consider motivations for which there is evidence. The dominant or primary purpose must be identified. If there is evidence of a predominantly proper purpose, the courts should not be concerned with other incidental motivations or desired results. In that case, a share issue for the purpose of diluting a majority shareholding block, so as to prevent that majority from rejecting a takeover bid favoured by the board, was held to be an exercise of power for an improper purpose, irrespective of whether the directors genuinely considered it to be in the best interests of the company. In *Re Jermyn Street Turkish Baths Ltd*,[374] an issue of shares, made to confer a predominant position on a 50% shareholder, was considered to be an exercise of power for a proper purpose, even though its purpose was not directly linked to the raising of capital, but rather to the securing of equity for cash deal that involved the allocation of control of the company to the investing shareholder.

273. In *Smith (Howard) Ltd v. Ampol Petroleum Ltd*, the court also articulated a rule equivalent to that described in US jurisprudence as the 'business judgment rule': The Court, in examining proper purpose in relation to the exercise of a power, must 'give credit to the *bona fide* opinion of the directors, if such is found to exist, and will respect their judgment as to matters of management'.[375] Further English decisions have reiterated this rule or approach. In *Regentcrest PLC v. Cohen*,[376] the

373. *Howard Smith Ltd v. Ampol Petroleum Ltd* [1974] AC 821.
374. *Re Jermyn Street Turkish Baths Ltd* [1971] 1 WLR 1042.
375. *Howard Smith Ltd v. Ampol Petroleum Ltd* [1974] AC 821, 835.
376. *Regentcrest plc v. Cohen* [2001] 2 BCLC 80.

court referred to Lord Green in *Re Smith and Fawcett Ltd.*[377] where it was stated that 'The principles to be applied are for present purposes free from doubt. They must exercise their discretion bona fide in what they consider – not what the court may consider – is in the interests of the company and not for any collateral purpose.'

274. The duty of a director to act in good faith regarding the exercise of a power delegated to him or her is now codified in section 228(1)(a) of the Companies Act 2014 which states:

> A director of a company shall act in good faith in what the director considers to be the interests of the company.

There is no statement of what is called the 'business judgment rule in the statute'. However, section 228 goes on to provide a number of specific rules which reflect existing case law. Section 228(2) states that:

> If a director of a company considers in good faith that it is in the interests of the company for a transaction … to be entered into … a director may restrict the director's power to exercise an independent judgment in the future by agreeing to act in a particular way to achieve this.

Furthermore, section 228(3) states that:

> Without prejudice to the director's duty under subsection (1)(a) to act in good faith in what the director considers to be the interests of the company, a director of a company may have regard to the interests of a particular member of the company in the following circumstances.
>
> (4) Those circumstances are where the director has been appointed or nominated for appointment by that member, being a member who has an entitlement to so appoint or nominate under the company's constitution or a shareholders' agreement.

These provisions recognise that it is possible for a director to 'fetter his discretion' as the older cases described it in certain circumstances.
However, in a recent High Court decision in *Keating v Shannon Foynes Port Company*[378] the court held that a company and its directors were not bound by the policies of a shareholder, even where, as in this case, the shareholder was the Irish state. The company had not paid additional performance related remuneration to the plaintiff, even though the possibility of such remuneration had been agreed in a contract of employment. The directors took the position that the shareholder (the State, as represented by the Minister) had stated policies against such remuneration. The plaintiff argued that the directors had duties to act in the best interests of the company and to comply with performance related pay requirements, which had been

377. *Re Smith and Fawcett Ltd* [1942] Ch.
378. *Keating v Shannon Foynes Port Company* [2022] IEHC 505.

contractually agreed with the plaintiff in a contract was acting in the best interests of the company. Failure to comply with a contract was a failure to act in the best interests of the company. In contrast the company had argued it was bound by the policies of the shareholder, particularly given the standing of the shareholder in this case. This argument was rejected by the court. In Irish law, there is some confusion between the principles set out in relation to this area of law and the enquiry under the *ultra vires* doctrine as to whether a power purportedly delegated to a board or a director is *ultra vires* the power of the company. The latter test involved exploring whether the exercise of a particular power, such as the power to borrow, is reasonably incidental to the business of the company. If this test is not met, then the power is regarded as being *ultra vires* and void. This test has been applied in numerous cases. For example, in *Parke v. Daily News Ltd*,[379] the making of *ex gratia* payments to the dependants of former employees, in circumstances where the company faced insolvency, was held by the court to have failed the *ultra vires* test as not being reasonably incidental to the business of the company. The court was unable to perceive a benefit for the company in the making of such payments.[380] However, the test for whether a particular director or board has exercised power in breach of their obligations *to the company* is whether the power is exercised in good faith and for the benefit of the company. If the particular exercise of the power fails this test, the director will be found to be in breach of his or her duties, but this does not affect the validity of the transaction per se. This distinction will no longer be so clear-cut following the abolition of the *ultra vires* rule under the Companies Act 2014. In *Nash v. Lancegaye (Ireland) Ltd*,[381] the board of directors sanctioned the issue of shares to secure a controlling interest for a particular director. In an action brought by a minority shareholder, the defendants argued that this issue of shares was in recognition of the individual's particular contribution to the company but primarily to raise much-needed capital. Dixon J. expressed himself to be unconvinced by the need for more capital and therefore was unconvinced that the power was exercised in good faith and for the benefit of the company.

G. The Duty of Skill and Care

275. A final area of obligation owed by directors to their companies is the common law obligation to exercise skill and care in the exercise of their duties. The duty of skill and care has been articulated in English and Irish company law in early cases such as *Re City Equitable Fire Insurance Co.*[382] The following principles are

379. *Parke v. The Daily News Ltd* [1962] Ch. 927.
380. Note that s. 52 of the 1990 Act includes an 'other stakeholder' provision permitting the directors to take into account the interests of employees in the exercise of their powers. These kinds of legislative provisions are therefore generally considered to be permissive, serving to broaden the scope of the directors' discretion, but s. 52 appears difficult if not impossible to enforce.
381. *Nash v. Lancegaye (Ireland) Ltd* (1958) 92 ILTR 11.
382. *Re City Equitable Fire Insurance Company Limited* [1925] 1 Ch. 407.

ascertainable from this decision. First, the duty of skill and care owed by each director relates to the circumstances of the individual appointee and the company.[383] Second, a director is not liable for mere errors of business judgment. As stated in the nineteenth-century, decision of *Lagunas Nitrate Co. v. Lagunas Syndicate*:

> If directors act within their powers, if they act with such care as is reasonably to be expected of them, having regard to their knowledge and experience, and if they act honestly for the benefit of the company they represent, they discharge both their equitable as well as their legal duty to the company.[384]

276. A director is not obliged to give continuous attention to board matters and finally in the same context, in the absence of grounds for suspicion or enquiry, the director is entitled to rely on the actions and expertise of others.[385]

277. In this area, the focus is less on the bona fides or honesty of a director than on the concept that there must be some minimum standard of competence below which a director should not fall. This idea or standard proved difficult to apply in company law as the courts and legislature were mindful of the fact that the term 'company director' is applicable to a broad range of individuals in companies varying both in terms of size and sectoral activities. However, in the more modern context, the courts and legislature have sought to establish some objective criteria. Accordingly, the traditional view is that negligence in and of itself will be insufficient to attract liability. Romer J. in the *City Equitable* case said that although a director must act honestly, he or she also must exercise some degree of skill and care. The question was what degree of care: 'For myself, I confess to feeling some difficulty in understanding the difference between negligence and gross negligence.'[386]

In the Irish decision of *PMPA Insurance Co. Ltd v. New Ireland Assurance Co. Ltd*, Kenny J. stated that 'the management of a company will not be interfered with unless it was in breach of Articles of Association, dishonest or grossly negligent'.[387]

These principles regarding the duty of skill and care of directors have been influenced in modern Irish company law by judicial consideration of the actions of directors under the directors' restriction and disqualification provisions introduced by the 1990 Companies Act, as amended by the 2001 Company Law Enforcement Act, and now re-enacted in Part 14 of the Companies Act 2014.[388] The extent to which there is cross-fertilisation between that area of law, primarily, but not exclusively, dealing with insolvency matters, and the standards discussed here, which arise because of shareholders' actions against directors in a solvent, ongoing situation, will continue to be clarified over time.

---

383. For an extreme example of variation, textbooks often refer to *Re Cardiff Savings Bank Ltd; Marquis of Bute's Case* [1892] 2 Ch. 100.
384. *Lagunas Nitrate Co. v. Lagunas Syndicate* [1899] 2 Ch. 392, 435.
385. *Jackson v. Munster Bank Ltd*, ex parte Dease (1885) 15 LR IR 356.
386. *Re City Equitable Fire Insurance Company Limited* [1925] 1 Ch. 407, 427.
387. *PMPA Insurance Co. Ltd v. New Ireland Assurance Co. Ltd* [1975] IR.
388. *See supra*, paras 251 forward.

One area that is particularly difficult for directors, particularly those holding what are termed non-executive directorships (although this term is not a legal term) is the question of the extent to which they are entitled to delegate to others in the company and the extent to which, when they delegate, as they must in larger companies, they must continue to supervise or monitor the activities of those to whom work is delegated. This issue arose in the older Irish case of *Jackson v. Munster Bank Ltd, ex parte Dease*,[389] in which a director who was primarily responsible for activities of the bank confined to one city was held responsible for failing to act to prevent abuses occurring in a branch in a different city. The fact that the defendant director had been notified of possible grounds for suspicion was held to be critical in that case. In *Dorchester Finance Co. Ltd v. Stebbing*,[390] the defendant directors who had carelessly signed blank cheques and who had not exercised any oversight function were held to be liable for losses caused to the plaintiff on foot of unenforceable loans. In *Barings Bank PLC (No. 5)*,[391] directors were disqualified for exhibiting serious failures of management and oversight regarding an incident of rogue trading, which effectively brought the bank to insolvency. These directors ignored audit recommendations to split the dealing and settlement offices in the Singapore branch of the bank. They oversaw the granting of requests for huge funding from Leeson without proper inquiry as to why such funding was necessary. The court found that there were effectively no internal management controls and stated that 'where delegation has taken place the board (and the individual directors) will remain responsible for the delegated function or functions and will retain a residual duty of supervision and control'. These principles have been incorporated into Irish law.[392]

278. In addition, the duties of skill and care which a director owes to his or her company have now been codified in section 228 Companies Act 2014 where section 228(1)(g) states that a director must:

> exercise the care, skill and diligence which would be exercised in the same circumstances by a reasonable person having both–
>
> (i) the knowledge and experience that may reasonably be expected of a person in the same position as the director; and
> (ii) the knowledge and experience which the director has.

389. *Jackson v. Munster Bank Ltd*, ex parte Dease (1885) 15 LR IR 356.
390. *Dorchester Finance Co. Ltd v. Stebbing* [1989] BCLC.
391. *Re Barings PLC* (No. 5) [2000] 1 BCLC 523.
392. *See* Nessa Cahill & Irene Lynch Fannon. In *Bloomsbury Professional's Guide to the Companies Act 2014* (Courtney ed., Bloomsbury 2015). *See also* the discussion in the Irish case law arising from the decisions in *Re Tralee Beef and Lamb Ltd.* [2008] 3 IR 347 and *Re Mitek Holdings* [2010] IESC 31.

H. Nominal Director

279. The terminology of nominal or non-executive director does not have specific legal significance in Irish law. One is either a company director or not, and each director owes the fiduciary duties arising from equity to the company. However, as regards the duties of skill and care, the expectations of a particular director will vary. The legislative provisions described above reflect that common law position. The law has moved from what might amount to a minimal set of obligations outlined under the authority of *Re City Equitable Fire Insurance,*[393] to imposing a minimum level of duty imposed on all directors under modern law. For example, in *Re Hunting Lodges Ltd,*[394] Carroll J. made some observations in relation to the role of a nominal or non-executive director that were criticised at the time but that were prescient in terms of standards largely accepted in modern company law. In that case, the court held that a director, regardless of whether he or she was executive or non-executive director, had a minimum set of obligations to which he or she must adhere. The Court cautioned that a person 'who continues as a director but abdicates all responsibility is not lightly to be excused'.[395] Keeping abreast of financial matters and ensuring that one is informed of financial statements was clearly a primary obligation. These minimum level of duties of skill and care have been reiterated in the context of modern company law provisions on restriction and disqualification.[396]

280. It is important to keep in mind that these standards were developed originally in the context of insolvency law and related statutory provisions. For example, the *Barings Bank PLC* case is a directors' disqualification case. The most usual outcome in these cases is a period of disqualification, whereas, in suits regarding an actual breach of director's duties, personal liability will be the outcome as it was in *Dorchester Finance* or the *Munster Bank* case. In the early 1990s, the incorporation of an objective element into the common law duties of care of a director began in earnest. In *Re d'Jan of London Ltd*[397] and *Norman v. Theodore Goddard,*[398] Lord Hoffman, or Hoffman J. as he then was, introduced an objective element into the duty of skill and care owed by directors to their companies in common law. It is not clear whether, aside from similar pronouncements made in the context of restriction and disqualification, these standards have been incorporated into Irish law. Therefore, the duty of skill and care as it is owed to a company may be quite subjective in character. However, in advising a director how to act or make decisions in an Irish context, decisions must and should be informed by the standards developed in the context of restriction and disqualification applications, which are discussed *infra.*

393. *Re City Equitable Fire Insurance Company Limited* [1925] 1 Ch. 407.
394. *Re Hunting Lodges Ltd* [1985] ILRM 75.
395. *Ibid.*, 85.
396. Cross reference.
397. *Re d'Jan of London Ltd* [1994] 1 BCLC 561.
398. *Norman v. Theodore Goddard* [1991] BCLC 1028.

I. Liability of Directors

281. In general and in the normal course of events, the duties of a director are owed to the company. As described above, this is now stated in section 227 of the Companies Act 2014. The company is therefore the proper plaintiff in enforcing such duties, a position that is not without its difficulties. A key issue regarding whether alleged breaches of directors' duties may be pursued is the possibility of ratification. Where an alleged breach is disclosed, the company can either absolve the director from liability by approving the breach, or it can choose to pursue the breach as the proper plaintiff to whom the duties are owed. If the company chooses to adopt the breach, the company, its board and its shareholders are bound by that. This raises the additional question of whether a breach is ratifiable by the company in this manner. Under Irish company law as with English company law, most breaches will be considered ratifiable – that is, capable of being approved once disclosed to the company. However, certain categories of actions are not ratifiable. In such instances, the company's cause of action against the director remains, regardless of whether the company purports to adopt or ratify the breach. Thus, a company cannot ratify an action of a director, which is a breach of duty amounting to a criminal act.[399] Similarly, acts that were *ultra vires* the company were not ratifiable for the obvious technical reason that it was not within the company's legal capacity to adopt such an act. It would seem that this principle is now moot given the new position regarding statements of objects in PLCs or activities in DACs where such statements are not to affect questions of the company's capacity. Beyond acts that are criminal and *ultra vires*, it becomes more difficult to identify what other conduct is not capable of ratification. It is relatively clear, however, that where an action of the director amounts to an expropriation of corporate property, these actions are not ratifiable, not capable of adoption by the company and therefore can be acted on in terms of suing a director for breach of duties.[400] Where the actions of directors are not ratifiable but where the majority of the shareholders and the board seek to adopt actions of the directors, a minority shareholder may have a remedy under the derivative action. Alternatively, an action under the Companies Act 2014, section 212, formerly section 205 of the 1963 Companies Act may provide redress for a shareholder.

1. Derivative Actions

282. The derivative action has roots stretching through case law to the eighteenth century,[401] but the doctrine as it currently stands in Ireland is principally drawn from a series of decisions from 1843 to 1901, of which the two most important are *Foss v. Harbottle*[402] and *Burland v. Earle*.[403] In *Foss*, the plaintiffs sued on

399. *Cockburn v. Newbridge Sanitary Steam Laundry* [1915] 1 IR 237.
400. *Cook v. Deeks* [1916] 1 AC 554; *Regal (Hastings) v. Gulliver* [1942] All ER 378.
401. *Charitable Corporation v. Sutton* (1742) 2 Atk. 400, 26 ER 642. See also *Hitchens v. Congreve* (1828) 4 Russ. 562, 38 ER 917.
402. *Foss v. Harbottle* (1843) 2 Hare 461; 67 ER 189.

behalf of themselves and all other shareholders in the company, except the defendants, alleging (among other things) that the defendants had purchased certain lands near Manchester, then formed a company and sold the land to that company at 'greatly increased and exorbitant prices'.[404] In addition to benefiting themselves, the suit alleged that the defendants had 'wasted and misapplied a considerable part of the monies belonging to the company'.[405] The defendants argued that the plaintiffs lacked standing to sue on behalf of the company. The Court thus had to consider 'whether the facts alleged in this case justify a departure from the rule which, prima facie, would require that the corporation should sue in its own and in its corporate character'.[406] Wigram V-C held that, '[i]f a case should arise of injury to a corporation by some of its members, for which no adequate remedy remained, except that of a suit by individual corporators in their private characters', then 'the claims of justice would be found superior to any difficulties arising out of technical rules respecting the mode in which corporations are required to sue'. The Court would, however, look for 'reasons of a very urgent character', before departing from the standard rule. In the present case, the plaintiffs lacked standing, because the general meeting had not addressed the question of whether to sue.

283. *Burland* involved a claim brought by minority shareholders to compel the directors to distribute as dividends a reserve fund that had accumulated over time. The plaintiffs contended that they had standing to bring the suit 'under the circumstances of an improper and oppressive use of their powers by the majority'.[407] Giving the judgment of the Privy Council, Lord Davey re-affirmed the rule that 'in order to redress a wrong done to the company or to recover monies or damages alleged to be due to the company, the action should prima facie be brought by the company itself'.[408] However, 'where the persons against whom the relief is sought themselves hold and control the majority of the shares in the company, and will not permit an action to be brought in the name of the company', 'the Courts allow the shareholders complaining to bring an action in their own names'.[409] But because in such an action, the plaintiffs cannot have a larger right to relief than the company itself would have if it were plaintiff, they cannot complain of 'acts which are valid if done with the approval of the majority of the shareholders, or are capable of being confirmed by the majority'.[410] Lord Davey added that the cases in which shareholders were allowed to bring such actions were 'confined to those in which the acts complained of are of a fraudulent character or beyond the powers of the company'. An example of this, said Lord Davey, citing *Menier v. Hooper's Telegraph*

403. *Burland v. Earle* [1902] 1 AC 83.
404. *Foss v. Harbottle* (1843) 2 Hare 461, 468; 67 ER 189, 193–194.
405. *Ibid.*, 471; 195.
406. *Ibid.*, 490–491, 202.
407. *Burland v. Earle* [1902] 1 AC 83, 89.
408. *Ibid.*, 93.
409. *Ibid.*
410. *Ibid.*

Works,[411] was 'where the majority are endeavouring directly or indirectly to appropriate to themselves money, property, or advantages which belong to the company, or in which the other shareholders are entitled to participate'.

284. The Irish Supreme Court[412] has approved the law as set out in *Burland* and reflected in more modern decisions of the English Court of Appeal.[413] Thus in *Balkanbank v. Taher*, the Supreme Court (*per* Hamilton C.J.) noted that the rule in *Foss v. Harbottle* 'is concerned with answering the question of who is the proper person to bring an action in respect of damage suffered by a Company. It states that the proper person is the Company itself'.[414] In the High Court decision of *Fanning v. Murtagh*,[415] the court considered that there were four (or perhaps five) 'exceptions to the rule in *Foss v. Harbottle*'. The principal 'exception' (properly so called) was stated as follows by the Supreme Court in *Balkanbank*: 'If a majority who are in control of a company commit a fraud on the minority, the minority, or an individual member acting on their behalf may maintain proceedings in respect of the fraud.'[416] As the Court noted, the word 'fraud' in this context does not necessarily connote dishonesty, let alone criminality, but rather is used 'more in the sense in which courts of equity were traditionally prone to use it'– that is, exercise of a power for a purpose other than the purposes for which it was entrusted, such conduct being described as 'a fraud on the power'.[417] Gross negligence is almost certainly sufficient to make out a case under this heading,[418] as too is ordinary negligence, at least where accompanied by an element of self-dealing.[419]

285. The other possible exception referred to in some authorities is that a derivative action should be permitted 'in the interests of justice'. In *O'Neill v. Ryan*,[420] the Supreme Court left open the question of whether an 'interests of justice' exception existed, but in *Glynn v. Owen*, Finlay Geoghegan J agreed with the extra-judicial view of Keane C.J. that 'the rule [... in Foss v. Harbottle ...] should not be applied in so rigorous a fashion ... as to lead to injustice', adding that it should not 'too broadly or liberally' be set aside, but only when 'a very strong case' has been made.[421] This approach was further affirmed by Irvine J. in *Fanning v. Murtagh.*

411. *Menier v. Hooper's Telegraph Works* (1874) LR 9 Ch App 350.
412. *O'Neill v. Ryan* [1995] ILRM 557; *Balkanbank v. Taher* (unreported, Supreme Court, 19 Jan. 1995).
413. *Edwards v. Halliwell* [1950] 2 All ER 1064, 1066; *Prudential Assurance Co. Ltd v. Newman Industries Ltd* (No. 2) [1982] 2 WLR 31.
414. *Balkanbank v. Taher* (unreported, Supreme Court, 19 Jan. 1995), 36. *Glynn and McCabe v. Owen and Others* [2007] IEHC 328, [2012] IESC 15.
415. *Fanning v. Murtagh* [2008] IEHC.
416. *Balkanbank supra* n. 411.
417. *Balkanbank* (*supra*), 36–37.
418. *Pavlides v. Jensen* [1956] Ch. 565.
419. *Daniels v. Daniels* [1978] Ch. 408, as approved by Finlay Geoghegan J. in *Glynn v. Owen* [2007] IEHC 328.
420. *O'Neill v. Ryan* [1993] ILRM 557.
421. *Glynn v. Owen* [2007] IEHC 328.

286. The case law suggests that a plaintiff seeking leave to proceed by way of derivative action must show that alleged wrongdoers control the voting power of the company in a general meeting and that it is accordingly futile to put the matter of whether the company should enforce the cause of action that the plaintiffs say exists.[422]

287. The procedure for a derivative action and the necessary exceptions to the rule in *Foss v. Harbottle* which provide grounds for the shareholder to acquire *locus standi* were summarised by Irvine J. in *Fanning v. Murtagh.*[423] In this case, the plaintiff had brought an action for oppression under what is now section 212 of the Companies Act 2014 but when the defendants sought to have this action dismissed the plaintiff, also initiated a derivative action on behalf of the company in question, Smart Telecom PLC which by the time of the action was EUR 50 million in debt and whose assets and liabilities had been acquired by the defendants through a vehicle called Smart Yuroe Ltd. The court noted that no Rules of Court were available to consider the nature of the action but adopted the approach outlined in the rules of the English court holding that for the plaintiff to proceed in this action and to acquire an indemnity for costs from the company, the plaintiff would have to show the following:-

(i) Evidence to support his claim to *locus standi* and to his right to relief claimed on behalf of the company.
(ii) Documentation of additional evidence to be brought to the court which is outside the plaintiff's knowledge or expertise.
(iii) An opinion from senior counsel that there was a reasonable chance of success based on the evidence set out at (i) and (ii)

288. Subsequently, Rules of Court have been passed to allow a plaintiff to bring this action in Irish law.[424]

289. The exceptional cases where a derivative action is available to a shareholder enabling him or her to sue on behalf of the company are enumerated as follows by Irvine J. in *Fanning v. Murtagh and Ors*:

(a) An act which is illegal or *ultra vires* to the company.
(b) An irregularity in the passing of a resolution which requires a qualified majority.
(c) An act purporting to abridge or abolish the individual rights of a member.

422. *Prudential Assurance Co. Ltd v. Newman Industries Ltd* (No. 2) [1982] 2 WLR 31.
423. *Fanning v. Murtagh* [2008] IEHC 277.
424. Order 15 R.S.C 1985 (as amended). *See* further Courtney para. 11.122.

(d) An act which constitutes fraud against the minority and the wrongdoers who are themselves in control of the company.[425]

290. As stated above, the fifth possible exception based on justice was considered in this decision. The court observed that the danger of accepting the proposition that there was an exception to the rule in *Foss v. Harbottle* based on justice might serve to support the 'very mischief that the rule sets out to eliminate' namely a shareholder embarking on litigation which involves the court hearing a 'full dress rehearsal' of a preliminary issue before deciding whether the plaintiff has the necessary *locus standi* at all.

291. There is a significant disincentive for potential plaintiffs to proceed by way of derivative action, since the benefit from any such action will flow to the company, not directly to the plaintiffs, and the plaintiff will carry the risk of incurring costs for himself and the company, as well as those of the defendant if he were to lose. As noted by O'Donnell J in *Glynn v. Owen* above, the issue of costs is a very significant problem in these kinds of cases. Recognising this difficulty, the courts have held that plaintiffs may apply to the Court for an order that the company must indemnify them against the costs of pursuing a corporate cause of action.[426]

292. Generally, as regards enforcement of directors' duties, the remaining difficulty is that the duties of a director are owed to the company. This means that the company must act as a plaintiff against a member of the board. As the decision to sue rests with the board acting on behalf of the company, it is not very often that this occurs, namely that the board will decide to sue 'one of their own' as it were. This will usually only happen where there has been a change of control in the company as in Regal Hastings, where the director has left the company as in *IDC v. Cooley* or where the company is in liquidation, or finally where a derivative action rests with the shareholder. For these reasons, what is called 'private enforcement' of directors' duties has been much less common and the more modern situation where directors are made accountable under modern legislation which provides for a type of public enforcement of directors' obligations is a much more common feature of company law in action. This phenomenon which we see in Irish law is also observable under UK Companies legislation.[427] Therefore, the modern legislation to which we now turn is extremely important in addressing standards of directorial behaviour.

---

425. *Fanning v. Murtagh and Ors* [2008] IEHC 277. Many aspects of this judgement have been cited with approval in subsequent decisions. *See Connolly v. Seskin Properties Ltd.* [2012] IEHC; *Kenny v. Eden Music, Lynch and Pender* [2013] IEHC 628 and *Saggart Motors Ltd. v. MC Motors Ltd.* [2019] IEHC 390.
426. *Wallersteiner v. Moir (No. 2)* [1975] QB 373; *Glynn v. Owen* [2007] IEHC 452 *Fanning v. Murtagh* [2008] IEHC 277. *See* further *Tomran Inc. William M. Passano Jr. et al., Baltimore City Circuit*, Matriacciani J. Court of Appeals of Maryland, 13 Dec. 2005. Irene Lynch Fannon, *A Transatlantic Case: The Derivative Action as a Corporate Governance Tool* 27 DULJ (2005) 1–27.
427. John Armour: 'Enforcement Strategies in UK Corporate Governance' in John Armour and Jennifer Payne (eds) *Rationality in Company Law: Essays in Honour of DD Prentice*. (Hart Publishing, 2009).

Before doing so it is worth noting however that where duties that directors owe to creditors is at stake, the company will very often be in an insolvency process of some kind and so the liquidator or relevant insolvency practitioner (in Ireland the most common alternative would be an Examiner) will be able to take action on behalf of the company against the directors. Therefore in many ways the duties to creditors could be more liable to enforcement than other duties which are typically at issue while the company is still a going concern. There has been some litigation in relation to the issue of when the duties that directors might owe to creditors take effect. A significant decision was handed down by the UK Supreme Court in the case of *BTI 2014 LLC v Sequana SA.*[428] Here directors of an insolvent company were sued by outstanding creditors in relation to a significant dividend which had been paid (within the normal rules for declaring dividends) almost 10 years before. The argument of the creditors was that directors had breached their duties in not taking account of the likelihood of insolvency which could be caused by the company's potential liabilities for polluting activity and because it was underinsured for these liabilities. The UK Supreme Court held that directors' duties owed to creditors did not arise unless the insolvency was at least probable at the relevant point of time. The duty arises when the directors know or ought to have known that the company was insolvent, bordering on insolvency or that insolvency was probable.

J. Obligations of Directors under Modern Legislation and Public

1. Enforcement

293. As with most common law jurisdictions, considerable change has been made to the enforcement of directors' obligations and more generally, standards of behaviour of directors and officers of companies by the enhancement of public law enforcement strategies. Beginning with the Companies Act 1990, extending through the McDowell Report of 1998 (the Working Group on Company Law Compliance and Enforcement) and the Company Law Enforcement Act 2001, Irish company law saw the introduction of disqualification procedures similar to those in the UK and Australia. In addition, Ireland followed the recommendations of the Cork Committee and introduced a restriction provision. These provisions are now contained in Part 14 of the 2014 Act.[429] In addition, changes have been made to the ODCE which was tasked under the Company Law Enforcement Act 2001 with the enforcement of various provisions. The body has now been established as a separate statutory body under the Companies (CEA) Act 2021.

294. Applications for restriction and disqualification orders under the provisions now enacted as Chapters 3 and 4 respectively of Part 14 of the Companies Act 2014 have generated considerable litigation in the Irish High Court with appeals to the

428. *BTI 2014 LLC v Sequana SA.* [2022] UKSC 25

429. *See* generally, Irene Lynch Fannon & Gerard N. Murphy, *Corporate Insolvency and Rescue* (Bloomsbury Professional, Dublin 2012) Chs 10 and 11. *See* Nessa Cahill, in Courtney (ed.) *Bloomsbury Professional's Guide to the Companies Act 2014* (Bloomsbury 2015) Ch. 8

Court of Appeal and in some cases, to the Supreme Court. The following sections provide a brief summary of the principles involved. Chapter 4 of Part 14 provides a mechanism by which a director of a company may be disqualified from acting as a director of any other company. Chapter 3 of Part 14 provides for the making of restriction orders against directors of insolvent companies and sets out certain conditions to be satisfied by the respondent director before s/he may become a company director, but does not represent an outright ban. However, it should also be borne in mind that the Court is free to attach such conditions as it sees fit to an order under Chapter 4 (a 'disqualification order'), with the result that a modified disqualification order may not be all that different from a restriction order.[430]

295. Chapter 4 section 838 envisages circumstances in which disqualification automatically follows certain events, including conviction of 'any indictable offence in relation to a company, or offences involving fraud or dishonesty'[431] and failure of a person disqualified in another State to inform the Registrar of Companies of that fact upon his or her appointment as director of an Irish company.[432] Apart from automatic disqualifications, Chapter 4 section 842 allows certain persons to apply to the Court in various circumstances for the Court in its discretion to decide whether to order disqualification. Applications may be made for disqualification on the grounds listed in section 842 viz. that the respondent:

(a) while promoter, officer, auditor, receiver, liquidator or examiner of the company, committed a fraud in relation to the company;
(b) while acting in any such capacity breached his duty to the company;
(c) has been the subject of a declaration of civil liability in respect of fraudulent or reckless trading;
(d) has, while promoter, officer, auditor, receiver, liquidator or examiner of the company, engaged in conduct making him unfit to be concerned in the management of a company;
(e) in consequences of a report of inspectors appointed by the Court, has engaged in conduct making him unfit to be concerned in the management of a company;
(f) has been persistently in default of statutory provisions requiring accounts, returns and documents to be sent to the Registrar of Companies;
(g) has been guilty of two offences in respect of failure to ensure compliance with section 286 of the 2014 Act (regarding books and accounts);
(h) was a director of a company at the date of sending to the company of a letter indicating intention of the Registrar of Companies under section 727 to strike the company off the Register for failure to file annual returns for three consecutive years and which was subsequently struck off under s. 733, or

430. Consider the order made in *Cahill v. Grimes* [2002] 1 IR 372.
431. Companies Act 2014, s. 838(1)(a) and (b) (for five years).
432. Companies Act 2014 s. 839.

(i) has been disqualified under the law of another State, and the Court finds that such conduct would have merited disqualification in this State, had it occurred here.

The Court, where satisfied on any of these matters, may, either on an application made to it or of its own motion, make a disqualification order against such person for such as it sees fit.[433] Most of the above categories of potential respondents – director, liquidator, receiver, etc. – are self-explanatory, but the term 'officer' has been held by the High Court to include a range of individuals who might be regarded as being in 'senior management' positions. The High Court 'recogniz[ing] the reality of the power and responsibility of senior management in large public or private companies who have particular expertise and authority', held that the section applied to 'those in a superior position in a company who may encourage, direct or acquiesce in defrauding creditors, customers, shareholders'.[434]

296. As to who may apply to the Court for a disqualification order, the Director of Corporate Enforcement (now the CEA) may apply under paragraphs (a)–(i) of section 842; the Director of Public Prosecutions may apply under paragraphs (a)–(g); the Registrar of Companies may apply under paragraph (f); and members, contributories, officers, employees, receivers, liquidators, examiners and creditors may apply under paragraphs (a)–(d).[435]

297. Many of the disqualification cases in Ireland have concerned the grounds under what was formerly section 160(2)(d) and (e) of the 1990 Act, now section 842(d) and (e), namely unfitness to be concerned in the management of a company. It has been held, that, in order to demonstrate unfitness, an applicant must prove conduct displaying a lack of commercial probity, gross negligence or total incompetence.[436] This standard is similar to that pertaining to English law. Two important decisions in the Supreme Court[437] and Court of Appeal[438] respectively provide clear guidance on the criteria which ought to be applied to these cases in light of the considerable divergence of approaches which has emerged in 20 years since the enactment of the original provisions. The Supreme Court for example in its decision in *ODCE v. McCann*,[439] reversed a decision of the High Court where the court had not disqualified the individual who had been pursued regarding events which had occurred more than 20 years prior to the hearing. The High Court had taken account of the relative youth of the individual (a qualified accountant at the time) and his

433. Companies Act 2014, s. 842.
434. *Director of Corporate Enforcement v. Boner* [2008] IEHC 151. *See also DCE v. D'Arcy* [2006] 2 IR 163.
435. Companies Act 2014, s. 844.
436. *Re CB Readymix Ltd; Cahill v. Grimes* [2002] 1 IR 372; *Director of Corporate Enforcement v. D'Arcy* [2006] 2 IR 163 both citing with approval the English decision in *Re Lo-Line Electric Motors Co.* [1988] BCLC 698.
437. *Director of Corporate Enforcement v. McCann* [2010] IESC 59.
438. *Director of Corporate Enforcement v. Walsh* [2016] ICEA 2.
439. *Infra* n. 649.

unblemished record since that time. However, in reversing this decision the Supreme Court set out the following principles:

298. The court should take account of the fact that the disqualification regime is flexible even to the point that the court may make an order for restriction of the director as an alternative. The purpose of the statutory regime is to deter directorial misbehaviour and to generally improve standards of corporate governance in the jurisdiction. The Supreme Court acknowledged that protection of the public from errant directors was also a stated function of the provisions (as had been enunciated in earlier English and Irish case law) but that this was neither the only nor the primary purpose of the statutory provisions. The Court also made it clear that the terms of the statute were paramount, and the decisions of the courts were not intended and should not be regarded as providing a 'gloss on the statute'. Finally, the Supreme Court stated that what was at issue in the particular case was the past conduct of the respondent at the particular time and that the court mistakenly gave more weight to the conduct of the respondent after that time as compared with past conduct which was the subject of the application.

299. In addition to this very heavily litigated ground for disqualification, it is worth noting that a promoter, officer, (and others already mentioned) may be disqualified under section 842(b) on the grounds that the individual has been guilty of 'any breach of his or her duty as such promoter, officer, statutory auditor 'and so on. The term 'officer' includes 'any director, shadow director or secretary of the company' under section 837 of the Companies Act 2014. It also includes individuals involved in positions of senior management in accordance with decisions of the courts.[440]

300. Chapter 3 of Part 14 of the Companies Act 2014 provides for the making of a restriction order against a director. This is a lesser sanction that disqualification and is used frequently. The consequence of a restriction order is that the respondent must comply with a set of conditions that must be met before the respondent may act, or be appointed, as director of any second or future company. In addition, the effect of the restriction order has an impact on the company itself. Where such an application is made, the onus is, unusually, on the person resisting the application to persuade the Court that he or she acted 'honestly and responsibly' in relation to the conduct of the affairs of the company, that he or she has co-operated to the extent reasonably expected with the liquidator of the company in relation to the conduct of the winding up of the company, and that there is no other reason why it would be just and equitable that he should be subject to [a restriction order]'.[441] The Supreme Court, albeit *obiter*, has expressed 'doubt as to whether this blanket reversal of the onus of proof, including a requirement to prove a negative proposition, is consistent with fundamental fairness and constitutional justice'.[442] However, this observation has not benefitted from any further argument in the following years. The default

---

440. *Re National Irish Bank: ODCE v. D'Arcy* [2005] IEHC 333.
441. Companies Act 2014, s. 819(2)(a)-(c).
442. *Re Tralee Beef and Lamb Ltd (In Liquidation); Kavanagh v. Delaney* [2008] 3 IR 347.

condition attaching to a restriction is that any subsequent company of which the respondent is a director must have a minimum allotted share capital of EUR 500,000 in the case of a PLC and EUR 100,000 in the case of any other company, with such restriction to last for five years,[443] but it is open to the Court to vary these conditions. Further restrictions apply to the subsequent company including the inability to avail of the private company exemption for financial assistance transactions under section 82 of the Companies Act 2014.

The Courts have adopted a range of criteria in deciding whether to impose a restriction order.

For some time, criteria which had been enumerated by Shanley J. in *La Moselle Clothing Ltd v. Soualhi*[444] were often adopted and were described as having achieved almost 'canonical status' by the Supreme Court in the later decision in *Tralee Beef and Lamb Ltd.*[445] These criteria included the following:

(a) The extent to which a director has or has not complied with any obligation imposed on him by the Companies Acts.
(b) The extent to which his conduct could be regarded as so incompetent as to amount to irresponsibility.
(c) The extent of the director's responsibility for the insolvency of the company.
(d) The extent of the director's responsibility for the net deficiency in the assets of the company disclosed at the date of the winding up or thereafter.
(e) The extent to which a director, in his conduct of the affairs of the company, has displayed a lack of commercial probity or want of proper standards.

However, in *Tralee Beef and Lamb*, an issue arose as to whether these criteria properly allowed for a consideration of the broader range of duties owed by directors. The High Court accepted the 'amplification', of this set of criteria by reference to directors' duties generally, namely, 'duties to the Company which are normally divided into duties of loyalty based on fiduciary principles, developed initially by the Courts of Equity, and duties of skill and care developed initially by the Common Law Courts from the principles in the law of negligence'. Though approving of this amplification in theory, the Supreme Court allowed an appeal in that case, because such amplification – or the respondent's compliance with his common law duties – had not been clearly part of the statutory scheme. In a subsequent decision, the Supreme Court has made it clear that the full range of obligations owed by directors can properly be the subject matter of consideration in such cases.[446] In any event, it is common now to consider the simplified criteria outlined by Clarke J. (as he then was) in *Re Swanpool Ltd.*[447]

443. Companies Act 2014, s. 819(3).
444. *La Moselle Clothing Ltd v. Soualhi* [1998] 2 ILRM 345; *Re Squash Ireland (Ltd)* [2001] 3 IR 35.
445. *Infra* n. 460.
446. *Re Mitek Holdings Ltd.* [2010] IESC 31. *See also Re Swanpool*: *McLaghlen v. Lennon* [2006] 2 ILRM 217.
447. *Ibid.*

301. The procedure governing applications for restrictions is unusual; it has been described by the Supreme Court as 'unique' and 'draconian'.[448] Under section 683 of the Companies Act 2014, the liquidator of every insolvent company must, issue proceedings, seeking a restriction order against each director of the insolvent company, unless relieved of the need to do so by the Director.[449] Failure to do so is an offence.[450] The Director may decline to relieve him or her of his or her duty to apply to the Court, and in such a case, the liquidator must nevertheless apply to the Court seeking a restriction order. The potential incongruity of such a scenario was the subject of adverse comment by the Supreme Court in *Tralee Beef and Lamb Ltd*[451] but was passed over without comment by the Court in the later case of *Dublin Sports Café Ltd.*[452]

302. A person against whom a restriction order is made may apply to the Court for relief, in whole or in part, from the order, or any conditions attaching thereto.[453] In an unusual provision, the legislation requires that such application must be made 'not more than one year after a declaration has been made in respect of him'. Although the original capitalisation requirement attaching to a restriction order was quite modest, this has been increased under the Companies Act 2014. However, once the subsequent company in which a restricted director is involved reaches this capital requirement 'the public may be, in practical terms, relatively unprotected from restricted directors who happen to have access to modest levels of wealth',[454] although not all would agree that EUR 100,00 is a modest amount. There is certainly a stigma in business circles attaching to a restriction order, and this reputational matter has been commented on by the courts on several occasions.[455]

303. Following the debate described above regarding the relevant criteria to be applied, it would seem that as regards restriction orders, the directors of companies must comply with a more clearly stated set of criteria as outlined by Clarke J. in *Re* Swanpool: *McLaghlen v. Lennon*[456] which include the following:

(1) Compliance with Companies Acts.
(2) Compliance with other duties.
(3) Duties which may arise under *Re Frederick Inns Ltd*,[457] namely duties owed to creditors as described [… in that decision.].

448. *Re Tralee Beef and Lamb Ltd (In Liquidation); Kavanagh v. Delaney* [2008] 3 IR 347.
449. Companies Act 2014 s. 683, s. 56(2).
450. Companies Act 2014 s. 683(5).
451. *Infra* n. 467.
452. *Re Dublin Sports Café Ltd; Fennell v. Long* [2008] IESC 66.
453. Companies Act 2014 s. 822. *See Re Ferngara Associates Limited: F & R Robinson v. Forrest* [1999] 1 IR 426; *Re CMC (Ireland) Ltd; Fennell v. Carolan* [2005] IEHC 340 (unreported, High Court, Finlay Geoghegan J., 1 Nov. 2005); *Re Xnet Information Systems Ltd; Stafford v. Higgins* [2006] IEHC 289 (unreported, High Court, O'Neill J., 10 Oct. 2006).
454. *Re Xnet Information Systems Ltd; Stafford v. Higgins* [2006] IEHC 289 (unreported, High Court, O'Neill J., 10 Oct. 2006), 19.
455. *See*, for example, *Xnet* (*supra*), 23; *Tralee Beef and Lamb* (*supra*), pp. 10–11.
456. [2006] 2 ILRM 217.
457. [1994] ILRM 87.

304. The Companies Act 2014 introduced a new procedure whereby an individual director may submit to a restriction or disqualification by providing an undertaking that he or she agrees to the terms of a restriction order or disqualification order.[458] The undertaking process is designed to prevent a multiplicity of applications to the Irish High Court and has been welcomed for that reason. The process is provided for in Chapter 5 of Part 14 of the Companies Act 2014.[459] Section 850 provides for a procedure which 'provides a person opportunity to submit to disqualification' and similarly section 852 provides for a procedure which 'provides a person opportunity to submit to restriction'. The process is initiated by the serving of a notice in both cases by the Director of Corporate Enforcement where 'the Director has reasonable grounds of believing' that the specified circumstances pertain to disqualification or restriction. Once the notice is served on the individual, a second notice period commences which gives the individual respondent a chance to consider his or her position, seek legal advice and decide whether to accept the undertaking or contest the allegations. The notice period is a period beginning on a day falling not less than twenty-one days after the date of the notice and ending 'immediately before the specified date' (date of commencement of the order). The legislation provides that during this period, no applications regarding disqualification shall be made during this notice period by the Director or 'every person aware of the notice' (section 851(1)). Similarly, during the notice period, no applications regarding restriction shall be made by the Director or 'every person aware of the notice' (section 853(1)). This process was designed to avoid the costs of High Court litigation and seems to be working effectively since its introduction following the commencement of the Companies Act 2014.

305. In addition to these changes, a new ground for restriction of directors has been introduced by section 34 of the Companies (CEA) Act 2021 which focuses on the director's failure to convene a general meeting to nominate a liquidator or failing to table a motion to nominate a liquidator or where the director has failed to provide notice of the meeting to employees in a winding up.

K. Conclusion

306. At present, the range of obligations owed by company directors to their companies is extensive under equitable principles and common law. In addition, there is considerable jurisprudence regarding the enforcement of directorial standards under modern legislation, which has a public law dimension to it as it is enforced and overseen by the ODCE, now the CEA, although it must be clarified that other parties are entitled to make disqualification applications as described above and the liquidator will make restriction applications. Generally, however, enforcement of company law provisions in Ireland has been particularly improved since 2001 when the Office of Corporate Enforcement was established under the

458. Companies Act 2014, Ch. 5 of Part 14.
459. *See* generally Nessa Cahill, *supra* n. 451 Ch. 8.

Company Law Enforcement Act of that year.[460] This office has now been created as a state agency with separate standing and increased powers under the CEA Act 2021. In fact, this area has led to a great deal of litigation in recent years. This public method of the enforcement of directorial standards has far outpaced the setting of standards through pronouncements and decisions in private law enforcement. The reason for this state of affairs is that the methods for privately enforcing directorial standards are limited to an action by the company or, in most unusual circumstances, an action by a minority shareholder. Actions against directors brought by the company as plaintiffs are still fairly uncommon in Irish law, so there is a dearth of jurisprudence in this area. Nevertheless, lack of private enforcement is counterbalanced by the rigour of the approach in the area of public enforcement. The following quotation is apt:

> It is of the greatest importance that any individual who undertakes the statutory and fiduciary obligations of being a company director should realise that these are inescapable personal responsibilities.[461]

III. Auditors

307. The principle role of the company auditor is to ensure that the company complies with the currently enforced accounting standards as set down by law. The auditor conducts his or her business with this obligation in mind. The principle mechanism to ensure adequate financial governance is through the auditors' report, which must be read at the AGM and should be made available to every member of the company as provided for in the Companies Act 2014, section 383. Under the Companies Act, shareholders are entitled to receive a report from an independent auditor as to whether the financial statements presented by the directors give a true and fair view of the state of affairs of the company and of its profits (or losses) for the period under review. The report also addresses whether these financial statements have been properly prepared in accordance with[462] the accounting provisions of the Companies Act. This obligation is subject to the exemptions which are now provided for in sections 370ff of the Companies Act 2014. These exemptions primarily apply to small and medium-sized enterprises. In circumstances where a company no longer qualifies as a small or medium enterprise for the purpose of these exemptions, then the directors must cause the company to deliver a copy of the revised statements with a directors' and auditor's report to the Registrar within twenty-eight days. The auditor has access to all books, accounts and vouchers and

460. Company Law Enforcement Act 2001, now re-enacted as Part 14 of the Companies Act 2014.
461. *Re Westmid Packaging Services Ltd; Secretary of State for Trade and Industry v. Griffiths and ors* [1998] 2 BCLC 646, 653 per Lord Woolf M.R. (approved in *Director of Corporate Enforcement v. Brennan* [2008] IEHC 132.
462. Companies Act 2014, s. 377(1)-(3).

is entitled to require from officers information and explanations that are within their knowledge.[463] Auditors are under a duty to carry out the audit with professional integrity.[464]

308. In addition to this primary role and obligation to the shareholders, the role of the company auditor under Irish company law has come under increasing scrutiny following the adoption of the Company Law Enforcement Act 2001, which is now re-enacted in the Companies Act 2014. In this context, auditors have a role in relation to public enforcement of company law standards. Where auditors form the opinion that the company being audited is contravening, or has contravened, its obligations to maintain proper books of account, they are obliged to serve a notice on the company informing it of that opinion. This obligation is required under the Companies Act 2014, section 392. Subsequently, the auditors may be required to share this opinion with the Registrar of Companies, who will in turn notify the Director of Corporate Enforcement. In addition, the auditors are required to make a report to the Director of Corporate Enforcement when, by virtue of carrying out an audit, information comes into their possession that leads them to form the opinion that the company, or an officer or agent of it, has committed an indictable offence under the Companies Acts. The use of auditors' reports has become a significant database on which to base activities relating to enforcement.[465]

309. A further issue that has arisen in modern company law is the extent of the obligations imposed on auditors where non-audit work is carried on by the same firm of which the auditor is a member or officer.

IV. Company Secretary

310. Section 129(1) of the Companies Act 2014 provides that the company must have a company secretary who may be one of the directors. However, where a particular transaction or act requires both the signature of a secretary and a director, the same person cannot perform both functions.[466] Section 129(4) of the Companies Act 2014 now provides that the directors of a company now have a duty to ensure that the person appointed as company secretary has the necessary skills and resources to discharge their statutory duties. Section 226(1) of the Companies Act 2014 also provides for the additional delegation of duties to the company secretary by the Board of Directors. Any such delegation shall be 'without derogation from the secretary's statutory or legal duties'. The Company Secretary is obliged to keep minutes of meetings of directors and any committees of directors. Any director can inspect minutes and copy in accordance with the Act. In addition, the Company Secretary is obliged to maintain the share register; to notify shareholders of meetings,

463. Companies Act 2014, s. 336.
464. Companies Act 2014, s. 390.
465. Companies Act 2014, s. 393.
466. Companies Act 2014, s. 134.

resolutions and so forth; to maintain all necessary information pertinent to the exercise by shareholders of their rights; and to ensure that this information is available for inspection.

V. Workers' Participation

311. See the general discussion at §6 in the General Introduction. Other than the types of consultative structures introduced in the context of particular legislation regarding collective redundancies, there is no structure in Irish company law, in keeping with common law structures generally, for the recognition of worker directors or worker representation on the boards of directors or on any other type of management board. As stated, 'administrative boards' are not a feature of corporate governance in Irish company law. There is a unitary structure of board management and no such concept as a two-tier board structure present in European countries. The only exception relates to state-owned companies, of which there are now very few operating in the profit sector. In this context, the Worker Participation (State Enterprises) Act 1988, facilitates the introduction of sub-board participative arrangements in a broad range of State enterprises, by agreement between the enterprise and the employee interests.

§6. Liquidation of the Company[467]

I. Grounds for Winding Up

312. The Companies Act 2014 maintains the distinction between voluntary liquidations and compulsory liquidations (otherwise court liquidations). However, the legislation has sought to achieve a streamlining of how all liquidations are conducted and also to shift the focus of how liquidations are conducted from official or compulsory (court) liquidations to voluntary liquidations. Liquidations are dealt with in Part 11 of the Companies Act 2014. The following reforms were made at that time:

(i) The applicability of the new SAP to the commencement of a members' voluntary winding up.[468]

(ii) Insolvency practitioners are to be regulated in Ireland for the first time.[469] In addition, new rules regarding remuneration of liquidators have been introduced.

(iii) Some changes have been made to the role of the creditors' committee of inspection.[470]

---

467. *See* generally, Thomas B. Courtney, (gen. ed.) et al. *The Professional's Guide to the Companies Act 2014* (Bloomsbury 2015) Chs 7 and 8. *See also* Irene Lynch Fannon & Gerard N. Murphy, *Corporate Insolvency and Rescue* (Bloomsbury 2012).

468. The SAP is outlined in Part 4, Ch. 7 of the Companies Act 2014. *Supra.*

469. Companies Act 2014, ss 633–635.

470. Companies Act 2014, ss 646(2), 666 and 667.

(iv) Liquidators' powers have been clarified.[471]
(v) Some changes have been made to avoidance provisions.[472]

A. *Voluntary and Compulsory Liquidations*

313. The distinction between voluntary liquidations (whether members' voluntary or creditors' voluntary liquidations) and official or compulsory liquidation rests on who exercises control over the process. A voluntary liquidation can either be a members' voluntary liquidation or a creditors' voluntary liquidation, depending on whether it is open to the directors to swear a declaration of solvency in accordance with the SAP described in the following paragraph. A voluntary liquidation will begin with passing a resolution pursuant to the constitution of the company.

314. A members' voluntary liquidation may be commenced using the SAP under the Companies Act 2014. This involves the passing of a special resolution and the swearing of a declaration by the directors of the company. The SAP[473] relies on a variety of forms of declaration depending on the purpose of the procedure. In this case, the declaration is to the effect that the company can pay its debts. Accordingly, the format of the declaration is outlined in section 207 of the Act. Section 207 provides that the relevant declaration will include a statement of the total amount of company's assets and liabilities at the 'latest practicable date' but not more than three months before the date of making the declaration, and will also include a declaration that the company will be able to discharge its debts within a period not exceeding twelve months after the commencement of the winding up.[474] Section 580(1) of the Companies Act 2014 provides that the company may pass a resolution to commence a voluntary winding up where a period expires or an event happens in accordance with the provisions of section 579(3)(a) and (b) where such period or event has been specified in the company's constitution.

315. A creditors' voluntary liquidation may commence *ab initio* under the provisions of section 586(2). This includes where the company resolves by ordinary resolution to wind up the company because it 'cannot by reason of its liabilities carry on its business'. Alternatively, a creditors' voluntary liquidation may commence through the conversion of a members' voluntary winding up to a creditors' voluntary winding up in the following three situations:

(1) where the court makes an order under section 582(2) of the Companies Act 2014 on foot of an application made by creditors to the court;

471. Companies Act 2014, s. 646(2).
472. Companies Act 2014, ss 603–608.
473. *See* generally Companies Act 2014, ss 201–211.
474. Companies Act 2014, s. 210 which imposes a significant civil sanction of personal liability for statement made regarding opinion as to solvency without reasonable grounds.

(2) where a creditors' meeting is held in accordance with section 584 of the Companies Act 2014 and a resolution is passed to convert a members' voluntary liquidation;
(3) where there is a default in the making of the statutory declaration of solvency or in the conduct of the SAP generally.[475]

316. In contrast, a compulsory or official liquidation begins with a petition to the High Court on the grounds described *infra*. If the petition is successful, the court will appoint a liquidator and the liquidation will proceed under the supervision of the High Court.

317. Section 569 of the Companies Act 2014 provides for the grounds upon which an application can be made to the court for winding up a company. This was called an official or compulsory liquidation, but now under the more recent 2014 legislation, such liquidations are referred to as court liquidations. Thus, in a court liquidation, the High Court, in answer to a petition to wind up the company, initiates the liquidation, appoints a liquidator and oversees the liquidation throughout the process. The most common ground on which the petition is based is section 569(1)(d) whereby the company is wound up because it is unable to pay its debts. The 2014 Act has increased the threshold level of indebtedness and provides that a company shall be deemed to be unable to pay its debts where a creditor makes a demand 'exceeding EUR 10,000' and this has not been paid within the twenty-one-day demand period.[476] Section 569(1)(f) allows a petitioner in an action for oppression to petition the Court to wind up the company as a remedy, and section 569(1)(e) refers to the possibility of a petition to wind up the company on 'just and equitable' grounds. This provision has covered a range of cases on the spectrum, from an alternative ground for the petitioner/creditor who seeks payment and who has petitioned under section 569(1)(d), to a member petitioning to have the company wound up in cases where there is a deadlock in the running of the company. Section 569(1)(g) was added in 2014 which gives the Director of Corporate Enforcement (now the Director of the CEA) *locus standi* to petition to wind up a company where the public interest requires this. There is no statement in the legislation as to what the public interest might entail but at the very least, the Director will petition to liquidate companies which have ceased to trade. Section 572(4) provides that the court may order that the company can be wound up as if it were a members' voluntary winding up where the order is made under paragraphs (a), (b), (c), (e) or (f) of section 569(1).

---

475. Companies Act 2014, s. 586(3)(c).
476. Sections 570(b) with 571(b) provides similarly that a company shall be deemed to be unable to pay its debts where two or more creditors representing in aggregate a value of indebtedness of at least EUR 20,000 make a demand for payment which is not met. Under the Companies (Miscellaneous Provisions) (COVID-19)) Act this threshold was increased to EUR 50,000 for the duration of the interim period which is now terminated.

II. Effects of Winding Up

A. Powers and Duties of the Liquidator

318. As described above, a liquidator is appointed either by the court in a court liquidation or by the members in a members' voluntary liquidation or by the creditors in a creditors' voluntary liquidation, the latter being the most common kind of liquidation. The main obligations of the liquidator are to pay all proven debts in accordance with the priorities described below, to wind up the company and to dissolve it in an orderly fashion. Under the Companies Act 2014, section 596, the liquidator must 'take into his custody or under his control' all the property to which the company appears entitled.

Under the Companies Act 2014, section 627, the liquidator has the power to sell the company's property. A liquidator also has standing to institute legal proceedings on behalf of the company, with a view to swelling the assets available for distribution to creditors, including proceedings claiming that certain transactions amounted to either fraudulent preferences of creditors or fraudulent dispositions of corporate property.

Some changes were made to the liquidation process in the 2014 Companies Act. Most significantly, there have been changes made to what were the Rules of the Court governing the process of liquidation. Indeed some provisions have been included as statutory provisions. Thus, Ord 74, r 22 regarding the service of the order for winding up is enacted under section 591(1) and Ord 74, r 24 is enacted under section 593. Similarly, section 617 enacts Ord 74, r 128 regarding the costs and expenses of the liquidation. Section 618 enacts in statutory form provisions of what was the old Table A under the Companies Act 1963 regarding distribution of assets in a members' voluntary winding up and section 619 goes on to apply the rules of distribution on bankruptcy to the winding up of insolvent companies, re-enacting section 284 of the 1963 Acts.

The creditors' committee (Committee of Inspection) has taken on a supposedly significant role as described in sections 646(2), 666 and 667 of the Companies Act 2014, although there is some scepticism about whether this has heralded real change. These changes were designed to give more control over the process of the liquidation to creditors. However, two observations must be made, first that the number of liquidations since the enactment of the changes is low and second, these committees are still dominated typically by one creditor so no real practical difference seems to have occurred. The following are the changes:-

The remuneration of liquidators will be agreed with the creditors' committee of inspection as provided for under section 646(2).

319. Section 666 provides that the committee of inspection in an official or court-ordered liquidation will be established on the initiative of the liquidator or alternatively, the liquidator can be directed to do so on the initiative of a minimum proportion of the creditors without court sanction.

Section 667 similarly empowers creditors, without recourse to the court, to appoint a committee of inspection in the case of creditors' voluntary winding up. It is worth recalling that the purpose of some of these provisions is to align more closely with the procedure in creditors' voluntary, members' voluntary and court liquidations.

320. Section 687 provides that creditors or contributories may override the wishes of the committee of inspection.

321. Section 687(2) provides that where there is a conflict between the wishes of the committee of inspection and the creditors or contributories, the wishes of the latter will prevail. To this end, section 687(3)(a) empowers the liquidator to convene meetings of the creditors and contributories to ascertain their wishes. Section 687(3)(b) goes on to provide that the liquidator must convene meetings of the creditors or contributories where they pass a resolution directing the liquidator or where such a request is made in writing by not less than one-tenth in value of the creditors or not less than one-tenth in value of the contributories.

B. Liquidators' Report

322. Section 682 provides for the liquidator to make a report and further secondary legislation has made certain directions regarding the content of the liquidators' report which requires, *inter alia*:

(i) Details regarding shadow directors and directors.
(ii) Details regarding the financial position of the company and the accuracy of the statement of affairs.
(iii) Details regarding the Committee of inspection.
(iv) Details regarding section 683 (restriction) and section 842 (disqualification) proceedings.

C. Regulation of Liquidators

Section 633 of the Companies Act 2014 represented an important change requiring that certain qualifications are necessary for appointment as a liquidator or provisional liquidator. Section 633(1) therefore provides that 'subject to ss 635 and 636 a person shall not be qualified for appointment as a liquidator of a company unless he or she falls within a paragraph of the Table to this section'. Section 519 applies these requirements to those acting as examiners discussed below under III – Pre-Insolvency Remedies. The Table referred to in section 633 includes the following individuals:

- Members of a prescribed accountancy body.
- Practising solicitor.
- Members of 'other professional body recognised by the Supervisory Authority'.
- Persons qualified under the laws of another EEA State.

– A 'person with practical experience of windings-up and knowledge of relevant law'.

This last category is described as limited and will be closely supervised by the Supervisory Authority.

The following sections describe the effect of a liquidation on particular creditors.

D. *Creditors' Rights*

323. The general principle is that debts owing on a winding up are paid *pari passu* out of the liquidated assets of the company.[477]

However, as described *infra*, the statute has assigned preferential status to certain types of debts – principally those owed to the Revenue and to employees. In all liquidations, the priorities of payments are governed by the provisions of Chapter 7, Part 11 of the Companies Act 2014 and specifically sections 617–623. Section 617 deals with costs of the winding up. The following priorities apply:

> First – The costs of the petition, including the costs of any person appearing on the petition whose costs are allowed by the Court.
> Next – The costs and expenses of any person who makes or concurs in making the company's statement of affairs.
> Next – The necessary disbursements of the Official Liquidator, other than expenses properly incurred in preserving, realizing or getting in the assets herein before provided for.
> Next –The costs payable to the solicitor for the Official Liquidator.
> Next – The remuneration of the Official Liquidator.
> Next – The out-of-pocket expenses necessarily incurred by the committee of inspection (if any).

The first series of payments out of the company's assets will thus be the expenses of the liquidation procedure, which will include costs of realisation of all the assets, fees of legal advisors and remuneration of the liquidator. When an examinership[478] has occurred prior to a winding up, the fees of an examiner and certified expenses once sanctioned by the court 'shall be paid in full and shall be paid before any other claim, secured or unsecured'.[479] In addition, liabilities incurred by the examiner which are treated as 'expenses properly incurred' shall be paid before any claim other than a claim secured by a mortgage, or other fixed charge.[480]

Of course, this necessarily implies that the examinership has not been successful, and the situation can be quite difficult for this reason.

477. Companies Act 2014, s. 618.
478. *Supra* para. 295.
479. Companies Act 2014, s. 554 (3).
480. Companies Act 2014, s. 554(4).

324. Once fees as described above are paid, the liquidator will distribute the assets in accordance with section 619 which provides that 'in the winding up of an insolvent company the same rules shall prevail and be observed … as are in force for the time being under the law of bankruptcy … ':

- Fixed charge holders are entitled to realise assets and to be paid in full from this realisation.
- The preferential creditors, accorded this status under relevant legislation will be paid before any other classes of creditors.[481]
- Floating charge holders will then be paid.
- Finally, the unsecured creditors will be paid, usually on a pro rata basis as there are often insufficient assets for unsecured creditors.

In the seminal case of *Salomon v. Salomon & Co Ltd.*,[482] as the House of Lords set down the robust principle of corporate personality, thus copper-fastening the effect of the statutory concept of limited liability, it also addressed the role of creditors and in doing so, pinned the creditors' position on a robust commitment to freedom of contract: *'Every creditor is entitled to get and to hold the best security the law allows him to take.'* Thus in Irish (as in English) law, the role of the commercial contract in securing the position of the creditor is extremely important. This is seen in relation to the extent to which a contract can be used to secure a broad range of assets, as we will see in our brief discussion of fixed charges on book debts and proceeds; in relation to the establishment of the receiver as an important insolvency process (see *infra*, paragraph xxx); and in relation to the use of retention of title clauses and other types of agreements to support an unsecured creditor. Even claims arising from the law of trusts are included as potentially affecting payments to creditors. In contrast, the role of statute in giving security to creditors is not as prevalent, except in relation to the implementation of the preferential category of creditors.

E. *Fixed Charges*

325. A charge is a contractual agreement that certain property be available as security to meet the performance of a liability, usually the payment of money.[483] A fixed or specific charge is one taken over 'ascertained and definite property or property capable of being ascertained and defined'.[484] This will often be an asset such as real property. As has been noted, assets subject to a fixed charge are 'permanently appropriated to the payment of the sum charged in such a way as to give the chargee a proprietary interest in the assets and to impose restrictions on the chargor's

481. Companies Act 2014, ss 621, 622.
482. *Salomon v. Salomon &Co. Ltd.* [1897] AC 22, 52 per Lord MacNaghten.
483. *Re Clare Textiles Ltd.*, [1992] NI 323 p. 2.
484. *Illingworth v. Houldsworth* [1904] AC 355. 358.

use of the asset'.[485] Fixed charges, as with other charges taken on company property, must be registered in the company's file pursuant to section 409 of the 2014 Act. Failure to register the charge with the CRO renders it void against the liquidator and any creditor of the company.[486] The Companies Act 2014 changed Irish law by introducing the option of a two-stage procedure regarding the registration of charges. Under this procedure, a lender or company may deliver notice of their intention to register a charge which must then be registered within a twenty-one-day notice period.[487]

F. Floating Charges

326. The floating charge is a common law concept peculiar to the corporate world and is not available over the assets of individuals in bankruptcy. The floating charge was defined by Lord MacNaghten in *Illingworth v. Houldsworth*[488] as 'ambulatory and shifting in its nature, hovering over and so to speak floating with the property which it is intended to affect until some event occurs or some act is done which causes it to settle and fasten on the subject of the charge within its reach and grasp'. The charge is said to 'crystallise' over the class of assets it has been floating above on the occurrence of certain events, known as 'crystallising events'.[489] These are the appointment of a receiver, the appointment of a liquidator or the commencement of a liquidation. A company's ceasing to carry on business is also a crystallising event.[490] Automatic crystallisation, (namely where a contract provides for a crystallising event in advance and outside of these public events), is a security measure attractive to lenders, but there are serious concerns about the viability of automatic crystallisation of charges when measured against some of the fundamental principles of insolvency law, such as the concept of public notification of creditors' rights to other creditors and to other stakeholders in the company.[491]

485. *In Re Spectrum Plus Ltd. (in liquidation)* [2005] 2 AC 680. A point worth noting is that, although the terms 'charge' and 'mortgage' are sometimes used interchangeably, there is a technical difference between them, inasmuch as a mortgage involves conveyance of legal title to the property involved subject to a right of redemption, whereas a charge merely gives the chargee the right to look to the charged property in satisfaction of the debt secured.
486. Companies Act 2014, s. 409(1). *See* generally Part 7 of the Companies Act 2014 regarding Charges and Debentures.
487. Companies Act 2014, s. 409(4).
488. *Illingworth v. Houldsworth* [1904] AC 355.
489. *Re Woodroffes (Musical Instruments) Ltd.* [1985] BCLC 227; *Re The Real Meat Co. Ltd* [1996] BCC 254.
490. *Re Woodroffes (Musical Instruments) Ltd* [1985] BCLC 227; *In re Sperrin Textiles Ltd* [1992] NI 323.
491. Although English case law has inclined toward approval of such clauses (cf. *Re. Griffin Hotel Co.* [1940] Ch. 87 and *Re Brightlife Ltd* [1987] Ch. 200), reservations have been expressed regarding approval of such clauses under Irish law. *See* Ronan Keane, *Company Law* 251 (4th edn., Tottel, 2007).

Crystallisation by notice is a variant of this practice and has been considered extensively by the Irish courts in *Re J.D. Brian Ltd.*[492] In this case, both the Irish High Court and subsequently the Supreme Court on appeal have approved the possibility of crystallisation by notice. The effect of this kind of crystallisation was also considered in this litigation and is considered *infra*. De-crystallisation is also a conceptual possibility enunciated and approved of in the Irish Supreme Court by *Re Holidair Ltd.*[493]

327. Floating charges face a particular challenge as to their validity in liquidations under section 597 of the Companies Act 2014. Historically, floating charges were often created at the last minute to secure assets and, as such, can be specifically open to challenge under section 597 of the Companies Act 2014. Similarly, floating charges can be challenged under the fraudulent preference provisions now contained in section 604 of the Companies Act 2014. (Formerly, section 286 of the Companies Act 1963, as amended by Companies Act 1990, section 135.) However, any transaction can be a fraudulent preference, so this is not a disadvantage peculiar to floating charges.

G. Preferential Creditors

328. Section 285 of the 1963 Companies Act created a class of preferential creditors, which has been increased by various amendments. Despite much discussion and consequent changes in neighbouring jurisdictions, particularly in the UK about the need to have classes of preferential creditors, these have been consistently retained in Ireland and are now found outlined in section 621 of the Companies Act 2014. In contrast, preferential status for Revenue debts (HMRC) was abolished in the UK in 2002 but was restored in 2020.[494] Preferential creditors will be paid in full after the fixed charge holders are paid and will be paid before any creditors with a floating charge. The provision seeks to protect vulnerable creditors such as employees in relation to outstanding wages and payments. Although there are a range of creditors protected under the Irish preferential creditors' list, generally, the most significant creditor protected under this legislation is the State in relation to unpaid taxes and various other payments due to the State by businesses that are incorporated. The effect of the growth of the categories and types of preferential creditors was to diminish the value of the floating charge because these creditors are given priority over floating charge holders. Consequently, lenders sought to extend

492. In the matter of *J.D. Brian Ltd* [2011] 3 IR 244. Finlay Geoghegan J. delivered a judgment regarding the issue of priorities, but unusually, and on request from the liquidator who indicated an intention to appeal, a second judgment was delivered regarding the effect of crystallisation. Both judgments are reported at [2011] 3 IR 244. In the matter of *J.D. Brian Ltd t/a East Coast Print and Publicity and Re East Coast Car Parts Ltd* [2015] IESC 62 (Laffoy J.). *See* further Irene Lynch Fannon, *The Floating Charge Debate: The Path to Clarity in Irish Law* 22 [2015] CLP 187–195.

493. *Re Holidair Ltd* [1994] I ILRM 481.

494. The Enterprise Act (UK) 2002 effectively abolished preferential status for all revenue and other debts, with the exception of preferential status being retained for employees. However, this priority status for revenue debts was restored in 2020 under the Finance Act (UK) 2020.

the reach and flexibility of the fixed charge, hence the extension of the concept of a fixed charge to book debts and more recently, the development of the concept of crystallisation by notice of floating charges. Broader issues regarding securitisation are explored currently in commercial practice, such as the charging of intangible assets, for example, and particularly, the charging of intellectual property rights such as patents.

H. The Extension of Classes of Assets Which Could Be Subject to a Fixed Charge

329. Because of the growth of classes of preferential creditors, it became common practice for lenders to seek to extend the range of assets over which they could take a fixed charge, as the floating charge became vulnerable to non-payment due to the extensive reach of the claims of preferential creditors. This is a result of the provisions of the legislation providing for preferential status. Section 285(7) (re-enacted as section 621(7)(b) of the 2014 Act) provides that where the assets of the company available for payment of general creditors are insufficient to meet the preferential debts, these debts will 'have priority over the claims of holders of debentures under any floating charge created by the company, and be paid accordingly out of any property comprised in or subject to that charge'.

330. To get around this provision, the creation of fixed charges over other assets, specifically book debts became common in Ireland and England during the mid-1980s. This practice was the subject of significant litigation primarily because the underlying conceptualisation of a fixed charge over the book debts of a company that is still actively trading is not without significant difficulties in the common law. The classic definition of book debts is 'debts owing to the company concerned with and arising out of the company's trade or business, which are entered, or commonly would be entered in the ordinary course of business, in well kept books of such trade or business'.[495]

331. During the extensive litigation arising out of this difficult concept, a significant feature became one of control.[496] The key question was whether the lender/creditor had obtained significant control over the disposal of the asset in question to render the charge a fixed charge or whether in fact, primarily due to the exigencies of the situation – namely the need for the company to have access to the asset to facilitate trading – control over the asset had rested with the borrower/debtor company. If the latter was the case, the fact that the company still exercised control over the asset presented difficulties in establishing the fixed nature of the charge. This

495. Schmitthoff (ed.), *Palmer's Company Law* 46-06 (24th edn., Sweet & Maxwell 1987).

496. *Re Keenan Bros Ltd* [1985] IR 401; *Siebe Gorman v. Barclays Bank Ltd* [1979] 2 Lloyds Reports 142; *Re Armagh Shoes Ltd* [1982] N.I. 59; *Re Wogan's (Drogheda) Ltd (under the Protection of the Court)* [1993] 1 IR 157; *Re Holidair Ltd* [1994] 1 IR 416; *In re Spectrum Plus Ltd (in liquidation)* [2005] 2 AC 680.

question is played out in many of the Irish decisions.[497] Nevertheless, the possibility of having a fixed charge over book debts was countenanced by the Irish courts. A second issue evolved as to the asset which was actually charged, and here a distinction evolved between a charge over the book debts themselves and the proceeds collected from the book debts. Where the lender/creditor did not specifically create the charge over the book debts and proceeds, the latter was eventually deemed to be free of the fixed charge.[498] The original litigation was driven by the relative positions of the commercial lender with a fixed charge over an asset such as book debts and the preferential creditor, usually the Revenue authorities. In Ireland, however, the litigation became even more significant because of the interplay between the significance of having a valid fixed charge over book debts and the necessity to fund an examinership if this were to lead to a genuine possibility of the rescue of a company. In litigation arising in the latter context, the court recognised the possibility of a charge that had crystallised into a fixed charge on book debts or proceeds on foot of the appointment of a receiver, de-crystallising on removal of the receiver following the appointment of an examiner.[499]

332. The decision of the House of Lords in *Re Spectrum Plus*,[500] held that although it is possible in law for a company to create a security consisting of a fixed charge over all its present and future book debts,[501] it would be extremely difficult to realistically exercise the necessary control over such an asset while still operating a trading company. This decision has cast considerable doubt over the efficacy of the fixed charge over book debts and/or proceeds and assets of this kind. It should be noted that the court specifically overruled the decision in *Siebe Gorman*[502] which is the basis for the creation of such a charge in both Irish and English law.

333. This area has been further litigated in Ireland with an important decision from the Irish Supreme Court in the case of *Re J.D. Brian Ltd t/a East Coast Print and Publicity* in July 2015.[503] This was an appeal from the decision of Finlay Geoghegan J.[504] in the High Court where it had been held that even though the concept of crystallisation by notice[505] of a floating charge was permissible under Irish

---

497. For example, *Re Keenan Bros Ltd* [1985] IR 401; *Re Wogan's (Drogheda) Ltd (under the Protection of the Court)*; *Jenkins v. Hill Samuel (Ireland) Ltd* [1993] 1 IR 157.

498. *Re Wogan's (Drogheda) Ltd (under the Protection of the Court)* [1993] 1 IR 157; *Re Holidair Ltd* [1994] 1 IR 416.

499. *Re Holidair Ltd* [1994] 1 IR 416.

500. *In re Spectrum Plus Ltd (in liquidation)* [2005] 2 AC 680.

501. *Ibid.*, 711–712.

502. *Infra* n. 511.

503. *In the matter of J.D. Brian Ltd t/a East Coast Print and Publicity and Re East Coast Car Parts Ltd* [2015] IESC 62 (Laffoy J.).

504. *In the matter of J.D. Brian Ltd* [2011] 3 IR 244. Finlay Geoghegan J. delivered a judgment regarding the issue of priorities, but unusually, and on request from the liquidator who indicated an intention to appeal, a second judgment was delivered regarding the effect of crystallisation. Both judgments are reported at [2011] 3 IR 244.

505. Note that no real distinction was made between the concept of automatic crystallisation and crystallisation by notice in these decisions. However, the actual clauses were crystallisation by notice clauses.

law, the consequences of such crystallisation would not affect the priority of preferential creditors under section 285 of the Companies Act 1963 (the '1963 Act').[506] The Supreme Court allowed the appeal from the High Court and made two important and significant decisions. First, that the charge in question had been 'converted into a fixed charge over the property of each company by virtue of the service of the crystallisation notice by the bank, prior to the commencement of the winding up of each Company'; and second that accordingly, the 'claims of the Bank as debenture holder to the funds realised from the assets the subject of the floating charges ... converted into fixed charges ... shall rank in priority to the preferential debts due by the Company identified by reference to s. 285(1)-(6) of the Act of 1963'.

334. The practical consequence of this decision was that where a lender created a floating charge over assets which could be crystallised on notice prior to liquidation, the charge converted to a fixed charge and therefore defeated the priority of the preferential creditor created by section 621. The effect of the Supreme Court decision was set aside by the Companies (Accounting) Act 2017 which is provided in sections 92 and 98(d) that State revenue debts 'shall have priority over the holders of debenture under any charge created as a floating charge by the company'. However, a hanging question remains following the Supreme Court decision and that concerns the general legal effect of crystallisation on a floating charge, which is a common law question of legal significance in all jurisdictions. In Ireland, the Supreme Court held that the effect of such crystallisation was to change the nature and priority of the original charge without any need for notification to the public registrar or to creditors generally, nor without any further registration requirement. This approach is certainly doubtful and was not the approach taken in the High Court.[507]

335. It is important to mention that the Examiner (*see* below) may apply to the court for permission to dispose of property subject to a floating charge. Section 530(1) Companies Act 2014 where this is likely to 'facilitate the survival of the company'. The access to assets subject to a floating charge which subsequently crystallises is preserved as section 530(1)(a) refers to property of the company which is 'subject to a security which, as created, was a floating charge'.[508]

I. The Unsecured Creditor

336. This creditor often has little hope of being paid in full after the fixed charge holder, the preferential creditors and the floating charge holder(s) have been paid. Thus, the supplier and other kinds of unsecured creditors have invented their own devices to deal with the difficult problem of not getting paid by companies and the

506. Now s. 621 of the Companies Act 2014.

507. *See* further Irene Lynch Fannon, *The Floating Charge Debate in Irish Law: The Path to Clarity*. 2015 Commercial Law Practitioner pp. 186–195. Irene Lynch Fannon, *Crystallisation of Floating Charges, Reform and Clarity*. 2016 Commercial Law Practitioner pp. 209-212.

508. *Re Holidair Ltd.* [1994] 1 ILRM 481 [1994] IESC 1; [1994] 1 IR 416.

consequences for their own solvency. Retention of title clauses are thus commonly found in supply contracts but are not always enforceable depending on the nature of the asset. Similarly, the recognition of a trust device to protect certain kinds of creditors, such as those ordering through mail or the Internet where deposits are paid for certain goods, is a possibility under Irish law, as it is under English law.

J. Unsecured Creditor Protection: Retention of Title Clauses; Liens

337. Retention of title clauses seeks to retain title in goods supplied until these goods are paid for. Therefore, although the goods may be in the possession of the creditor company, the retention of title clause purports to permit recovery of the goods supplied or indeed recovery of mixed goods to the value of the goods supplied. In addition, retention of title clauses seeks to follow the proceeds arising from the sale of goods so supplied. The possible validity of such clauses was recognised in the English decision of *Aluminium Industrie Vassem v. Romalpa Aluminium*[509] and in Ireland in *Frigoscandia (Contracting) Ltd v. Continental Irish Meats Ltd.*[510] However, over time, the conceptual difficulties inherent in these clauses from a common law perspective cast some doubt over the possibility of such clauses being valid once the clauses purported to follow mixed goods or proceeds.[511]

The decision in *Carroll Group Ltd v. G & J.F. Bourke Ltd*[512] represents a clear statement of the law of retention of title clauses as it applies in Ireland. While a simple retention of title clause over identifiable products in the possession of the liquidator or receiver will be enforceable in the majority of cases, difficulties may arise when the retention of title clause follows goods into manufactured or mixed goods or proceeds of the sale of goods.[513] Despite much subsequent litigation, this decision is still 'beyond doubt … the leading authority on proceeds of sale clauses at the time of the High Court judgment was that of Murphy J. in Carroll, a case in which the Court concluded that the relevant proceeds of sale clause did not create a fiduciary relationship between the buyer and seller but rather confined the seller to a charge over the funds received in respect of the resale of its goods, which required registration'.[514] The key issue is that where the assets are complex and ownership must be followed in a mixed asset or indeed funds, the right to trace or

509. *Aluminium Industrie Vassem v. Romalpa Aluminium* [1976] 1 WLR 676.
510. *Frigoscandia (Contracting) Ltd v. Continental Irish Meats Ltd* [1982] ILRM 396; cf. *Kruppstahl A.G. v. Quitman Products Ltd* [1982] ILRM 551.
511. *Re Peachdart Ltd* [1983] BCLC 225 (clause purporting to follow leather into manufactured handbags held to be invalid); *Carroll Group Ltd v. G & J.F . Bourke Ltd* [1990] ILRM 285 (clause held to be valid insofar as it purported to retain title over identifiable products, cigarettes, but invalid to the extent it purported to follow proceeds of sale); *Re Bond Worth* [1980] Ch. 228 (again, a clause purporting to follow mixed goods was held to be invalid). *See* further *Thyssen v. Armour Edelstahlwerke A.G.* [1991] 2 AC 339, in which the House of Lords limited the effectiveness of such clauses, and 'Bradgate: Retention of Title in the House of Lords' (1991) 54 LQR 726 for a commentary on the decision in *Armour*.
512. *Carroll Group Ltd v. G & J.F . Bourke Ltd* [1990] ILRM 285.
513. Irene Lynch Fannon & Gerard N. Murphy, *Corporate Insolvency and Rescue* 356 (2nd edn., Bloomsbury 2012).
514. *See Unitherm Heating Systems Ltd. v. Wallace* [2015] ICEA 191.

follow those assets depends on the concept of beneficial ownership which implies the creation of a charge. A second difficulty is that if this right held by the unpaid supplier diminishes as payment is made, then the conceptual analysis of the agreement leads towards the establishment of a charge. This approach is specifically described in *Re Bond Worth Ltd.* where the court observed that 'any contract which, by way of security for the payment of a debt, confers an interest in property defeasible or destructable upon payment ... must necessarily be regarded as creating a mortgage or charge ... .'[515] The difficulty is that at present, these rights are not registrable rights under Irish or English law and are thus void as against the liquidator and other creditors. It is worth noting that simple retention of title clauses does not create a registrable charge even though it has been suggested in the UK that all contracts containing retention of title clauses should be registrable as charges.[516]

K. Unsecured Creditor Protection: Trust Devices

338. The *Quistclose* trust, called after the decision that validated it, allowed for an unsecured creditor to recover funds when such funds had been forwarded for a specific reason. In *Barclays Bank Ltd v. Quistclose Investments Ltd*,[517] a loan was made to a company on the agreed condition that it would be used to pay an already declared dividend. The loan was paid into a special bank account opened specially for the purpose. The bank knew that the money was borrowed and that the account would be used only for the purpose of paying the dividend. Before the dividend could be paid, the company went into voluntary liquidation. The lender sought to recover the amount of the loan on the basis that, where funds were forwarded for a sufficiently clear reason and where the reason could not be achieved, there was a resulting trust in favour of the creditor. As a result, the bank, being on notice, was a constructive trustee of the money. This claim was upheld by the House of Lords. An example of the consequences of this decision is to be seen in *Re Kayford Ltd*,[518] in which a court upheld the creation of a *Quistclose* trust in these circumstances: A mail order company paid money received from customers (either full payment in advance or deposits) into a particular account, withdrawing the money only if and when it later delivered the goods, with the intention of protecting the funds remaining in the account from general distribution in the event of insolvency. Such customers would normally be regarded as unsecured creditors in relation to such deposits and would not normally receive any money in most insolvent liquidations. As has been emphasised in more recent case law,[519] the key issue in relation to a *Quistclose* trust is whether the parties intended the money to be at the free disposal of the recipient or whether instead, the parties came to an arrangement that the

515. [1980] Ch. 228.

516. David Sheehan: *Registration and Re-Characterisation of Retention of Title Clauses* University of Leeds March 2018.

517. *Barclays Bank Ltd v. Quistclose Investments Ltd* [1970] AC 576.

518. *Re Kayford Ltd* [1975] 1 All ER 604; 'Michael Bridge: The Quistclose Trust' (1992) *Current Issues in Insolvency Law* (London: Stevens and Sons, 1991); *see* Irene Lynch Fannon, Jane Marshall & Rory O'Ferrall, *Corporate Insolvency, and Rescue* (Butterworths 1996), Chs 4 and 7.

519. *Twinsectra v. Yardley* [2002] 2 AC 164; *Cooper v. PRG Powerhouse Ltd* [2008] BCC 588.

money be used exclusively for a stated purpose. The necessary implication of money being advanced for a sole or exclusive purpose is that otherwise, the money is to be returned to the lender.

339. In *Re Farepak Food and Gifts Ltd,*[520] Mann J. considered whether a *Quistclose* trust had arisen where customers had prepaid for Christmas hampers. He decided that this type of trust had not arisen based on the facts of the case as there was no contract of loan between the parties. Mann J. stated that:

> crucially, there is no suggestion that the money ought to have been put on one side by Farepak pending the transmutation from credited money to goods or vouchers. If there were a Quistclose trust then that obligation would have been inherent in it, but the business model would have made no sense. It would have required Farepak to have kept all the customer moneys in a separate account from January until November, untouched until the time when the goods or vouchers were acquired and then sent out. That is completely implausible. It would turn Farepak into a very odd savings organisation. Even banks do not have to do that.

L. Transfer of Undertakings Regulations

340. The Transfer of Undertakings Regulations was introduced into Irish law by virtue of an EU Directive designed to protect the position of employees of an undertaking where part or the entirety of that undertaking was transferred to another. Essentially, the rights of the employees and the corresponding duties of the employer are transferred to the purchasing entity. The European Communities (Protection of Employees on Transfer of Undertakings) Regulations 2003 (S.I. 131 of 2003) apply to any legal transfer of an undertaking, business or part of a business from one employer to another employer. Such transfers include mergers. The Regulations, which came into operation on 11 April 2003, revoke and replace the Regulations of 1980 (S.I. 306 of 1980) and the amending Regulations of 2000 (S.I. 487 of 2000), which had been in operation since 3 November 1980 and 21 December 2000, respectively. The Regulations implement an EU Directive, currently Council Directive 2001/23/EC (12 March 2001). An issue arose in relation to insolvency proceedings in Ireland, particularly whether the Regulations were applicable to receiverships or examinerships. The essential principle is that the contractual rights of the employees do not transfer when the original employer is subject to proceedings whereby it may be adjudicated bankrupt, or wound up for reasons of insolvency, by order of the High Court. However, if the sole or main reason for the institution of bankruptcy or insolvency proceedings is the evasion of an employer's legal obligations under the Regulations, then the Regulations apply to a transfer concluded by such an employer.

520. *Re Farepak Food and Gifts Ltd* [2006] ALL ER 265.

M. Transactional Avoidance: Swelling the Assets

341. Transactional avoidance provisions are provided for in a range of provisions of different legal provenance, some derived for example from individual bankruptcy law and others derived from more modern provisions.[521] First section 602 of the Companies Act 2014 re-enacts sections 218 and 255 of the 1963 Act concerning the invalidation of dispositions made after the commencement of the winding up. Section 604 invalidates what were called 'fraudulent preferences' but replaces the term 'fraudulent' with 'unfair preference'. Nevertheless, proof of an intention to prefer is still required. Section 608 is of newer provenance having first appeared as section 139 of the 1990 Act. Although not specifically described as an anti-deprivation principle, despite the considerable discussion engendered about this common law principle since the English decision of Belmont Park,[522] it would seem that section 608 may indeed be a rule which operates in a similar manner. In *Re Chatelaine Thudichum,*[523] transactions were successfully challenged on the grounds that these transactions had the effect of perpetrating fraud on the creditors. In the same decision, the same transaction was unsuccessfully challenged as an unfair preference. Further decisions on this provision are few but include *Devey Enterprises Ltd v. Devey and Devey* where Laffoy J observed that 'strangely, despite the fact that twenty years have elapsed since section 139 (the previously enacted provision from the 1990 Companies Act) was enacted, it has been the subject of very little judicial consideration'. She went on to refer to the summary of the provision provided by MacCann and Courtney in their annotation of the Companies Acts:

> In order to set aside a disposition of assets the liquidator does not have to prove that the company intended to defraud its creditors. Rather, he has the lower evidential burden of merely establishing that the effect of the disposition has been to defraud the creditors. However, in *Re Comet Food Machinery Co Ltd*[524] the Supreme Court observed, albeit obiter, that the section could be invoked if it were established that assets had been diverted with a view to frustrating a judgment against the company. This is hardly a controversial observation since, in such circumstances, the disposition would not only have had the effect of defrauding the creditors; rather, it would have been intended to defraud them.

521. At present there are attempts to harmonise these provisions at EU level. *See* further Reinhard Bork & Michael Veder: *Harmonisation of Transactions Avoidance Law* (Intersentia, 2021. The contributors on Ireland are Irene Lynch Fannon and Matthew Chippin. Recommendations made by the authors of this work are reflected in the new INSOL III proposed Directive on Harmonising Certain Aspects of Insolvency Law (COM(2022) 702 final / 2022/0408 (COD)) (updated 25 May 2023) (COM(2022)).
522. *See Belmont Park Investments Pty Ltd. v. BNY Corporate Trustee Services Inc.* [2011] 3 WLR 521. R. Goode, *Principles of Insolvency Law* 703 (4th edn., Sweet and Maxwell 2011) for a discussion of this principle in English law.
523. *Re Chatelaine Thudichum* [2008] IEHC 58.
524. *Re Comet Food Machinery Co Ltd* [1999] 1 ILRM 475.

342. Further discussion of this provision arose in *Re Tucon Process Installations Ltd.*[525] In that case, the action under section 139, now section 608 was brought by the company against the Bank of Ireland, with a view to recovering payments which had been made by debtors of the company into its bank account. These payments were made following the commencement of the winding up and so the company sought to have the monies paid to the bank (which had reduced its overdraft with the bank) to be set aside and monies paid into a pool for the general creditors. The issue of whether the company had *locus standi* arose. The statute specifically refers to the liquidator, contributory or creditor having standing. Hunt J. therefore acceded to the argument that the company had no *locus standi*. His decision on this point was upheld on appeal with Costello J. noting that this argument regarding standing of the company had not been argued before the court neither in *Le Chatelaine Thudichum* nor in *Devey Enterprises Ltd.*

343. Despite the holding that the appellant had no *locus standi* to bring the matter before the court, Costello J. went on to consider the argument regarding the provisions as the High Court had also done so. In this part of the judgement, it was held that the payments in question were not in breach of the terms of the statute as they were payments from debtors of the company reducing the company's overdraft with its bank and reducing the liability of the debtors. The payments were made in the 'ordinary course of business' and to a legitimate creditor and would not be regarded as payments made which perpetrated fraud on the creditors. However, it should be noted that there are unresolved issues concerning the timing of the payments.

III. Pre-insolvency Remedies: Restructuring and Turnaround

344. This section considers two procedures under Irish law. The first, receiverships is a remedy attaching to a secured creditor to appoint a receiver. This can be viewed simply as a way of enforcing security or can be viewed as a means by which a business facing financial difficulties can be sold without going into liquidation. The second process, examinerships was created under statutory framework in 1990 and is explicitly modelled on Chapter 11 of the US Federal Bankruptcy Code. It is now reflective of the provisions of the EU Preventive Restructuring Directive 1023/2019 and was the template for the transposition of that Directive which was added to as a process by the EU (Preventive Restructuring) Regulations 2022.

A. Receiverships

345. A receiver is normally appointed on foot of a debenture document. A receivership is generally based on a contractual relationship between the lender and the company. A number of events usually entitle a debenture holder to appoint a receiver:

---

525. *Re Tucon Process Installations Ltd.* [2015] IEHC 312 and IECA 211.

- Where there is a failure to pay the principal sum.
- Where there is a failure to pay an instalment on the loan.
- Where the company is otherwise unable to pay debts.
- Where the company ceases to trade.
- Where a winding up has commenced – Where the company jeopardises the security.
- Where there is a breach of the debenture agreement.

346. The powers of the receiver are now enumerated under section 437 of the Companies Act 2014. This section is modelled on section 420 of the Australian Corporations Act 2001 and gives certain specific powers to receivers in addition to any powers conferred by order or instrument. Section 439 repeats the existing obligation imposed on a receiver by section 316A of the 1963 Act as inserted by section 172 of the 1990 Act to 'exercise all reasonable care to obtain the best price reasonably obtainable as at the time of sale'.[526] Accordingly, the receiver is liable to the company for negligence in relation to the sale of assets where he or she fails to meet this standard of care. If surplus assets are generated, they should be paid to the company. Due to a number of controversial issues arising in relation to the exercise of their powers by receivers, the CLRG considered further regulation of receivers, particularly in relation to receivers appointed over individually held assets (as distinct from receiverships where the appointment is to the assets of a company). Nevertheless, the same principles will apply. No steps have been taken to implement the recommendations of the Review Group to date.[527]

B. Corporate Rescue Examinerships

347. This insolvency process was introduced in Irish law under the Companies (Amendment) Act 1990. Between 1990 and the mid-1990s, a series of decisions of the courts highlighted some unsatisfactory aspects of the legislation, which were changed and amended by the Companies (Amendment No. 2) Act 1999. In general, there was a view that the original legislation had set too much emphasis on rescue weighed against having due regard to pre-existing negotiated rights between the company and its creditors .[528] At the time of writing, renewed interest in rescue processes has been ignited with the passing of the Preventive Restructuring Directive and its transposition by June 2023, at the latest, by all member states of the EU.[529] Interestingly, this type of robust preventive restructuring framework is or has not

526. Irene Lynch Fannon, *Bloomsbury Professional's Guide to the Companies Act 2014*, 204 (Bloomsbury, 2014), Ch. 7.
527. *See* Report of the Review Group on the Regulation of Receivers, March 2019 www.clrg.org http://www.clrg.org/publications/report-of-the-company-law-review-group-on-the-regulation-of-receivers.pdf (Accessed June 2023).
528. For a general discussion of both the early phase of the examinership legislation and its development through the 1990s and beyond *see* Irene Lynch Fannon & Gerard N. Murphy, *Corporate Insolvency and Rescue* (2nd edn., Bloomsbury Professional, Dublin, 2012). Chs 12 and 13.
529. *See* Directive 2019/1023 The Preventive Restructuring Directive. *See also* Christoph Paulus and Reinhard Damamm : *European Preventive Restructuring: Article by Article Commentary* (Beck/

been part of most jurisdictional frameworks in the EU, despite its presence in Ireland. It is assumed that US influence in Ireland explains the provenance of the examinership legislation which is modelled on Chapter 11 of the US Federal Bankruptcy Code. Indeed, one of the titles given to an actor in Chapter 11 is Examiner, hence the title given to the Irish legislative framework.

348. Part 10 of the Companies Act 2014 largely repeats existing examinership law. Since its original passing, a significant concern has been the fact that the rescue process has not generally been availed of by small companies. The Companies (Miscellaneous Provisions) Act, 2013, introduced a change to the law in order to facilitate access by small private companies (as defined in section 350 of the Act) to the examinership process. Small private companies may apply directly to the Circuit Court (where according to the Department of Justice, legal fees are 30% less than the High Court) to have an examiner appointed, and not be required to apply to the High Court first, as is currently the case. This makes the process cheaper and more accessible to the SME sector. Some cases have been heard already under this legislation, the first concerning the appointment of an examiner to Cell Bridge Playzone in April 2014 leading to the rescue of the company which employed twenty-seven employees.[530] This possibility has been re-enacted in section 509(7)(b) of the Companies Act 2014. Despite some early success, this initiative did not bear fruit. During COVID-19, a specific effort has been made to redraft a rescue process more suitable for smaller companies. The framework for this legislation was set out by the CLRG in its Report in 2020[531] and this led to legislation called the Companies (Rescue Process for Small and Micro Companies) Act 2021.

Despite the significance of the examinership process as a rescue vehicle for certain kinds of Irish companies, it transpires that following the Great Recession, examinerships were not as successful as expected. There was a decrease in figures from 2009 to 2010 due to a lack of investments available. Sixteen companies availed of the process in 2010 compared with thirty-seven in 2009. Nevertheless, it has been reported that in 2012 alone, almost 1,000 jobs were saved in small and medium size companies due to successful examinership petitions. This was an increase of over 65% on 2011 figures. It does not account for the number of jobs saved in large companies in 2012 such as Eircom. In 2014, twenty-seven companies went into examinership. By year end, seventeen had returned to normal status, one had entered creditors liquidation, two entered receivership and seven companies were in examinership.[532]

Hart/Nomos, 2021). The author is a contributor to this work. In Ireland the implementation of this Directive has occurred under the European Union (Preventive Restructuring Directive 1023/2019) Regulations 2022. The Irish Examinership process is an important template regarding the introduction of this type of process in Europe and contains most if not all of the provisions of a 'robust restructuring process' envisaged as one of the options of implementation.

530. (2014) *Irish Independent* 3 April.

531. www.clrg.org, http://www.clrg.org/clrg/publications/the-company-law-review-group-s-special-report-on-the-rescue-of-small-business.pdf.

532. Companies Registration Office Report 2014.

349. Under section 519 of the 2014 Act, in order to be appointed as an examiner, one must be qualified to act as a company's liquidator. Section 542(6)(b) has been inserted on foot of the High Court decision in *Re McEnaney Construction Ltd [2008] IEHC 43*. Under this provision, the court is now allowed to authorise a reduction in the capital of a scheme of arrangement or compromise.

350. The examinership process is commenced on application to the High Court by a petitioner which may be the company, the directors of the company, a creditor or prospective or contingent creditor of the company (including an employee), or members of the company holding not less than one-tenth of such of the paid-up capital of the company as carries voting rights at general meetings as per section 510 of the 2014 Act. The Court may make an order to appoint an examiner when it appears to the Court that the company is, or is likely to be, unable to pay its debts, where there is no winding up of the company and where the court is satisfied that there is a 'reasonable prospect of survival'. Following the appointment of an examiner, the company is under the protection of the Court from its creditors for seventy days, but the examiner may also apply to the Court for extensions of up to thirty further days, in order to finalise his report and any proposed scheme of arrangement aimed at ensuring the survival of the company. At the end of the period of examinership, if the examiner presents a scheme of arrangement, the Court must decide whether or not to confirm proposals put forward by the examiner and the Court may, of its own motion or on the application of the examiner, extend protection for a further period while it considers its decision. Generally, no enforcement proceedings may be brought against the company while the company is under the protection of the Court. As regards a receivership, a receiver may be removed, following the appointment of an examiner under the provisions of section 522 of the Act.

C. *Issues Surrounding Examinerships*

351. As noted previously, some particular issues regarding the operation of the examinership process came under scrutiny in the 1990s. These are outlined and considered in the first report of the CLRG, published in December 1994. Arising from the recommendation of that group, the following matters were addressed in the 1999 Act: the requirement that an application for the appointment of an examiner had to be supported by a financial report from an independent accountant; that in considering matters arising in relation to the appointment of an examiner, the court would have regard (*inter alia*) to this report; and that the court must consider that there is a reasonable prospect of the company and its business surviving before an examiner could be appointed. The term 'independent accountant' under the 1990 Act has been replaced with 'independent expert' as per section 511 of the current legislation. In addition, the length of the examination period was shortened to seventy days, (which can be extended to 100 days on application to the court) and certain rights the examiner seemed to have under the original legislation to deal with assets that were charged were curtailed.[533] In particular, it was not possible for the examiner to deal with assets subject to a fixed charge. Furthermore, the dramatic power the examiner seemed to have under the original legislation to repudiate any contract that was detrimental to the company under the provisions was confined to contracts entered into in the course of the examinership, thus rendering the effect of that particular legislative provision to be entirely different from what seemed to be originally envisaged.

D. Outcome of Examinership

352. Despite those amendments, the examinership continues, in situations where it is viable, to deliver on the original goals envisaged in the legislation, in that it can facilitate corporate rescue and turnaround. A most important feature of the legislation is that it provides a legislative framework to facilitate the deferral of payment of some creditor's claims or indeed a sensible settlement of creditor's claims for less. It also provides a breathing space for a company to facilitate the sourcing of additional investment. Throughout the examinership period and at its culmination, the creditors of all classes are protected by the legislative requirements regarding the Court's role in overseeing the final scheme of arrangement. When the examiner's report is placed before the Court, any creditor or member whose claim or interest would be impaired if the proposals were implemented may appear and be heard. The Court shall not confirm any proposals, unless at least one class of creditors whose interests or claims would be impaired by implementation of the proposals has accepted the proposals, or if the sole or primary purpose of the proposals is avoidance of payment of tax due. The Court must also be satisfied (1) that the proposals are fair and equitable in relation to any class of creditors or members that has not accepted the proposals and whose interests would be impaired and (2) that the proposals are not unfairly prejudicial to the interests of any interested party. In more recent caselaw, the courts have articulated what is meant by unfair prejudice and have developed what is described in the context of the Preventive Restructuring Directive (2019/1023) as a 'best -interests-of-creditors test'. Effectively this test requires that any particular creditor or class of creditors who has not agreed to the compromise or agreement may object on the grounds that their interests are not as well-protected as compared with other creditors in this current scenario as compared with how they would fare on this comparative test in alternative scenarios such as a receivership or liquidation. An application of this test by the Irish Supreme Court can be seen in *Re McInerney Homes Ltd.* where the court approved the High Court's refusal to approve the compromise.[534] In essence, the issue at the confirmation hearing was whether the proposal was unfairly prejudicial to the banks. In this regard, the judge adopted a test with which the parties agreed. He considered (in

533. At present under the Companies (Miscellaneous Provisions) (COVID-19) Act 2020, the possible duration of an examinership has been extended by an additional fifty days. These measures have been extended to December 2023.

534. *See Re McInerney Homes Ltd.* [2011] IESC 31. *See* further Irene Lynch Fannon: Guest Editorial *International Insolvency Review* October 2019 for a consideration of this approach in an EU context. *See* further the JCOERE Project, an EU Commission – DG Justice (No. 800807) funded project for which the author was Principal Investigator. www.ucc.ie/en/law/JCOERE for further information on the implementation of the Preventive Restructuring Directive 1023/2019.

paragraph 4.3) that 'it would require exceptional circumstances before a court could approve a scheme of arrangement where secured creditors could be shown to be worse off under the scheme than under the alternative methods by which the value of the secured creditors' security could be realised.' The court continued, in citing the lower court with approval: 'The judge [in the lower court] … pointed out that under this proposal, as under many, if not all examinership proposals, the unsecured creditors would be paid an amount which was calculated as being more than that which they would receive under a liquidation. He suggested that if such a proposal nevertheless required that another class of creditors (in this case the secured creditors) receive something less than they would receive under receivership or liquidation, then that would by itself be a reason to conclude that there was unfair prejudice to the creditors, unless the disparity was justified by strong reasons. This approach was not contested on this appeal.'

353. A second issue which has recently arisen is whether a company which has already received the benefit of a renegotiated debt restructuring may apply to have an examinership appointed with a view to obtaining a second restructuring. In *Re Kitty Hall Ltd and Ors and the Companies Acts,*[535] the Court of Appeal, noting that surprisingly, this issue had never been argued before held that there was no bar to the appellant making this application noting that the case highlighted 'the interesting clash of 'important policy values' which lie behind corporate rescue, and whether the court should uphold 'settlement agreements on the one hand and the effective operation of the examinership process … on the other'.

354. In that vein, recent cases highlight that applications to have an examiner appointed and indeed adopting a rescue process generally can be open to applications being made where the purpose of the application may not be to rescue the corporate entity but to restructure the entity with different controlling interests. Whether this is pursued as part of a genuine rescue attempt or as part of a different set of motivations is one where the court will have to exercise discretion. The court referred to this issue in *O'Flynn v. Carbon Finance*:[536]

> [It is] … submitted to the Court that the petitioner is using the examinership process for an improper purpose, namely as a means of wresting control of the underlying assets … by engineering a situation of insolvency and default events to enable the bringing of a petition. The petition itself appears to acknowledge the aim of transferring ownership at paras. 8.7, 9.4 and 11.3 and it was also acknowledged … in submission. The matter of whether this is a valid complaint or a matter to be considered by the Court would appear a matter for the Court's consideration in the exercise of its discretion at the hearing of the petition … .

535. *Re Kitty Hall Ltd and Ors and the Companies Acts* [2017] IECA 247.
536. *O'Flynn v. Carbon Finance* [2014] IEHC 458. *See also Re Ina's Kitchen Desserts Ltd.* [2020] IEHC 644. In both cases an Examiner was not appointed and the company was not put into examinership.

355. Objections may be raised, at a hearing for the Court's consideration of an examiner's report, by a member or creditor whose interest or claim would be impaired by the proposals before the Court, on the grounds that: (a) there was a material irregularity at a meeting held for consideration of the proposals by members or creditors; (b) acceptance of the proposals at such meeting was obtained by improper means; (c) the proposals were put forward for an improper purpose; and/or (d) that the proposals unfairly prejudice the interests of the objector. A person who voted in favour of the proposals may only object on the grounds that acceptance of the proposals at such meeting was obtained by improper means or that, subsequent to the vote, he or she became aware that the proposals were put forward for an improper purpose. The Court, having regard to such provisions and to any objections raised, may confirm or reject the proposals in full or confirm the proposals subject to modifications.

356. An important development in relation to Irish restructuring law occurred during the reorganisation of Norwegian Air during 2020 and 2021. The company availed of both an Irish examinership process governed by Part 10 of the Companies Act 2014 and a scheme of arrangement process under Part 9 of the Companies Act 2014 (described in the next section). A key difference is that Examinerships are covered by the EIR Recast and therefore the concept of COMI is important in determining jurisdiction. The Irish High Court held that its jurisdiction to appoint an examiner to a company extended to a non-Irish debtor company that did not have its centre of main interests (COMI) in Ireland, or any other EU country, but which was related to another company (e.g., a parent, subsidiary or sister company) that (i) had its COMI in Ireland, (ii) was in examinership and (iii) where the debtor had a 'sufficient connection' to Ireland. The court held that NAS (the parent company of a range of subsidiaries with connection to Ireland), 'has a real and deep connection to the State'. The connections included substantial direct and indirect Irish subsidiaries of NAS and its wider commercial operations located in the State. The Irish High Court endorsed and adopted the sufficient connection test set out in the leading decisions of the English High Court in *Re Drax Holdings Ltd* and *Re Rodenstock* in the context of English law schemes of arrangement. In addition to recognising the court's broad jurisdiction to appoint an examiner, the decision bolsters the view that the Irish courts have jurisdiction to approve Irish law schemes of arrangement under Part 9 of the Companies Act 2014 (Part 9 Schemes) for non-Irish companies with a sufficient connection to the jurisdiction.[537] Effectively in considering the process available under the Examinership process and the English style Scheme of Arrangement provisions available in Irish law (described in the next section), Irish law has a multiple range of options available to a debtor company or group.

537. *Re Norwegian Air and Ors.* [2020] IEHC 664.

§7. MERGERS AND TAKEOVERS

I. Introduction

357. Chapter 1 of Part 9 of the Companies Act 2014 replaces sections 201–204 of the Companies Act 1963, (as amended) which is designed to facilitate compromises and arrangements, including mergers, takeovers and other restructuring, providing a company law framework underpinning this activity. The general actions considered here are also subject to public law regulation in terms of competition law, and notification where companies are listed. These are considered below. These are referred to as 'schemes of arrangement' or 'reconstructions'– between a company and either its members or its creditors or both. Schemes of arrangement under sections 450–454 present an alternative to the type of restructuring which occurs in examinership,[538] and sometimes in receiverships but the provisions also apply in solvent situations regarding mergers, takeovers and voluntary reconstructions.[539] During the Great Recession, the equivalent provisions have been extremely popular in the United Kingdom and have proved to be an attractive restructuring device, not only for English companies but also for non-English companies seeking to avail of schemes in England.[540] The structure of any scheme is not pre-determined and the sparsity of the legislative framework provides a great deal of flexibility in the type of rearrangement of interests which can occur which can include creditors agreeing to convert loan capital into share capital (i.e., debt into equity) or the deferral of enforcement of creditors' claims. A scheme of arrangement may involve, for example, reorganisation of capital or rescheduling of debt.[541] In addition to examinerships, the scheme of arrangement process presents an alternative to a creditors' (or a members') voluntary winding up but is available in non-insolvent situations as well.

II. Restrictions on Mergers and Takeovers: The Legal Framework

358. A takeover, merger or other reconstruction of a company or a group is conducted under a company law framework described as a scheme. A proposed scheme must be approved by a majority in number 'representing three-fourths in value of the creditors or class of creditors or members or class of members, as the case may be', voting on the proposal either in person or by proxy at a duly called meeting.[542] The scheme must also be approved by the company in a general meeting or by its

538. *Supra* paras 296–301.

539. *See* generally Lyndon MacCann, *Corporate Restructuring: Schemes, Mergers and Divisions*, in *Bloomsbury Professional's Guide to the Companies Act 2014* (Courtney ed., Bloomsbury Professional 2015). *See also* Irene Lynch Fannon & Gerard N. Murphy, *Corporate Insolvency and Rescue* (Bloomsbury Professional 2012), Ch. 14.

540. *See* generally Jennifer Payne, *Schemes of Arrangement* (Cambridge University Press, 2013).

541. *See*, for example, *Re McEnaney Construction* [2008] IEHC 43 (scheme for reduction of capital in examinership).

542. Companies Act 2014, s. 450(1). Previously such meetings could only be called with court approval but now these meetings can be convened by directors of the company.

board or, where appropriate, by its liquidator or receiver.[543] When a meeting of creditors or members is summoned under section 450, section 452 provides that with every notice summoning such a meeting must be sent a statement explaining the effect of the proposed arrangement and stating any material interests of the directors, whether as directors, creditors, members or otherwise, and the effect thereon of the proposed arrangement. Furthermore, the Court may order meetings of creditors and/or members to be held to consider proposals; at any such meetings, affected parties must be segregated into appropriate classes 'confined to those persons whose rights are not so dissimilar as to make it impossible for them to consult together with a view to their common interest'. Failure to do so may result in the Court refusing to sanction a proposed scheme.[544] A scheme proposed under section 450 must be sanctioned by the Court before it can take effect. The Court only approves schemes where the applicable statutory provisions and procedures have been complied with; the prescribed majorities (of members or creditors, as the case may be) have held the necessary meetings and have bona fide approved the scheme; and the scheme is fair and equitable.[545] The Court will not intervene, however, merely on the basis that, applying its own business judgment, it would have come to a different conclusion as to whether to approve the scheme.[546] In approving a scheme, the Court may impose such conditions or modifications as it sees fit, in order to ensure that the scheme is fair and equitable.[547] Under section 451, the Court has more extensive powers to stay all proceedings in being against the company and restrain any further such proceedings for such period as it sees fit. An application for a stay may be made by the company, the directors, a member or creditor, or where the company is being wound up, the liquidator.[548] A scheme becomes binding once the provisions of sections 453 and 454 of the Companies Act 2014 are complied with. These conditions include approval by the Court under section 453 and registration under section 454. The scheme then becomes binding on all creditors or members or any particular class thereof, on the company and where relevant the liquidator and contributories of the company.[549]

---

543. *Re Savoy Hotel Co.* [1981] 3 WLR 441; *Re Oceanic Steam Navigation Co. Ltd* [1938] 3 All ER 740.
544. As occurred in *Re Pye (Ireland) Ltd* (unreported, High Court, Costello J., 12 Nov. 1984 and Supreme Court, 11 Mar. 1985). *See* further Irene Lynch Fannon, Jane Marshall & Rory O'Ferrall, *Corporate Insolvency* (Butterworths 1996), Ch. 12. *See also* McCann, *supra* n. 531 at p. 174 and Irene Lynch Fannon & Gerard N. Murphy: *Supra* n. 531.
545. *Re John Power and Sons Ltd* [1934] IR 412; *Re Dorman Long and Co. Ltd* [1934] Ch. 635; *Carruth v. Imperial Chemical Industries Ltd* [1937] 2 All ER 422.
546. *Re London Chartered Bank of Australia* [1893] 3 Ch. 540.
547. *Re Canning Jarrah Timber Co. (Western Australia) Ltd* [1900] 1 Ch. 708.
548. Companies Act 2014, s. 451.
549. Companies Act 2014, s. 453.

A. Public Law Regulation of Takeovers and Mergers

359. The Competition Acts 2002–2014[550] govern the public regulation of takeovers, mergers and other acquisitions. This legislation was amended in 2022 with the passing of the Competition (Amendment) Act 2022 which transposed the ECN+ Directive.[551] The Competition and Consumer Protection Act 2014 replaced the Competition Authority with the Competition and Consumer Protection Commission (hereinafter referred to as 'the Commission' in this section). Consequently, mergers and acquisitions meeting certain criteria must be notified to this Commission under the terms of the Competition Acts 2002–2014. Section 16 of the Competition Act 2002 (as amended)[552] provides that notification is required where a transaction involves:

- the merger of two or more previously independent undertakings; or
- a sole or joint acquisition of direct or indirect 'control' of the whole or part of an undertaking ('control' for the purpose of this definition existing where decisive influence is capable of being exercised with regard to the activities of an undertaking.); or
- an undertaking acquiring all or a substantial part of the assets, including goodwill, of another undertaking, with the result that the first undertaking effectively replaces the second undertaking in the business concerned.

Section 18 (as amended)[553] provides that, in order to require notification, it must be the case that:

- the aggregate turnover of two or more of the undertakings involved is not less than EUR 50 million;
- the turnover in the State of each of two or more of the undertakings involved is not less than EUR 3 million; In addition, under section 18(5) (as amended) the Minister for Enterprise, Trade and Employment, where he or she is of opinion that exigencies of the common good so require, may, after consultation with the Commission, by order specify a class or classes of merger or acquisition to be subject to the requirement of notification. Receiverships, liquidations and intra-group transactions are exempted from the definition of qualifying mergers and acquisitions.

360. The previous Authority (now the Commission as described above) considers that an undertaking carries on business in the State where it (a) has a physical

550. Section 1 of the Competition and Consumer Protection Act 2014 provides that the Competition Acts 2002–2012 and Parts 3 and 4 of the present act may be cited together as the Competition Acts 2002–2014.
551. The Competition Act 2021 is designed to implement provisions of what is known as the ECN +Directive. This will, amongst other developments provide for increased criminal sanctions. *See* Directive 2019/1 described at https://eur-lex.europa.eu/legal-content/EN/TXT/?uri=CELEX%3A32019L0001.
552. Competition and Consumer Protection Act 2014, ss 1(5), 6 and 53(c).
553. Competition and Consumer Protection Act 2014, s. 55.

presence (such as by having an office or agency) and either makes sales or supplies services to customers on the island of Ireland or (b) has made sales into the island of Ireland of at least EUR 2 million in its most recent financial year. 'Turnover in the State' has been interpreted as referring to turnover generated through services supplied or sales made to customers within the jurisdiction. A qualifying merger or acquisition below the financial thresholds may be voluntarily notified to the Commission. One possible reason for voluntary notification would be to obtain advance clearance from the Commission, where a possible competition concern is envisaged. It also bears noting that, under section 18(9) of the 2002 Act, (as amended)[554] it is an offence to fail to notify a qualifying merger or to fail to supply required information. A person guilty of such an offence is liable to fines of up to EUR 3,000 (on summary conviction) or EUR 250,000 (on indictment).

1. Notification

361. Notification, where made, must be in writing to the Commission within one month of the date of conclusion of the agreement or making of a formal public bid, and the notification must contain full details of the agreement or bid. It is open to parties involved in any such transaction to seek a meeting with Authority staff, prior to notification. Once notification is made, short details of the same are published online, and third parties may make submissions. Section 19 (as amended)[555] provides that a merger or acquisition notified to the Commission may not be put into effect until (a) the Commission determines that it should be put into effect; (b) the Commission makes a conditional determination; or (c) specified time periods have elapsed without the Commission informing the notifying parties of a determination. Within thirty working days commencing on the date of notification (or the date of response to any formal request for information), the Commission must inform the notifying parties, and any third parties who made submissions, as to its determination – either to allow the transaction or to initiate a full investigation. The merger or acquisition is deemed to be cleared where the Commission does not meet this time limit. If approved, the merger or acquisition must take place within twelve months of receipt by the Commission of the notification (or receipt of further information). If it elects to initiate a full investigation, the Commission must within 120 working days from the date of notification (or request for further information) make a determination – that the merger or acquisition may proceed, that it should take effect, or that it should take effect subject to conditions.

362. The substantive test used by the Commission in its analysis is whether the merger or acquisition will have the effect of substantially lessening competition in markets for goods or services in the State. This is similar to the US standard and varies only slightly from the test used in the EC Merger Regulation (i.e., whether a transaction 'significantly impedes effective competition').

554. Competition and Consumer Protection Act 2014, s. 56.
555. Competition and Consumer Protection Act 2014, ss 56 and 58.

2. Appeal

363. A notifying undertaking may appeal a decision of the Commission that a merger or acquisition shall not take effect, or a decision that it shall take effect only subject to certain conditions, to the High Court. Issues of fact and law – to a degree – may be dealt with on appeal. As far as practicable, the Court shall rule on any such appeal within two months. The appeal process is described in section 24 of the Competition Act 2002 as amended.

3. Special Circumstances

364. Previously, the Competition Act of 2002, contained special provisions relating to 'media mergers'. These have been repealed by section 7 of the Competition and Consumer Protection Act 2014.

365. Where a merger or acquisition has been put in place otherwise than in accordance with the procedures outlined *supra*, it is open to the Commission or third parties to bring proceedings alleging breach of sections 4 and/or 5 of the Act, (as amended) which prohibit anti-competitive agreements and abuse of a dominant position, respectively.

B. EU-Wide Mergers: The Role of the European Commission

366. The above position in Irish law is similar to the jurisdiction exercised by the European Commission in respect of large EU-wide mergers and acquisitions under Council Regulation (EC) No. 139/2004 of 20 January 2004 on the control of concentrations between undertakings (the EC Merger Regulation), which summarised and recast the original 1989 Regulation and subsequent amendments. The EC Merger Regulation applies to transactions it terms as having 'a Community dimension', namely those where (a) the combined aggregate worldwide turnover of the undertakings involved exceeds EUR 5 billion, and (b) the aggregate Community-wide turnover of at least two of the undertakings exceeds EUR 250 million. In the alternative, where a transaction does not meet those criteria, it will be deemed to a Community dimension where: (a) the combined aggregate worldwide turnover of the undertakings involved exceeds EUR 2.5 billion; (b) in each of at least Member States, the combined aggregate turnover of all the undertakings is at least EUR 250 million, provided that in each of those three or more Member States, the combined aggregate turnover exceeds EUR 25 million; and (c) the aggregate Community-wide turnover of at least two of the undertakings concerned is more than EUR 100 million. The Commission appraises transactions having a Community dimension as thus defined. The Regulation, in Article 2(2), provides that, in order to be declared compatible with the common market, a proposed 'concentration' (i.e., merger) must 'not significantly impede effective competition in the common market or in a substantial part of it, in particular as a result of the creation or strengthening of a dominant position, shall be declared compatible with the common market'. There is not sufficient space here for detailed consideration of the Regulation, but it should be noted that the Regulation has been amended by Commission Regulation (EC) No. 1033/2008 (Official Journal L 279, 22 October 2008, 3–12).

367. At the time of writing deadline for transposing the 'Mobility Directive' (Directive (EU) 2019/2121) has now passed. Ireland, along with many other Member States, has not yet implemented this directive which amends some of the existing rules on EU cross-border mergers and will also facilitate cross-border conversions and divisions of EU companies. The new regime enhances the existing framework for EU cross-border mergers. Transitional arrangements for cross-border mergers currently underway will need to be considered mergers commenced under the current regime but completed after transposition are not dealt with in the directive. It appears that transitional measures may vary across Member States.

C. The Role of the Irish Takeover Panel

368. In addition to the foregoing, the Irish Takeover Panel supervises takeovers and certain other 'relevant transactions' involving companies listed on the recognised Irish stock exchanges. The Panel was established by the Irish Takeover Panel Act 1997[556] and is incorporated as a company limited by guarantee. The Panel is designated as the competent authority under the European Communities (Takeover Bids (Directive 2004/25/EC)) Regulations 2006 (S.I. 255 of 2006) for the purposes of Article 4(1) of the EC Takeover Bids Directive. Nothing in sections 450–454 of the Companies Act 2014 regarding schemes of arrangement prejudices the jurisdiction of the panel within the meaning of the 1997 Act, although the Court and the Panel are each required to have due regard to the exercise of the other's powers under the respective legislative frameworks.[557] Indeed, Order 75, Rule 24 of the Rules of the Superior Courts provides (see Rules of the Superior Courts (Takeover Schemes) 2005 (S.I. 688 of 2005)) that: (a) the Court may direct the Registrar to invite the Panel to provide to the Court 'such form as the Court may request, any report or other information which appears relevant to the exercise of the Court's jurisdiction' under sections 450–454; and (b) the applicant or moving party in any such court proceedings must promptly provide the Panel with copies of any motion or petition and details of the terms of any court order, including promptly upon perfection a true copy of same.

---

556. *See also* European Communities (Cross Border Merger) Regulations 2008. Directive 2004/25/EC, a Directive of the European Parliament and the Council of 21 Apr. 2004 (on takeover bids) and subsequent European Communities (Takeover Bids (Directive 2004/25/EC)) Regulations 2006 (S.I. 255 of 2006).
557. Companies Act 2014 ss 450–454.

369. The Panel is responsible for making Rules to ensure that takeovers (including takeover bids as defined in the 2006 Regulations) and other relevant transactions comply with the General Principles set out in the Schedule to the 1997 Act. Under section 5 of the 1997 Act, the principal objects of the Panel are to monitor takeovers and other 'relevant transactions', so as to ensure compliance with the 1997 Act and any Rules made by the Panel. Section 8 provides that rules made by the Panel may be for the purposes of: (a) specifying, by reference to matters such as the amount of securities acquired, offers, agreements or transactions as 'relevant transactions' for the purposes of the Act; (b) ensuring that takeovers and other relevant transactions comply with the scheduled principles and the rest of the Act; (c) providing, in the interests of shareholders, for the manner in which such transactions and related activities are to be carried out; and (d) specifying circumstances in which a person shall be presumed, until the contrary is established to the satisfaction of the Panel, to be acting in concert with another person in regard to a takeover or other 'relevant transaction'.[558]

370. Under section 9(1) of the 1997 Act, the Panel may of its own volition or on the application of any interested person make a ruling as to whether any activity or proposed activity, with respect to a takeover or other relevant transaction, complies with the scheduled principles and any Rules under section 8, and any such ruling shall have immediate effect. Section 9(2) allows the Panel, to ensure compliance with any Rules and with the scheduled principles, to direct any party to a takeover or relevant transaction to do, or refrain from doing, anything specified in the direction. Under section 12, the Panel may apply to the Court in a summary manner for enforcement of any such direction. Section 10 provides that the Panel may, on its own initiative or at the request of a party to a takeover or relevant transaction, enquire into the conduct of any person, where it has reasonable grounds for believing that a breach of the scheduled principles or any Rules made under section 8 has occurred or may occur. Following an enquiry into the conduct of any person under this section, if it so thinks fit, the Panel may (publicly or otherwise) advise, admonish or censure such person in relation to his or her conduct. A person whom the Panel advises, admonishes or censures may appeal to the Court, which may, as it sees fit, approve or annul the decision; if the latter, the Court may direct a fresh enquiry or publicise notice of its decision. Section 11 provides that, in exercise of the powers conferred on it by sections 9 and 10, the Panel may hold hearings; for the purpose of any such hearing, the Panel shall have the same powers as the Court in respect of: (a) enforcing attendance and their examination, and (b) compelling the production of documents. Likewise, a witness before the Panel shall be entitled to the same immunities and privileges as if he or she were a witness before the Court.

Under Regulation 10 of the European Communities (Takeover Bids (Directive 2004/25/EC)) Regulations 2006 (S.I. 255 of 2006), the Panel may specify circumstances in which it is enabled to grant derogations from, or waive, any rules under that section.

---

558. *See* further www.irishtakeoverpanel.ie.

1. Protective Measures

371. Where an offer has been made to acquire shares in a target company and at least 80% in value of the shares affected has been so acquired, a remaining minority shareholding may be compulsorily acquired, as permitted by and subject to the provisions of sections 457–459 of the Companies Act 2014. The provisions of section 457 set out the requirements underpinning the right of the offeror whose offer has 'become binding or been approved or accepted in respect of not less than 80% in value of the shares affected' to acquire the remaining 20% shareholding and sets out a time limit of six months in which such acquisition takes place. Section 459(5) includes the minority shareholding block to apply to the court for an order contrary to the compulsory acquisition order envisaged in the section.

372. Once the requirements are complied with, section 457(3) states that:

> the offeror shall be entitled to acquire the beneficial ownership of all or any of the remaining shares affected from the dissenting shareholder or shareholders on–
>
> (a) the same terms as have become binding or been approved or accepted as mentioned in subsection (2), or
> (c) where an application is made under section 459(5)(a), any different terms that the court specifies.

If no such application is made, the offeror then becomes entitled to acquire beneficial ownership of said shares. The Supreme Court has held that, where a dissenting shareholder applies to the Court opposing compulsory acquisition, he or she bears the 'heavy' burden of persuading the Court that the proposed transaction is unfair.[559] The Court will pay 'great attention' to the views of the majority who have accepted the bid,[560] although such views will not carry as much weight where the approving shareholders are associated (whether directly or indirectly) with the offeror company as would acceptance by shareholders wholly independent of the offeror company. It is not enough for a dissenting shareholder to argue that a more attractive scheme, contract or offer could have been put forward; rather it appears that to succeed in persuading the Court to intervene, it must be shown that the proposal is 'obviously unfair, patently unfair, unfair to the meanest intelligence'.[561]

Under sections 457(6) and 457(7)(4), an offeror company acquiring the beneficial ownership of not less than 80% in value of the shares in the offeree company is obliged to give notice of that fact within thirty days of the date of such acquisition to all other shareholders, and any such other shareholder may, within three months of such notice being given to him or her, require the transferee company to acquire his or her shares.

559. *Walls v. PJ Walls Holdings Ltd* [2008] 1 ILRM 1; *Re Fitzwilton PLC* [2000] 2 ILRM 263.
560. *Duggan v. Stoneworth Investment Ltd* [2000] 1 IR 563.
561. *Walls v. PJ Walls Holdings Ltd* [2008] 1 ILRM 1.

§8. HOLDING COMPANIES AND SUBSIDIARIES

I. Introduction

373. The doctrine of corporate personality has been considered *supra* (*see* Part I, Chapter 1, §2, IV). One of the most significant effects of corporate personality in modern commercial life is to be seen in relation to groups of companies. Once corporations had legal personality, it was inevitable that a corporation would be permitted to become the owner of shares in another company. As a result, groups of companies now include a parent or holding company and many subsidiaries and related companies. A firm commitment to the doctrine of corporate personality underpins these structures, this commitment having been further reiterated in recent decisions such as *Prest* in England and Wales and *O'Donnell v. Bank of Ireland and Ors.*[562] But in Ireland, a line of case law recognises the possibility that this doctrine can be set aside in certain circumstances concerning groups. These cases are usually described as cases where the courts have disregarded separate corporate entities in groups in 'the interests of justice' or where a 'single economic entity' is recognised. This line of analysis began with the English case of *DHN Ltd v. London Borough of Tower Hamlets*,[563] followed in Ireland by the cases of *Power Supermarkets Ltd v. Crumlin Investments Ltd*[564] and *State (McInerney & Co. Ltd) v. Dublin County Council.*[565]

374. Following these cases, the courts in both jurisdictions retreated from the adoption of this analysis as a remedy for all 'injustices'. The following two cases serve to illustrate how the courts continue to reiterate the robustness of the principle of corporate personality and its operation in a group structure to maximise the effect of limited liability. In *Adams v. Cape Industries PLC*,[566] the plaintiffs sought to have the group structure disregarded in some of its parts, to enable the significant liabilities of one company in relation to injuries caused through the mining of asbestos to be met by the parent company of the group. This application was refused. Involuntary creditors who had obtained judgment in Texas could not enforce that judgment against the principal company in the group, which was incorporated in London.

Similarly, a return to orthodoxy is evidenced in the Irish Supreme Court in *Allied Irish Coal Supplies Ltd v. Powell Duffryn International Fuels Ltd.*[567]

375. Nevertheless, the Irish courts have specifically retained the possibility of disregarding separate corporate structures within a group where the interests of justice require it, although this concept has been severely curtailed. In the judgement

562. Considered below in text accompanying fns. 593 *ff.*
563. *DHN Ltd v. London Borough of Tower Hamlets* [1976] 1 WLR 852.
564. *Power Supermarkets Ltd v. Crumlin Investments Ltd* (unreported, High Court, Costello J., 22 Jun. 1981).
565. *State (McInerney & Co. Ltd) v. Dublin County Council* [1985] ILRM 513.
566. *Adams v. Cape Industries PLC* [1990] Ch. 433.
567. *Allied Irish Coal Supplies Ltd v. Powell Duffryn International Fuels Ltd* [1998] 2 ILRM 61.

of the High Court in *Fyffes PLC v. DCC PLC,*[568] Laffoy J. reviewed the relevant authorities in this area, beginning with *DHN v. London Borough of Tower Hamlets,* described *supra.* In *Fyffes,* the plaintiff sought to disregard the various group entities and regard the companies at issue in relation to the defendants as a single economic entity to underpin the alleged infringement of the rules on insider dealing and market abuse outlined at the time of the trades in question by Part V of the 1990 Companies Act.[569] Laffoy J. held, following this argument that the companies involved should be regarded as a single economic entity, in the particular circumstances concerning an interpretation of the statutory interpretation of the legislation prohibiting insider dealing:

376. This decision, insofar as it dealt with the doctrine of corporate personality was appealed and affirmed in the Supreme Court.[570] It was observed in the Supreme Court that the decision of the High Court was so thoroughly and clearly reasoned that only one aspect of the decision was appealed. The analysis of the corporate personality doctrine was further followed in a more recent decision of the Supreme Court in *O'Donnell and Ors v. Bank of Ireland &Ors.*[571] This case is somewhat similar in its facts to the similarly authoritative restatement of the doctrine of corporate personality from the UK Supreme Court in *Prest v. Petrodel.*[572] In conclusion, difficulties surrounding the application of the single entity argument relating to groups of companies remain.

II. Groups and the Agency Question

377. In *Firestone Tyre & Rubber Co. Ltd v. Lewellin,*[573] a US company, Akron, the parent of the appellant, had established the appellant company, Brentford, as a subsidiary in the UK. Brentford manufactured tyres for sale to distributors in Europe. Distribution contracts entered into by Akron with distributors and with Brentford were used to support a claim that, for tax purposes, Brentford did not carry on business as a separate entity in the UK. The House of Lords rejected this argument based on the facts of the case, holding that the appellant was carrying on the business in the UK as an agent of the US parent company and was therefore subject to taxation under UK law. In *Smith, Stone and Knight Ltd v. Birmingham Corporation,*[574] the plaintiff company operated a paper manufacturing business and subsequently acquired a paper waste management business. Although a subsidiary company was created, called the Birmingham Waste Co. Ltd with a view to operating the business, the plaintiff parent company retained ownership of the property

568. *Fyffes PLC v. DCC PLC* [2005] IEHC 477 (unreported, High Court, 21 Dec. 2005). This decision on the issue of liability for insider dealing was successfully appealed to the Supreme Court by Fyffes. The Supreme Court found that trading had occurred where the defendant was in possession of price sensitive information: [2007] IESC 36.
569. Since repealed and replaced by Ch. 1 of Part 23 of the Companies Act 2014.
570. [2007] IESC 36.
571. [2014] IESC 77.
572. [2013] UKSC 2013.
573. *Firestone Tyre & Rubber Co. Ltd v. Lewellin* [1957] 1 WLR 464.
574. *Smith, Stone and Knight Ltd v. Birmingham Corporation* [1939] 4 All ER 116.

held by the original business and retained ownership of the business from the date of acquisition. Atkinson J. held that the waste management business was still owned by the parent company and operated by its agent, the subsidiary, with the result that the parent company could claim compensation for both the loss of land and business on foot of a compulsory purchase order made by the defendant corporation.[575]

III. Groups and Liability for Debts

378. Real injustices are sometimes visited on plaintiffs where groups have organised themselves to avoid liability in the manner described in *Re Southard* and *Adams v. Cape Industries PLC*. For example, it can be the case where creditors of one subsidiary may not be paid on insolvency even as other companies in the group 'prosper to the joy of the shareholders' as described by Templeman J in *Re Southard Ltd*.[576] The injustice is particularly aggravated when we consider the plight of the involuntary tort creditor left without an unsatisfied judgment, as occurred in *Adams*, but there are other egregious examples.[577] Irish law has attempted to address this situation with the enactment of sections 599 and 600 of the Companies Act 2014 (formerly sections 140 and 141 of the Companies Act 1990).[578]

379. The sections provide for contribution and pooling orders respectively. In relation to section 599, an application can be made to the High Court whereby companies related, as defined in the legislation,[579] to the company in liquidation may be

575. A similar result was achieved in *D.H.N . Food Distributors v. Tower Hamlets London Borough Council* [1976] 1 WLR 852.
576. *Re Southard & Co. Ltd.* [1979] 1 W.L.R. 1199
577. The Irish Company Law Review Group considered the case of the restructuring of a prominent Dublin Department store, Clerys, whereby a new holding company restructured the business into an operations subsidiary and a property own subsidiary. The former was liquidated with loss of employment, significant loss to creditors who had been concession stand owners in the Department store and who had contributed to the refurbishment of the premises and even loss of customer deposits including deposits for goods from some employees. The Report of the CLRG issues in 2017 considered the possible application of ss 599 and 600 to the fact scenario and made some observations but no suggestions for specific reform. *See* Report of the Company Law Review Group on the Protection of Employees and Unsecured Creditors. 2017. http://www.clrg.org/publications/clrg%20adhoc%20committee%20report.pdf Following further incidents and consequent political pressure the Company Law Review Group has reconsidered this provision and has made some suggestions to change toe provision in accordance with the provisions as they were originally conceived.
578. Similar provisions are present in the New Zealand Companies Act (NZ) 1993, ss 271–272. It seems that Ireland and New Zealand are the only common law jurisdictions with these type of provisions. *See* further *Re Frederick Inns Ltd.* [1994] IRLM 387. (deal with this somewhere else?).
579. Companies Act 2014 s. 2(10) and 2(11) provide a definition of relatedness for the purposes of ss 599 and 600 as follows: that other company is its holding company or subsidiary; or more than half in nominal value of its equity share capital (as defined in s. 7(11)) of the Companies Act 2014) is held by the other company and companies related to that other company (whether directly or indirectly, but other than in a fiduciary capacity); or more than half in nominal value of the equity share capital (as defined in s. 7(11)) of the Companies Act 2014) of each of them is held by members of the other (whether directly or indirectly, but other than in a fiduciary capacity); or that other company or a company or companies related to that other company or that other company together with a company or companies related to it are entitled to exercise or control the exercise of more than

ordered to contribute to the debts of the company. Alternatively, under section 600, an application can be made to the High Court to order that the assets of two or more related companies in liquidation be pooled. These orders will be made where it appears to the Court that it is 'just and equitable' to do so. In relation to section 599 where a parent company might be ordered to contribute to the assets of a related insolvent company, the consideration of whether it is 'just and equitable' to make the order includes the consideration of three specific issues: (a) the extent to which the related company took part in the management of the company being wound up; (b) the conduct of the related company towards the creditors of the company being wound up; and (c) the effect such order would be likely to have on the creditors of the related company concerned Under section 600 where two or more related companies are in liquidation, the court may order that the assets of the companies be pooled if the criteria set out in the legislation are satisfied. There have been no cases – or at least no cases resulting in written judgments of the Court – where such orders have been made. In accordance with section 599, the application for a contribution order may be made by a liquidator, creditor or contributory of a company in liquidation. The court may grant a contribution order for 'an amount equivalent to the whole or part of all or any of the debts provable in that winding up'. Under section 600 of the Companies Act 2014 (formerly section 141 of the Companies Act 1990), the High Court can again make an order pooling the assets of two or more related companies in a group. Effectively, the order will provide that 'the companies shall be wound up together as if they were one company'. The court may make such an order where it appears 'just and equitable' to do so, and again similar criteria are mentioned to which the Court shall have regard.[580]

In its review of these provisions in the 2017 Report, the CLRG also noted that there was a final condition which an applicant for a contribution order had to prove, namely that the liquidation of the insolvent company was attributable to the actions or omissions of the second company.[581] It was noted that this was a particularly strict provision and distinguished the Irish provisions from the similar, but more flexible provisions found under the NZ Companies Act 1980,[582] under which there had been successful litigation.[583] However, overall the CLRG Report did not see its way to recommending an amendment to section 599.[584] However, following particular incidences of aggressive group restructuring which left employees in particular, but also additional creditors, without full payment while valuable group-owned assets were retained in separate but related companies, the CLRG returned

---

one half of the voting power at any general meeting of the company; or the businesses of the companies have been so carried on that the separate business of each company, or a substantial part thereof, is not readily identifiable; or there is another company to which both companies are related.

580. Companies Act 2014, s. 600(6) – '(a) the extent to which any of the companies took part in the management of any of the other companies; (b) the conduct of any of the companies towards the creditors of any of the other companies; (c) the extent to which the circumstances that gave rise to the winding up of any of the companies are attributable to the actions or omissions of any of the other companies; (d) the extent to which the businesses of the companies have been intermingled'.

581. Companies Act 2014, s. 599 (5).

582. Now s. 271a of the NZ Companies Act 1993.

583. *Lewis Holdings Ltd v. Steel & Tube Holdings Ltd* [2015] NZCCLR 5.

584. *Infra* n. 598 CLRG Report, 2017 51–52.

to this question and in a recent Report in 2021 recommended changes to this legislation which would render it more effective. These changes are now incorporated in the Employment (Collective Redundanies and Miscellaneous Provisions) and Companies (Amendment) Bill 2023 currently being considered by the legislature.

IV. Groups and Accounts and Taxation

380. In the context of groups, one of the most significant features of Ireland's economy is the success of its policies in attracting significant Foreign Direct Investment (FDI) in terms of the location of multinational subsidiaries. The taxation position of subsidiaries of multinationals is described in general *infra* on the principle that the taxation of a subsidiary is treated in much the same way as the taxation of a single Irish resident company. Some specific issues regarding groups are mentioned in the preceding section. Members of a group may surrender current-year trading losses, excess charges on income, excess management expenses (in the case of investment companies) and excess capital allowances. In this context, the relevant definition is that two companies are members of a group if one is a 75% subsidiary of the other or both are 75% subsidiaries of a third company. Note that a company is a 75% subsidiary of another company where not less than 75% of the ordinary share capital is owned directly or indirectly by that company. Group relief is available to Irish companies, subject to certain conditions, in respect of trading losses incurred by their non-Irish subsidiary companies that are resident in the EU Member States and EEA States with which Ireland has a double taxation treaty.

§9. Taxation

I. Introduction

381. In general, a company will be subject to corporation tax regarding the taxation of corporate profits as calculated in accordance with the relevant accounting principles and taxation acts. It will also be subject to capital gains tax as described *infra*. In relation to the distribution of dividends, these will be taxed as income for those in receipt of the dividends but also note the provisions regarding withholding tax as described *infra*. Provisions regarding the taxation of groups are described in the previous section in brief.

II. Corporate Income and Capital Gains

382. A company resident in Ireland is liable to pay corporation tax on its worldwide profits, not just its Irish source profits, whether or not these profits are repatriated into Ireland. In groups of companies, the corporate personality principle will treat each company as a separate entity for these purposes. Accordingly, a non-resident company, such as a European or US multinational, trading in the State through a branch or agency is liable to pay Irish corporation tax on the profits of its

Irish subsidiary company wherever these profits arise. Foreign profits of Irish resident companies are subject to double taxation relief under Part 35 Taxes Consolidation Act, 1997. Ireland has a significant and extensive array of double taxation agreements, which have operated significantly to its advantage in relation to its attractiveness as a location for FDI.

383. During the 1990s, Ireland operated a significantly advantageous tax regime for manufacturing and other companies as part of its successful mission of attracting significant multinational investment and location in Ireland, usually referred to as FDI policies. Companies engaged in manufacturing had their profits taxed at an effective rate of 10%. Although the corporate tax rate has been increased and the 'manufacturing rate' is in the process of being phased out, it remains in existence for some companies with regard to manufacturing activities that were carried on before 23 July 1998 (or grant approved on or before 31 July 1998) until it expires on 31 December 2010 – that is, for accounting periods ending on or before 31 December 2010 as provided for in Part 14 Taxes Consolidation Act, 1997. The current corporate tax rate is 12.5% which is applicable to all companies regardless of sectoral activity.

384. In recent years, Ireland has become the focus of some concern regarding its corporate structure from the United States, from the OECD and from the European Commission. In the case of the United States, the Obama administration sought to address the activities of US companies in utilising particular jurisdictions to reduce their US tax liability. Ireland was one of the jurisdictions which became the subject of a US Senate enquiry. The OECD had also expressed concerns regarding the activities of certain multinational corporations.[585] In addition, the EU Commission expressed concern about the nature of competitiveness in the EU and in particular, the operation of very low corporate tax rates in certain jurisdictions, again Ireland was one such jurisdiction. Following various initiatives and investigations, the Irish government made its strategy clear:

(i) Under EU law, member states have the right to set their own tax rates – a guarantee that was clarified during the Lisbon and Nice treaty debates in Ireland. Ireland clearly wishes to continue the low corporate tax rate of 12.5% – a matter which has full public support, but at the same time, the government had to make it clear it would not tolerate manipulation of these rules by multinational corporations seeking to gain particularly favourable and undesirable outcomes.

(ii) In 2014, the Minister for Finance, Michael Noonan announced a government crack down on corporate schemes which were effectively being designed to evade global tax liabilities. A particular scheme described as the 'double Irish' was a particular target. Although the Government was described in the Irish media as responding to international pressure, in particular, the opening of a

585. www.oecd.org. The OECD has launched its BEPS project in 2015. (Base Erosion and Profit Sharing Project). On 27 Jan. 2016, thirty-three countries formally agreed to support this project including Ireland.

European Commission investigation into two specific tax rulings granted to Apple, there was a clear strategy on the part of the Government to pre-empt any pressure to increase the Irish corporate tax rate by demonstrating a robust attitude to existing tax provisions.[586]

There are currently in effect three rates of corporation tax as follows:

- 12.5% rate on trading companies. The relatively low rate of tax for Irish resident trading companies is still an important element in Ireland's FDI policy. This tax rate has been increased to 15% as a result of global agreement under OECD initiatives as of October 2023. The Government of Ireland is therefore clearly intent on staying within globally agreed parameters;
- 25% rate for non-trading income and income from certain excepted trades. This rate applies to non-trading income including income chargeable under Case III (e.g., discounts, interest, foreign income), Case IV (patent royalties) and Case V (rental income from land and buildings in the State) of Schedule D of the Taxes Consolidation Act, 1997. Also included at this rate is income from activities that consist of working minerals, petroleum activities, and dealing in or developing land, other than construction operations;
- 20% rate for company capital gains and profits from dealing in residential development land. Companies' capital gains (other than gains from development land) are computed as capital gains tax to a corporation tax at the rate of 20%, which mirrors the general capital gains tax rate pursuant to section 21(3) and section 78 Taxes Consolidation Act 1997 (as amended by successive Finance Acts). Gains realised by companies from disposals of development land are chargeable to capital gains tax;
- Finally, the Irish Minister for Finance announced in October 2015 that a new corporate tax rate of 6.5% would be made available to corporations where the income was directly related to results of R &D conducted in Ireland. Known as the 'knowledge box' tax, it seems that this initiative will come under review from the EU.[587]

385. In 2018, the European Commission–DG Competition took action against the Irish government and Apple Inc. claiming that Ireland had given illegal state aid to Apple Inc. in the form of a 'sweetheart tax deal' which allowed the company as

---

586. As described in the Irish Times:

> The pre-emptive move arguably made sense in relation to the upcoming OECD rules on base erosion profit shifting (Beps) – Ireland would have had to bow to pressure on new standards sooner or later – but the controversy over Ireland's corporate tax regime opens up broader questions about the EU's jurisdiction over tax issues.

Suzanne Lynch Controversy over 'double Irish' Raises Issues of EU's Power over Tax Regimes (Irish Times 17 Oct. 2014).

587. Irish Times (17 Oct. 2014, Dublin).

a group to pay less than 1% tax on profits from European sales. The amount in question was EUR 13 billion. Ireland and Apple Inc. appealed this decision while arranging for the amount allegedly owed by Apple to be placed in escrow. In 2020, the General Court held in favour of both parties against the Commission. This matter is under appeal. It should be noted that the Commission was at pains to point out publicly that the issue was not the corporate tax rate of 12.5% per se but the actual unusual arrangements between the Irish government and Apple Inc.[588] The appeal was heard by the CJEU in May 2023 with judgement expected later in the year.

386. In the meantime, the Biden Administration has led a campaign against US corporations avoiding tax by use of different jurisdictions, different tax rates and favourable tax rules. At a recent G7 meeting, the intent of the US administration to campaign for a globally imposed tax rate at a minimum of 15% received considerable support. In addition, work on agreeing to a harmonisation of rules on the tax base has continued.[589] Ireland is fully compliant with all EU Directives in this area and has expressly conveyed its willingness to support OECD initiatives.

III. Dividends and Other Distributions

387. Dividends and other distributions made by Irish resident companies are liable to Dividend Withholding Tax except where these are made to qualifying non-resident persons or excluded persons under section 172D Taxes Consolidation Act, 1997. Dividends received by Irish resident companies from other Irish resident companies are not chargeable to Corporation Tax, because such dividends are already subject to tax within the dividend-paying company. In the group and multinational context, it is worth noting that section 43 of the Finance Act, 2008, made a change to the taxation of foreign dividends received by companies within the charge to Irish tax, where these dividends are received from companies that are resident for tax purposes in EU Member States or in countries with which Ireland has a tax treaty. Such dividends that are paid out of trading profits are now, on election, chargeable to tax here at the 12.5% rate of corporation tax (from the date of election) instead of at the 25% rate. Where dividends do not qualify to be charged at the 12.5% rate, they will continue to be charged at the 25% rate. Where a dividend is paid partly out of trading profits and partly out of other profits, the part of the dividend that is paid out of trading profits of the dividend-paying company will be taxable at the 12.5% rate. The change applies with respect to a dividend received on or after 31 January 2008.

588. *See* further Irene Lynch Fannon, 'Apple Tax: The Core Issues' in (eds) Gammage C. & Novitz T.: *Sustainable Trade and Finance* (Elgar, 2019).

589. https://www.nytimes.com/2021/05/20/business/economy/global-minimum-tax-corporations.html. Heralded as a global agreement to 'tax the world' the outcome from the G7 meetings is a surprisingly ambitious step from the Biden administration.
https://www.nytimes.com/2021/06/07/business/dealbook/g7-tax-yellen.html?searchResultPosition=4.

Chapter 2. The Private Company

§1. What Makes this Type of Corporation Different?

388. As described in Part I, Chapter 1, Irish company law applies to both public and private limited companies. There is no specific statute directed at the different circumstances of the smaller private company, which can often simply be a 'one-man' company or family-owned business. However, the Companies Act 2014 which consolidates and, in other cases, reforms Irish company law has placed the legislative emphasis very clearly on the private company limited by shares as the main type of company used by Irish business. As described above, the Act addresses private companies limited by shares in Parts 1–14. Further Parts then tailor these provisions to fit the appropriate type of company. Of most relevance here is a PLC.

Section 9 of the Act sets out the structure of the legislation stating the following:

> Subject to subsection (3) and(4) all of the law in this Act in relation to private companies limited by shares is to be found in Parts 1–14 (or instruments under them) and Schedules 1 to 6 … .

One of the much-publicised features and heralded reforms of the new Irish private company limited by shares is that it has full legal capacity. A second type of private company limited by shares may continue to specify business activities. Such companies are now called designated activity companies or DACs. DACS are really a variant of the private company limited by shares. Following Parts 1–14 dealing with the standard-form private company limited by shares, later Parts of the legislation deal with other types of companies. For example, Part, 16 and Part 17 then deal with what are now called DACS – private companies limited by shares with designated activities- and PLCs-public companies limited by shares. Accordingly, in relation to DACs section 964(1) of the Companies Act 2014 states:

> The provisions of Parts 1 to 14 apply to a DAC except to the extent that they are disapplied or modified by–
>
> (a) this section; or
> (b) any other provision of this Part.

Similarly, section 1002 of the Companies Act 2014 states that:

> The provisions of Parts 1–14 apply to a PLC except to the extent that they are disapplied or modified by–
>
> (a) this section, or
> (b) any other provision of this Part.

A Table is provided in this section for ease of reference.

There are two additional specific types of companies recognised by this new Companies Act 2014 which are perhaps worth mentioning for those practitioners with niche areas of practice. These are *External Companies* regulated in Part 21 of the 2014 Act and *Investment Companies* regulated in Part 24. In relation to the former, External Companies, the key distinction here is between a 'branch' of an external company and a 'place of business' of an external company. This distinction determines registration and filing obligations of the related enterprise, so that only a branch of a foreign-registered company must be registered in Ireland under section 1302 of the Act. Investment Companies regulated in Part 24 are PLCs established for the collective investment of funds in property. Nevertheless, for the sake of consistency, this monograph has adopted the structure adopted in monographs from other jurisdictions. Accordingly, Part 1 Chapter 1 deals with public limited companies and Part 1 Chapter 2 deals with private companies.

The previous chapter indicated, where relevant, when rules applied differently to private companies. This chapter focuses on these particular principles and notable exemptions.

§2. In What Respect Is There a Different Treatment of This Corporation?

I. Incorporation

389. As described in Part I, Chapter 1, it is now possible to incorporate a limited liability company in Ireland with just one member under the European Communities (Single-Member Private Limited Companies) Regulations 1994.[590] This is a company limited by shares. The requirements for incorporation and registration of this kind of company are set out in Part 2 of the Companies Act 2014. The number of members is set at a maximum of 149 under section 17(4). It is possible to have only one director in such a company under section 128(1) which states that 'A company shall have at least one director.' At least one director must be resident in the State, and the company must, under the requirements of the Companies (Act No. 2) 1999, carry on an activity in the State. A person must be over 18 to be appointed a director of a company.[591] Regardless of how many directors a company has, Irish law does not specifically distinguish between executive and non- executive directors. Each director will still be subject to a minimum standard of behaviour first adumbrated in Irish law in *Re Hunting Lodges Ltd.*[592] Although criticised at the time as over-stepping the very *de minimis* obligations normally expected of a nominal or non-executive director, these principles are now clearly part of Irish law as elucidated in the case law on director disqualification and restriction provisions. This latter series of cases is one of the most developed areas of modern Irish company law.[593]

---

590. *See supra*, paras 15 and 60.
591. Companies Act 2014, s. 131(1). This provision should be read in tandem with the new consent on appointment procedures which apply to directors.
592. *Re Hunting Lodges Ltd.* [1985] ILRM 75.
593. *See supra* part 1, Ch. 1 s. 4, III, 6.

II. Establishing the Members and Their Contribution

A. *Numbers of Members Required, Minimum Capital Requirements*

390. Private companies' articles must limit the number of members to 149 or less, not including existing employees or former employees who, while in the employment of the company were, and still are, members of the company.[594] In addition, as described *supra*, the minimum number of members of a private company is one. The Companies Act 2014 has changed the rules in this regard relating to public companies which are now also permitted to have just one member. This is in keeping with further flexibility available regarding the formation of public limited companies whereby the minimum issued share capital requirement has been reduced to EUR 25,000.[595] There is no minimum capital requirement for private companies limited by shares. Perhaps the only exception to these permissive rules for private limited companies is where a company must comply with additional capitalisation requirements as a result of taking onto its Board a restricted director pursuant to the provisions of Chapter 3 of Part 14 of the Companies Act 2014. The private company in this situation must have a minimum fully paid-up share capital of EUR 100,000. For PLCs in the same situation, the minimum capital is increased to EUR 500,000 and each share must be paid for in cash.[596]

B. *Consideration for Shares; Valuation; Fraudulent and Worthless Consideration*

391. In private companies, even though from a creditor's point of view, the issues may be even more crucial, the 'adverse interest' is not apparent in terms of the shareholders themselves. Under Irish company law, this lack of regulation regarding the valuation of private company shares represents a considerable lacuna in the protection of creditors from asset or value stripping in private companies. For example, in a management buy-out of a company when the management, or indeed another interested party, receives ownership of the company in return for services rendered to the company or in return for an asset conveyed, there is no legislative provision for an independent valuation of such service or other asset. Accordingly, there is little to protect the overall wealth of the company from the creditors' point of view. In many respects, therefore, this legislation, designed as it is primarily to protect creditors as all capital maintenance provisions are, does nothing to protect the value of private companies, a crucial part of the Irish economy.

III. Formal Incorporation Documents

A. *The Objects Clause and the* Ultra Vires *Doctrine*

392. As noted in Part I, Chapter 1, §2, *supra*, under Irish law the private company limited by shares has been divided into two categories, first the limited liability

594. Companies Act 2014, s. 17.
595. Companies Act 2014, s. 1010.
596. Companies Act 2014, s. 819(3).

company and second, the designated activity company. The former will have full legal capacity as described in section 38 of the 2014 Act which states:

> 38 (1) Subject to subsection (2), notwithstanding anything contained in this constitution a company shall have, whether acting inside or outside of the State –
> (a) full and unlimited capacity to carry on and undertake any business or activity, do any act or enter into any transaction; and
> (b) for the purposes of paragraph (a), full rights, powers and privileges.
> (2) Nothing in subsection (1) shall relieve a company from any duty or obligation under any enactment or the general law.

These companies will be described as limited liability companies (LTDs) and the company name will be followed by the suffix LTD. In the alternative, a private company limited by shares may may wish to continue with a clause specifying its activities. Such a company will be described as a DAC and the company name will be followed by the suffix DAC.

Section 38 does not apply to DACs nor to PLCs. The relevant provision in relation to DACs, section 972(1) of the Act provides that:

> A DAC shall have the capacity to do any act or thing stated in the objects set out in its memorandum.

A really important feature, however, is that the statement of the company's activities in its objects clause will form the basis of a rule of internal discipline only and will not have any effect whatsoever on contracts or actions affecting the company's external relationships. Section 973(1) of the Act provides that:

> The validity of an act done by a DAC shall not be called into question on the ground of lack of capacity by reason of anything contained in the DAC's objects.

The internal discipline rule is summarised as follows:

- A member of a DAC may bring proceedings to restrain the doing of an act which, but for subsection (1), would be beyond the DAC's capacity but no such proceedings shall lie in respect of any act to be done in fulfilment of a legal obligation arising from a previous act of the DAC.
- Notwithstanding the enactment of subsection (1), it remains the duty of the directors to observe any limitations on their powers flowing from the DAC's objects and actions by the directors which, but for subsection (1), would be beyond the DAC's capacity may only be ratified by the DAC by special resolution.
- A resolution ratifying such action shall not affect any liability incurred by the directors or any other person; if relief from any such liability is to be conferred by the DAC, it must be agreed to separately by a special resolution of it.
- A party to a transaction with a DAC is not bound to enquire as to whether it is permitted by the DAC's objects.

This section gives effect to the recommendation in the First Report of the CLRG that private companies limited by shares should be granted the legal capacity of a natural person with the consequent effect that the doctrine of *ultra vires* is disapplied. The note states that the section is modelled on subsection 16(1) of the New Zealand Companies Act, 1993. Stating that nearly 90% of Irish-registered companies were private companies limited by shares and the majority of these were closely held companies, the review group arrived at a belief that such companies should not be required to set out any objects or powers and such companies should be empowered with the capacity of a natural person. The position relating to PLCs is described in Part 1, Chapter 1.

B. Authority

393. An issue which has always been related to the issue of *ultra vires* in the past is the question of the authority of a company's agents. So regardless of whether the company has full legal capacity or not, it is still possible that a third party may be caught by entering into a transaction with an agent of the company who does not have the authority to enter into such a transaction. Conversely, the company may suffer from being bound by the unauthorised actions of a particular person, holding him or herself out as an agent. The question is not one of legal capacity but one of authority of an agent and whether the authority of that agent is actual, ostensible, or held out authority and whether there is reliance on such authority. The decision in *Ulster Factors Ltd v. Entonglen Ltd.*[597] exemplifies these problems very well. Leaving aside the question of capacity, the issue of authority of agents is also dealt with in the Companies Act 2014. Section 40 of the 2014 Companies Act provides that a) the 'board of directors of the company; and b) any registered persons' shall be deemed to have authority to exercise any power of the company and to authorise others to do so. Any person who is authorised by the Board to bind the company must be registered. (This provision is similar to that which has pertained under the European Companies Regulation 1973 and complies with EU Regulations).

However, where a person is given limited authority by the Board to bind the company, for example, to borrow on behalf of the company up to a particular limit, say EUR 100,000, that person is not registered or registrable.[598] These provisions seem to go only half way in addressing the sorts of difficulties which arise. The non-registration of the person with limited authority only indicates that this person has less than full authority, but the third party may still be exposed to misrepresentation of his or her actual authority by such a person and the company may still be exposed to liability on foot of such misrepresentation where there is reliance. Section 39(6) and section 40(9) to section 40(11) address this problem. Section 39(6) states that

597. [1997] IEHC 34.

598. Companies Act 2014, s. 39(1) 'Where the board of directors of a company authorises any person as being a person entitled to bind the company (not being an entitlement to bind that is, expressly or impliedly, restricted to a particular transaction or class of transactions), the company may notify the Registrar in the prescribed form of the authorisation and the Registrar shall register the authorisation.'

'the provisions of a company's constitution with regard to a person's office or powers shall not, in themselves, be taken as an authorization by the board of the directors of the company of the person as a person entitled to bind the company'.

Section 40(9) provides that where a question of ostensible authority arises, no 'reference shall be made to the company's constitution'.

Section 40(11) states that the section is 'in addition to, and not in substitution for, the Rule in Royal British Bank v Turquand' otherwise known as the 'indoor management rule'. In the past, a third party might have relied on the Articles of Association to create the appropriate authority for an agent, but this possibility is excluded from now on. In cases where an agent has some authority in relation to a particular transaction but not full authority to bind the company, it would seem that a third party will be on notice that a particular agent does not have full authority due to the lack of registration of that person. However, the precise limitations on a person's authority will not be apparent. How the limitations of that authority are to be established is left unanswered except that the Rule in Turquand's case will still apply. The nature of the enquiries a third party might have to make is not clear. In other words, the act does little or nothing to resolve the kinds of problems which have occurred in the extensively discussed case law on this issue.

C. *Articles of Association*

394. Apart from the issue of capacity and the abolition of the *ultra vires* doctrine for private companies limited by shares, a second much-heralded reform is that private companies limited by shares will no longer have a Memorandum of Association nor a set of Articles of Association. Instead, this company will have a 'constitution'.[599] This constitution shall state the company's name, that it is a private company limited by shares, that the liability of the member is limited and a statement as to capital. Section 19(2)(a) states that the constitution shall 'be in a form in accordance with the form set out in Schedule 1 or as near to it as circumstances permit.' Instead of having a document which was usually referred to as the Articles of Association which set out the governing rules for each company, the Companies Act 2014 has 'created a series of statutory defaults so that companies will no longer be required to make provision for standard administrative matters'.[600]

Therefore, unless the constitution of a particular company opts out of particular statutory provisions, the rules governing the internal governance of a private company limited by shares will be found throughout the Companies Act 2014. Parts 3 and 4 of the Act will be particularly relevant in this regard. So, for example, provisions relating to basic governance matters such as the authority of the Board which were provided for in Article 80 of the standard-form Articles of Association in Table A are now included as provisions of the Companies Act, in this case section 158. The authority of the Managing Director which used to be provided for in standard-form Articles of Association is now described in section 159. In contrast,

599. Companies Act 2014, s. 19.

600. *See* Courtney, *Companies Act 2014: The Anatomy of the Act*, in *Bloomsbury Professional's Guide to the Companies Act 2014* (Courtney ed., Bloomsbury Professional 2015).

section 967(1) of the Companies Act 2014 states that 'the constitution of a DAC shall be in the form of a Memorandum of Association and Articles of Association which together are referred to in this Part as a "constitution"'. Section 967(2) goes on to state that the Memorandum of Association shall state the name, that the company is a DAC, its objects, that the liability of its members is limited and a capital clause. Schedules 7 and 8 of the Act set out the form of this constitution for a DAC limited by shares or a DAC limited by guarantee respectively. The same situation applies, however, in relation to the relationship between default provisions of the Companies Act 2014 and what would have hitherto been described as Articles of Association. Section 968 describes 'mandatory' and 'optional' provisions of Parts 1–14 of the Companies Act and goes on to state that the Articles of a DAC may contain regulations in relation to the DAC but so far as these regulations do not exclude or modify any optional provisions of the Companies Act 2014 these will apply. Finally, section 968(5) provides that articles of a DAC 'instead of containing any regulations in relation to the DAC, may consist solely of a statement to the effect that the provisions of the Companies Act 2014 are adopted'.

IV. Legal Personality and Constitutional Structures

395. In relation to lifting the corporate veil, all of the issues relating to larger companies apply also in principle to smaller private companies. However, on the facts of various cases, when a company is smaller, it may be easier to establish an agency relationship[601] or to draw close connections between the company and the individual controlling the mind and will of the company in the context of attributing criminal intent[602] or some other human attribute, such as residence. Nevertheless, it is important to bear in mind that the necessary facts must be proven and that there is no *per se* agency relationship between any company and its owner; nor should a company be considered to be the same legal entity as its owner simply because it is a smaller entity with few or no countervailing shareholders or directors. This is particularly relevant in relation to smaller private companies limited by shares which are formed as subsidiaries of holding companies.[603]

V. Promoters

396. Discussion of the law relating to the fiduciary obligations of promoters to their companies is applicable to private limited companies. However, one of the difficulties regarding private companies in relation to this area of law, a difficulty that arises equally in relation to the enforcement of directors' duties, is that the duties are owed to the company, and therefore the company is the proper plaintiff regarding enforcement of these obligations. As a small private company is usually controlled by its founders (promoters) or controllers (directors), the expectation that the

601. *Lee v. Lee's Air Farming Ltd* [1961] AC 12.
602. *D.P.P. v. Kent & Sussex Contractors Ltd* [1944] 1 KB 146.
603. *Fyffes plc v. DCC and Ors.* [2005] IEHC and [2009] IESC.

company will act as a plaintiff is, in most cases, unrealistic. A third-party intervention usually occurs before such cases are litigated; this third-party intervention is often a liquidation, receivership, examinership or restructuring. In the case of *Hopkins v. Shannon Transport Systems Ltd,*[604] the litigation arose due to the refusal of a government department to pay grant aid that had originally been made available to the company and the consequent action on the part of the plaintiff to secure such payment. The court held that the plaintiff had been in breach of fiduciary duties, which he owed as a promoter to the company, and that the transaction was voidable at the instance of the company. However, the second type of activity that typically gives rise to a consideration of the position of a company promoter – namely the raising of capital through the issuing of a prospectus – does not normally apply in the private company context as usually such shares are listed or issued on a public market.

VI. Share Capital

397. Under Irish law, the private company limited by shares may adopt a complex or straightforward structure as is considered appropriate. Thus, it is common to find in private companies that there may be two classes of shares, ordinary shares and preference shares, that are commonly made available to original subscribers, promoters, venture capitalist investors and so forth. The use of preferential shares is also common in a venture capital context. Private companies may issue redeemable shares unless prohibited from doing so in its constitution.[605]

VII. Capital Movement

398. A discussion of pre-emption rights in the context of private companies is considered *infra* in the section on Share Transfer.

VIII. Capital Maintenance

A. Introduction

399. All of the capital maintenance provisions discussed in Part I, Chapter 1, apply in principle to private companies. However, to a great extent, capital maintenance rules take on an air of unreality as they apply to smaller private limited companies due to the fact that there is no minimum capital requirement under Irish company law and many private limited companies have little issued capital. In fact,

604. *Hopkins v. Shannon Transport Systems Ltd* (High Court, unreported, 10 Jan. 1972).
605. Companies Act 2014, s. 66(4). *See* further Companies Act 2014, s. 102(1)(d) and Companies Act 2014, ss 105–116.

many are undercapitalised. One of the consequences of this fact is that some of the rules work in unusual ways. The financial assistance prohibition in section 82 of the Companies Act 2014 is a case in point.

B. Financial Assistance Transactions

400. The provision by a company of financial assistance in the acquisition of its own shares is generally prohibited under section 82(2) of the Companies Act 2014. Such financial assistance includes loans; guarantees from the company to potential purchasers; security from its assets to secure loans entered into between a bank and the purchaser, for example; and any other securitised transactions. These provisions will catch any transaction that displays these characteristics. For a PLC, some limited exceptions address specific situations, covering such matters as payment of dividends, discharge of lawfully incurred debts, and lending by financial institutions in the ordinary course of business, but, generally, these transactions are prohibited. Accordingly, various kinds of transactions that might serve to facilitate restructuring in a private company may involve the acquisition of a controlling interest by a director or investor whether an existing shareholder or otherwise. When the acquisition of a controlling interest is financed in part or directly or indirectly through use of the company's assets, such transactions are in breach of section 82 of the Companies Act 2014, as described previously. Thus, for example, a simple guarantee secured by reference to the company's assets supporting personal borrowing on the part of such an investor will be a breach of section 82. However, section 82(5) permits financial assistance if this is only 'an incidental part of some larger purpose of the company.'[606]

It is possible, however, to provide financial assistance for the acquisition of shares if the SAP outlined in section 82(6)(a) as described in sections 202 and 203 is followed. However, the SAP is only available to PLCs in limited circumstances and this provision is excluded by virtue of section 1002(3). Effectively there remains a blanket prohibition on such transactions for PLCs. What was considered an exemption provided for private companies is now a default provision which is not extended to PLCs. The SAP in this context[607] requires the following consent process:

(i) The passing of a special or unanimous resolution as outlined in section 202(1)(a)(i) having been passed not more than twelve months prior to the activity.

(ii) Where the resolution is not unanimous, the resolution must normally stand for a waiting period of thirty days before the transaction. However,

---

606. *See* further Companies Act 2014, s. 211(2). *See* further W. Johnston, *Taking Security, the Summary Approval Procedure*, in *Bloomsbury Professional's Guide to the Companies Act 2014* 145–153 (Courtney (gen. ed.) Bloomsbury 2015). This 'larger purpose' exemption has been part of English law since 1985. *See also Wallersteiner v. Moir* [1974] 3 All E. R. 217.

607. Companies Act 2014, s. 203.

if more than 90% of the nominal value of each class of issued shares votes in favour of the resolution, this waiting period does not apply.[608]

(iii) A declaration made by the directors in accordance with the terms of section 203 of the Companies Act 2014.

401. The consequences for breaching the terms of the private company exemption are severe. The transaction will be voidable at the instance of the company against a party with notice of the nature of the transaction or with notice of non-compliance. The meaning of notice is important. In *Bank of Ireland Ltd v. Rockfield Ltd*,[609] McWilliam J. in the High Court, citing Lindley L.J. in *Manchester Trust v. Furness*,[610] held that notice of the transaction or notice of non-compliance must be actual for the transaction to be held to be void against the third party. However, in applying this doctrine to the facts, the Court held that there must be a limit within this principle where the court would not condone what was described as 'wilful blindness'. On appeal to the Supreme Court, the Court reiterated the basic principle but applied it to the facts in hand in a stricter, more literal way, finding that as the plaintiff notice did not have actual notice, it was entitled to enforce the transaction. The Court observed that there was no room for any form of constructive notice in commercial transactions. Further consideration of similar notice issues was considered in later cases such as *Eddison v. Allied Irish Bank PLC*[611] and *Lombard and Ulster Bank v. Brookhouse School*.[612] In both cases, the essential principles were reiterated, emphasising that a transaction in breach of the section would be void against parties with *actual* notice of the breach.[613] When non-compliance with the terms of the private company exemption was found, the transaction would be similarly void. However, for the transaction to be void, the enforcing party would have to be fixed with *actual* notice of the non-compliance.

In more recent case law such as the decision in *CH (Ireland) Inc. v. Credit Suisse Canada*,[614] the courts have taken a slightly different approach to parties who failed to appreciate the significance of various pieces of information available in the course of the transaction. As observed by McCracken J. in that case, because a clear statement of fact directly informed CSC of the nature of transaction, the Court cannot protect parties who may not have appreciated the relevance of the statement that

---

608. Companies Act 2014, s. 211(2). *See* further W. Johnston, *Taking Security, the Summary Approval Procedure*, in *Bloomsbury Professional's Guide to the Companies Act 2014* 145–153 (Courtney (gen. ed.) Bloomsbury 2015).

609. *Bank of Ireland Ltd v. Rockfield Ltd* [1979] IR 21.

610. *Manchester Trust v. Furness* [1895] 2 Q B 539.

611. *Eddison v. Allied Irish Bank PLC* (unreported, High Court, Costello J., 24 Jul. 1985).

612. *Lombard and Ulster Bank v. Brookhouse School* (unreported, High Court, Costello J., 2 Jun. 1987); cf. Irene Lynch Fannon, *Financial Assistance in the Purchase of Its Own Shares by a Company – s. 60 of the 1963 Companies Act*, 1 Dublin U. L. J. 14 (1988).

613. *Eccles Hall Ltd. v. Bank of Nova Scotia, Paramount Enterprises Ltd and O'Keeffe* (3 Feb. 1995, unreported) HC.

614. *CH (Ireland) Inc. v. Credit Suisse Canada* [1999] 4 IR 542. A further point worth considering in this context is that in the original decision of *Bank of Ireland Finance v. Rockfield, supra* n. 607, s. 539 the decision of McWilliam J might be more defensible considering this was not entirely a commercial transaction, but concerned the conveyance of a mortgage on property.

amounted to a breach of company law. Finally, where a company gives financial assistance in breach of section 82, there is a provision for criminal liability whereby 'every officer of the company who is in default' shall be liable to conviction of an offence. In *Re Cognotec Ltd.*,[615] a loan of EUR 10 million was made to Cognotec Holdings from the Bank of Ireland with this loan being secured by guarantees from Cognotec Ltd. (the company at the centre of the litigation in this case) and Cognotec (Ireland) Ltd. The EUR 10 million was then passed to Cognotec (Ireland) Ltd. to buy shares held by AM Software in Cognotec Ltd. All parties to the transaction recognised that the guarantee from Cognotec Ltd. amounted to financial assistance within the meaning of the provision and so it was agreed that the private company exception would be availed of. However, unknown to the Bank of Ireland, the required statutory declaration from directors under the then-existing framework was not completed. (A similar declaration continues to be required under what is now called the SAP). As a result, the transaction and the loan were potentially void. Furthermore, at a subsequent meeting of the directors which was allegedly held in Jerusalem on 19 March 2010, a decision was made to renege or alter this transaction. However, there was some doubt as to whether this meeting ever took place. In any event, the Bank sought to appoint a receiver on foot of the loan (debenture) document in light of the continued financial difficulties of the company. It was at this point that the company sought a declaration that the entire loan was in breach of the financial assistance provisions and was therefore void, meaning that the purported appointment of the receiver was also void. The key question was whether the Bank of Ireland had notice of the non-compliance with the provision. Effectively did the Bank of Ireland have notice that the directors of the company had not completed the declaration required under the provision? The court held that the requisite notice was actual notice and that the Bank did not have notice of the non-compliance. Consequently, the company could not seek a declaration that the transaction was void as against the Bank.

IX. Shares and Share Transfer

402. The free transferability of shares is an important feature of a PLC. In private limited companies, some restrictions can be placed on the transfer of shares, and these are commonly found in the Articles of Association. Under the reform of the Companies Act 2014, these provisions will no longer be found in the Articles of Association as such. As explained, the constitution of the company will contain mandatory and optional provisions derived from the Act itself.

The following rules apply:

- Unless the constitution of a private company provides otherwise (whether this is an ordinary private company, a LTD or a DAC) the directors will have discretion to refuse to register share transfers.[616]

615. [2010] IEHC 309.
616. Companies Act 2014, s. 95(1).

- In addition, the creation of pre-emption rights that oblige shareholders to offer their shares to existing shareholders was commonly found in the Articles and Memoranda of Association.
- Pre-emption rights on the allotment of shares in private companies are now contained in section 69(6) of the Companies Act 2014. Section 69(8) recognises that the constitution of a company can make alternative provisions.[617]

A. *Directors' Refusal to Accept Registration*

403. Traditionally in private companies, the directors were entitled under the Articles of Association to refuse to register the transfer of shares. This discretion is now provided for in section 95(1) of the Companies Act 2014. This provision states that 'save where the constitution of the company provides otherwise – (a) the directors of a company may, in their absolute discretion, and without assigning any reason for doing so, decline to register any transfer of any share'.

Over time, the courts have had occasion to scrutinise the exercise of this power by directors. The exercise of the director's power in this regard is subject to the normal principles applying to the exercise of any power by directors, namely that the power must be exercised in good faith, for its proper purpose and for the benefit of the company.[618] The statutory provision above which reflects standard-form clauses in older Articles of Association clearly states that the directors are not obliged to give reasons for their decision, and the general wisdom is that they are best advised not to do so. It may be open to some doubt as to whether the right not to give reasons for a decision would find favour under Irish law generally. An important underlying principle in this area is the countervailing principle that a shareholder has a right to transfer his or her shares and the exercise of the director's power to refuse to register a transfer must be considered against the backdrop of preserving that right. See a discussion of these principles in *Re Copal Varnish Ltd*,[619] *Re Swaledale Cleaners Ltd*[620] and *Re Zinotty Properties Ltd*.[621]

B. *Pre-emption Rights*

404. Pre-emption rights were commonly found in the Articles of Association of private companies, ensuring the closed nature of the company. Thus, the standard-form articles contained in the Companies Act 1963 provided the following: 'The company is a private company and accordingly – (a) the right to transfer

617. However, the subsequent statement in s. 69(11) as to the relationship between these subsections is not entirely clear. The pre-existing provision was contained in s. 23(10) of the 1983 Act.
618. *See*, for example, the judgment of Green M.R. in *Re Smith and Fawcett* [1942] Ch. 304, and *see* further *supra* paras 163–167 for a general discussion of these principles.
619. *Re Copal Varnish Ltd* [1917] 2 Ch. 349.
620. *Re Swaledale Cleaners Ltd* [1968] 3 All E. R. 619.
621. *Re Zinotty Properties Ltd* [1984] BCLC 375.

shares is restricted in the manner hereinafter prescribed.'[622] Pre-emption rights are now contained in section 69(6) of the Companies Act 2014 with similar language.

X. Shareholders, Management and Control

A. Shareholder Meetings

405. The law relating to shareholders' meetings is now completely codified in Irish law and is contained in Chapter 6 of Part 4 of the Companies Act 2014. The case law interpreting these rules which would have hitherto been contained in both legislation and provisions of the Articles of Association is still relevant. The normal rules described in Part I, Chapter 1, §4 regarding the conduct of meetings in principle apply equally to private companies. However, when there are significantly smaller numbers of shareholders, procedures will of necessity be less formal. It is thus possible for private companies to conduct their business through informal consent procedures. The following principles now apply under the reforms in the Companies Act 2014:

i) Repeating the exemptions provided for under the European Communities Regulations of 1994 it continues to be possible for 'single-member' companies to dispense with holding an AGM.[623] This also applies to DACS[624] and to other types of private companies such as companies limited by guarantees (CLGs).[625]
ii) Common law decisions in England recognized the possibility of a resolution being validly passed if unanimously agreed to by all the shareholders in a situation where the resolution was circulated to each without a meeting being actually held. This possibility was also approved of under Irish law in the case of *Buchanan v. McVey*.[626] As with English company law, this principle has now been codified.[627]
iii) Section 193 of the Companies Act 2014 provides more detail on this provision, for example that the resolution can consist of several signed documents.[628] The provisions also specify when the resolution is deemed to be passed, namely when the last member signs.[629]

622. Companies Act 1963, First Schedule, Table A, Part II, Art. 2.
623. Companies Act 2014, s. 175(3) and (4).
624. Companies Act 2014, s. 988.
625. Companies Act 2014, s. 1202.
626. *Buchanan v. McVey* [1954] IR 89.
627. Companies Act 2014, s. 193.
628. Companies Act, 2014, s. 193(3).
629. Companies Act 2014, s. 194(4)

Chapter 1. Partnership under the Partnership Act of 1890

§1. PERSONALITY

424. Unlike a limited company, traditional partnerships have no separate legal personality. Whereas separate corporate personality for limited companies developed in the mid-to the late nineteenth-century, for a considerable time before that 'English law … always refused to see anything in a partnership, however large, beyond a mere aggregation of individuals.'

§2. LIABILITY

425. Unlike limited company shareholders, partners do not enjoy financially limited liability. These are the most important consequences of distinguishing between whether a business has been incorporated as a company or is more properly regarded (by accident or design) as a partnership. The partnership is liable for acts of all partners done as part of the ordinary course of the firm's business. Under section 9 of the 1890 Act, every partner in a firm is liable jointly with the other partners for all contractual debts and obligations of the firm incurred while he or she is a partner. The members of a firm are (jointly and severally) liable for any wrongful act or omission of any partner acting in the ordinary course of the business of the firm, or with the authority of his or her co-partners causing loss or injury to a third party.

426. Liability extends to acts done by a partner *qua* partner 'in the ordinary course of the business of the firm'. Liability does not begin until the partnership (i.e., principals for which a partner may be said to be agent) has come into existence, but extends (under section 38) until after dissolution of the firm. The phrase 'in the course of the ordinary business of the firm', or similar term occurs in section 5 and the other specific instances of liability contained in the 1890 Act (for example in sections 5, 6, 10, 11, 13 and 15).

427. A partnership agreement frequently outlines the nature of the firm's business. This will be evidence of what is the firm's ordinary course of business, but such an agreement will not usually be exhaustive or treated in law as conclusive as to what constitutes the ordinary course of a firm's business, unless expressly stated as such. Partners – in trading and non-trading partnerships – have been held to have ostensible or implied authority to do the following things on the firm's behalf: conduct legal proceedings; open a bank account; sign cheques; enter contracts within the ordinary sphere of the firm's business; sell goods belonging to the firm or purchase; appoint, employ or remove employees or agents; receive payment of firm debts; and release firm debts.[656] The common law distinguishes between partners in trading firms from those in non-trading firms and holds that certain acts (such as

656. *See* further Michael Twomey & Maedbh Clancy: *Partnership Law* (Bloomsbury, 2019) 220–221.

borrowing) are within the implied authority of partners in trading firms, but not partners in non-trading firms.[657] Similar reasoning is applied in considering questions of liability arising in the ordinary course of business.

428. Under section 5 of the 1890 Act, where a partner acts in the ordinary course of the firm's business, but without authority, the firm is bound, unless the third party alleging a wrong either (a) knows the partner has no authority or (b) was not under the impression that he was dealing with a partner at all. Likewise, section 8 provides that, where partners agree on restrictions on the authority of one or more partners, no act done in contravention of such agreement binds the firm with respect to persons having notice of the agreement.

429. Although partners cannot escape liability solely on the basis that a wrong was primarily caused by a fellow partner, the case law suggests that partners do not have to contribute to losses where fellow partners' conduct amounts to recklessness, wilful misconduct or fraud, unless, of course, the former have authorised or ratified the conduct in question.[658]

430. As with company directors, acts of a partner done without authority may be retrospectively ratified by the principal on whose behalf the partner acted – that is, the firm. A firm may not retrospectively ratify an act by a partner before the firm came into existence, but, once in existence, the firm may prospectively adopt the transaction. Partners ratifying or adopting a transaction must have knowledge of the act.[659]

§3. Contribution and Distribution of Profit

431. The 1890 Act, section 2(3), makes the sharing of profits prima facie evidence of partnership and provides further, in section 35(e), that a partner may apply to the Court for dissolution of the partnership where the underlying business 'can only be carried on at a loss'. Therefore, it would seem that business ventures designed with the intention of creating losses cannot come within the definition of a partnership. However, on similar facts in the case of *MacCarthaigh (Inspector of Taxes) v. D.*,[660] *O'Hanlon J.*, though expressing 'some reservations ... [as to whether] the arrangement entered into ... should properly be regarded as a partnership at all', held that, since the case had come before him by way of a case stated by the Revenue Appeal Commissioner, he was bound by the Commissioner's finding that there had been a partnership, as this was 'a primary fact' that bound an appellate court.

657. *Ibid.*, pp. 221–224.
658. *Ibid.*, p. 324.
659. *Marsh v. Joseph* [1897] 1 Chs 213, 246.
660. *MacCarthaigh (Inspector of Taxes) v. D.* [1985] IR 73.

432. In terms of finances, the following default rules apply, subject to contrary (express or implied) agreement between the partners:

- All partners are entitled to share equally (rather than in proportion to capital contributed) in the capital and profits of the business, and must also contribute equally toward losses, whether capital or otherwise, sustained by the firm.[661]
- Where partners agree to share profits unequally and make no specific provision, losses are shared in the same proportion.
- The rates of interest on a partner's capital contribution and on loans by a partner to the firm are, respectively, 0% and 5%.[662]
- No partner is entitled to remuneration for acting in the partnership business.[663]

It is important 'not to confuse such a partner who receives a preferential appropriation of profit with a "salaried partner". The latter is simply an employee of the firm who is held out to the world as a partner. He is not "carrying on the business in common" with the partners but is employed by them'.[664]

In practice, partnership agreements typically provide that a partner may draw down money from the firm in anticipation of year-end profits, that at the end of the year, that partner is entitled to (or if the amount is negative must repay) the entire profit to which he would have been entitled, *less* drawings.

§4. Management[665]

433. The relations of partners to one another are governed in the first instance by the partnership agreement. The 1890 Act provides a default template that applies 'only to the extent that its provisions have not been excluded or modified'.[666] Each partner is an agent of his fellow partners, and a principal for each of his fellow partners. Accordingly, it is unsurprising to find that the statute provides that the firm must indemnify each partner in respect of payments made and personal liabilities incurred by him in the ordinary course of the business of the firm, or in 'anything necessarily done for the preservation of the business or property of the firm'.[667]

I. Fiduciary Duties

434. Partners must act with utmost good faith in their dealings with one another. A partnership agreement is a contract *uberrimae fidei*, irrespective of its terms.[668]

661. 1890 Act, s. 24(1). The reference in s. 24(1) to partners 'shar[ing] equally in the capital' of the business must be read to mean capital profit, due to s. 44(b)(3).
662. 1890 Act, s. 24(4) and 24(3).
663. 1890 Act, s. 24(6).
664. Law Society of Ireland, Business Law, 23.
665. *See* Law Society of Ireland, Business Law 18–25 (2006).
666. Michael Twomey & Maedbh Clancy: *Partnership Law* (Bloomsbury, 2019)
667. 1890 Act, s. 24(2).
668. *Const v. Harris* (1824) Turn & R 496, per Lord Eldon ('In all partnerships, whether it is expressed in the deed or not, the partners are bound to be true and faithful to each other.').

The court will construe partnership agreements in light of this overarching duty.[669] This overarching duty of good faith founds the following aspects of fiduciary duty codified in sections 28–30 of the 1890 Act:

- Partners are bound to render true accounts and full information of all things affecting the partnership to any partner or his legal representatives.
- Every partner must account to the firm for any benefit derived by him without the consent of the other partners from any transaction concerning the partnership, or from any use by him of the partnership property, name or business connection, including transactions occurring after the dissolution of the firm by a partner's death or bankruptcy, up until the affairs of the firm have been completely wound up.[670] This duty extends to a liability to account to the firm for secret profits made in a personal capacity, in circumstances where no demonstrable harm has been done to the firm.[671]
- If a partner, without the consent of the other partners, carries on any business of the same nature as, and competing with that of the firm, he must account for and pay over to the firm all profits made by him in that business.

435. At common law, a *former* partner is free to compete with the partnership, provided he does not use the partnership's property, name or business connection. Therefore, partnership agreements often include no-competition clauses under which partners agree, in the event that they leave the firm, not to compete with it in a specified area and for a specified time. However, such clauses must not breach competition law.[672] Two years appears to be the outer temporal limit of such clauses, which is consistent with the dictates of competition law.[673]

II. Duty of Care

436. Partners owe each other a duty of care in the conduct of the firm's affairs. The baseline standard of care imposed on a partner is uncertain. The matter is not addressed in the 1890 Act. As a joint report of the English and Scottish Law Commissions has noted, nineteenth-century cases adopted a variety of expressions, such

---

669. *Green v. Howell* [1910] 1 Ch. D. 495 (C.A.) (power to expel a partner for breach of specified articles may not be exercised other than in good faith, such as where a partner is expelled in order to allow the purchase of his interest on unfavourable terms) and *Law v. Law* [1905] 1 Ch. D. 140 (C.A.) (where one partner negotiates with another to purchase the latter's share in the business, and the prospective purchaser knowingly enters the negotiations with greater knowledge regarding the partnership accounts, the prospective vendor must be put in possession of all material facts relating to partnership assets of which the prospective purchaser is aware).

670. *See*, for example, *Don King Productions Inc. v. Warren* [1999] 2 All ER 218 and *Taylor v. Masons* [2001] EWCA Civ 2106.

671. *Bentley v. Craven* (1853) 18 Beav 75 (partner bought sugar at discount and resold to company at market price; ordered to account to firm for profits so earned, despite the fact that the firm would have had to pay market price in any event) and *Boston Deep Sea Fishing & Ice Co v. Ansell* (1888) 39 Ch. D 339.

672. *See* Competition Acts 2002–2014.

673. *See* Law Society of Ireland, Business Law, 21–22.

as 'culpable negligence' and 'want of reasonable care', without closely analysing the nature and extent of the duty.[674] In a more recent case, Woolf J. has spoken of a duty to act 'without culpable negligence' and 'not … below the standards of a reasonable businessman in the situation in which he found himself'.[675] The Law Commission's report also found that there are 'few reported cases of partners attempting to sue each other in negligence'.[676] Recent Scottish authority has held that the standard of care must be objective rather than subjective.[677] In a later case, the New South Wales Supreme Court has held that the ordinary negligence standard does not apply between partners, holding that wilful misconduct or gross or culpable negligence before the partner at fault is liable,[678] but such a view has recently been rejected by the Chancery Division of the High Court of England and Wales, in favour of a duty to exercise reasonable care requiring compliance to an objective standard, albeit that a partner should not be liable for a failure due to want of a larger share of prudence or skill than he possesses.[679]

III. Obligation to Take Part in the Management of the Firm

437. Subject to contrary (express or implied) agreement, every partner 'may take part in the management of the partnership business'.[680] Contrary agreement may permissibly locate powers of management of the firm in a subset of partners. A further default rule provides that 'difference[s] arising as to ordinary matters connected with the partnership business may be decided by a majority of the partners, but no change may be made in the nature of the partnership business without the consent of all existing partners'.[681] Unanimity is therefore required for any change in the partnership business; it is also required for the introduction of a new partner[682] and for an agreement permitting expulsion of a partner to be decided by a majority, rather than (as is otherwise the default position) unanimously.[683]

IV. Other Instances of Agency

438. As well as general acts of a partner done in the ordinary course of the firm's business or with the express, implied or ostensible authority of the firm, a firm is

674. The Law Commission and the Scottish Law Commission, Partnership Law (2003) (Law Com No. 283) (Scot Law Com No. 192), Ch. 11.7, 183 (Citing *Bury v. Allen* (1845) 1 Coll 589, 604; 63 ER 556, 562; and *Thomas v. Atherton* (1878) 10 Ch. D 185, 199 and 202).
675. *Winsor v. Schroeder* (1979) 129 NLJ 1266.
676. The Law Commission and the Scottish Law Commission, The Law Commission and the Scottish Law Commission (*supra*, n. 1), 183.
677. *Ross Harper & Murphy v. Banks* [2000] SLT 699.
678. *Lane v. Bushby* [2000] NSWSC 1029.
679. *Tann v. Herrington* [2009] EWHC (Ch) (unreported, Bernard Livesey QC sitting as a Judge in the Chancery Division, High Court of England and Wales, 10 Mar. 2009).
680. 1890 Act, s. 24(5).
681. 1890 Act, s. 24(8).
682. 1890 Act, s. 24(7).
683. 1890 Act, s. 25.

also liable where a partner: executes acts or instruments (section 6 of the 1890 Act), misapplies property (section 11) or commits a breach of trust (section 13). Section 13 is an interesting provision, in that it provides an exception to the general rule of vicarious liability, inasmuch as it exempts partners from liability where a co-partner, who happens to be a trustee, employs trust property 'in the business or on the account of the partnership' in breach of trust. The section provides that a partner will not be able to rely on this exemption if he or she has notice of the breach of trust. Section 16 provides that a firm is deemed to be on notice of a fact relating to 'partnership affairs' where one partner is deemed to be on notice of that fact. (This raises a question as to whether notice would be imputed automatically for the purposes of section 13 in the case of a breach of trust, but interpreting sections 13 and 16 together in that way would risk emptying section 13 of meaning, and normal principles of statutory interpretation would suggest that such an interpretation should be avoided.)

439. Another important provision is section 15 of the 1890 Act, which provides that an admission or representation made by any partner in the ordinary course of business concerning partnership affairs is evidence against the firm.

440. Finally, there is the issue of post-dissolution liability. Section 38 provides that 'the authority of each partner to bind the firm, and the other rights and obligations of the partners, continue notwithstanding the dissolution so far as may be necessary to wind up the affairs of the partnership, and to complete transactions begun but unfinished at the time of the dissolution, but not otherwise'.

§5. Transferability and Dissolution[684]

I. Occurrence of Dissolution

441. A partnership is automatically dissolved, without the intervention of the Court, in the following circumstances (cf. sections 32–34 of the 1890 Act):

(a) If entered into for a fixed term, by the expiration of that term.
(b) If entered into for a single adventure or undertaking, by the termination of that adventure or undertaking.
(c) If entered into for an undefined time, by a partner giving notice to the others of his intention to dissolve the partnership. The partnership is dissolved from the date mentioned in such notice, or, if no date is specified, on receipt of notice, unless the articles provide for some other date.[685] (d) By the death of a partner, unless (as is often the case) the articles provide otherwise.
(d) By the bankruptcy of a partner, unless the articles provide otherwise.
(e) At the option of the other partners, if one partner suffers his share in the partnership property to be charged by the Court in respect of his separate debt.

684. *See* Law Society of Ireland, Business Law, 35–44.
685. *See also* 1890 Act, s. 26.

(f) By the happening of an event making it unlawful for the business of the firm to be carried on, or for the members of the firm to carry it on in partnership;[686] or where the partnership is formed to carry on intrinsically illegal activity, such as crime.

On the occurrence of any of these events, the partnership automatically dissolves. In circumstances such as the death or bankruptcy of a partner, though the partnership dissolves in theory, the remaining may in practice choose to carry on as before. This is known as a *technical* dissolution: the partnership is not in any real sense ended, but simply reforms and continues as before.[687] On the other hand, the parties may, on the occurrence of such an event, choose to wind up the partnership. This is a *general* dissolution. On the termination of a partnership, any surviving partner may apply to the Court to have the partnership wound up.[688] Winding up a partnership is the responsibility of the partners: The Act does not provide for an office holder to carry out such a function, but partners may apply to the Court for a receiver, if necessary, to preserve partnership assets.[689] The list of circumstances set out *supra* (taken from sections 32–34) is, with one exception (namely, illegal partnerships), default rules around which the firm may contract. Thus, written partnership agreements may provide, for example, that the death or bankruptcy of a partner (or dissolution by notice under sections 26 and 32(c)) will not trigger dissolution.

442. Further circumstances are set out in the 1890 Act, section 35, in which a partnership is not automatically dissolved, but in which a partner may apply to the Court for dissolution, namely:

(a) Where a partner is found lunatic by inquisition, or is shown to the satisfaction of the Court to be of permanently unsound mind.
(b) Where another partner becomes in any way incapable of performing his part of the partnership contract.
(c) Where another partner is in the opinion of the Court guilty of conduct that, having regard to the nature of the business, is calculated to pre-judicially affect the carrying on of the business.
(d) Where another partner wilfully or persistently breaches the partnership agreement, or otherwise so conducts himself in matters relating to the partnership that it is not reasonably practicable for the other partner(s) to carry on.
(e) When the business of the partnership can only be carried on at a loss.
(f) Whenever in any case circumstances have arisen, which, in the opinion of the Court, render it just and equitable that the partnership should be dissolved.

---

686. This provision has been strictly interpreted; thus, a solicitor's inadvertent failure to renew his practising certificate has been held to dissolve his partnership. *See Hudgell Yeates & Co. v. Watson* [1978] 2 All ER 363.
687. There can be no technical dissolution where an event occurs making it unlawful for the business of the firm to be carried on, or for the members of the firm to carry it on in partnership.
688. 1890 Act, s. 39.
689. *Hurst v. Bryk* [2002] 1 AC 185, 196 per Lord Millett.

II. Consequences of Dissolution

443. As noted *supra*, on the dissolution of a partnership, any remaining partner is entitled to apply to have the firm's property applied in payment of the firm's debts and liabilities, or to have the firm wound up – and thereby instigate a general dissolution.[690] As also noted above, this is only a default rule. The partners may agree to exclude its application. Where a general dissolution occurs, the partners retain authority to bind one another, 'so far as may be necessary to wind up the affairs of the partnership, and to complete transactions begun but unfinished at the time of the dissolution, but not otherwise'.[691] Once the firm is in general dissolution, the firm's debts and liabilities will be ascertained and discharged, and the firm's assets will be sold as necessary to raise sufficient funds for that purpose. The assets of the firm, including the sums, if any, contributed by the partners to make up losses or deficiencies of capital, shall be applied in the following order: (1) in paying debts and liabilities of the firm to third parties; (2) in repaying advances made by partners to the firm; (3) in paying to each partner rateably what is due from the firm to him in respect of capital; and (4) the ultimate residue, if any, shall be divided among the partners in the proportion in which the profits are divisible.[692] Losses, including losses and deficiencies of capital, shall be paid first out of profits, next out of capital, and finally, if necessary, by the partners individually in the proportion in which they were entitled to share profits.[693] Partners may agree to share surplus assets and/or contribute to losses in a different ratio than the default ratio set out in the legislation (i.e., in the same proportion as their entitlement to profits),[694] but (predictably) may not by contract alter the rule that creditors are to be paid off first.[695]

III. Outsiders

444. Persons dealing with the firm are entitled to treat all apparent members of the firm as still being partners, unless and until they have notice of a change.[696] A public notice in *Iris Oifigiúil* (today's equivalent of the Dublin Gazette) shall be notice for persons who had not previously dealt with the firm,[697] but the remaining partners must individually notify existing customers.

690. 1890 Act, s. 39.
691. 1890 Act, s. 38.
692. 1890 Act, s. 44(b).
693. 1890 Act, s. 44(a).
694. 1890 Act, ss 24(1) and 44(b).
695. *See* Law Society of Ireland, Business Law (2006), 39.
696. 1890 Act, s. 36(1).
697. 1890 Act, s. 36(2).

IV. Retirement

445. The 1890 Act does not provide a default mechanism that a partner may use to retire from a firm, other than by dissolving the partnership on notice.[698] As noted *supra*, such dissolution opens the prospect of an application for the winding up of the firm.[699] Therefore, retirement is an important and necessary subject of any written partnership agreement.

446. A partner who retires from a firm does not thereby cease to be liable for partnership debts or obligations incurred before his or her retirement.[700] The remaining partners may agree to indemnify the retiring partner in respect of such debts and obligations. A retiree is not liable for debts or obligations incurred by the partnership after his retirement, as the agency relationship has ended.[701] (The same applies where a partner dies or becomes bankrupt.) However, there is an exception to this proposition in the case of existing customers or creditors – that is, persons who were aware of a partner's connection with the firm before that partner's retirement: They must have notice of the retirement, before the retiree is released from liability in respect of them.[702] The only other way a retiring partner may be liable for post-retirement debts is if he 'knowingly suffers himself to be represented' as a partner in the firm.[703] Where a person (by retirement, death or bankruptcy) ceases to be a partner, 'and the surviving or continuing partners carry on the business of the firm with its capital or assets without any final settlement of accounts as between the firm and the outgoing partner or his estate, then, in the absence of any agreement to the contrary, the outgoing partner or his estate is entitled at the option of himself or his representatives to such share of the profits made since the dissolution as the Court may find to be attributable to the use of his share of the partnership assets, or to interest at the rate of 5% per annum on the amount of his share of the partnership assets'.[704]

§6. Taxation

447. Detailed treatment of the application of Irish tax law to partnerships is beyond the scope of this work. The following few points may, however, be of passing interest. Partnerships are tax-transparent: Tax is assessed on the partners separately and not on the firm,[705] unlike in a company where both the firm (on its profits) and its members (on their dividends) are taxed. This flows from the fact that a partnership is not a separate legal entity, but is rather a collection of individuals. So,

698. 1890 Act, ss 26 and 32(c).
699. 1890 Act, s. 39.
700. 1890 Act, s. 17(2).
701. 1890 Act, s. 36(3).
702. 1890 Act, s. 36(1).
703. 1890 Act, s. 14(1).
704. 1890 Act, s. 42(1). *See Meagher v. Meagher* [1961] IR 96.
705. Taxes Consolidation Act (TCA) 1997, s. 1008(1). *See*, for example, TCA 1997, s. 30, as regards capital gains tax.

too, do other tax advantages to the partnership as a form of business organisation. For example, partners' social insurance contributions are less than the combined rate paid by employers and employees.[706] Structuring a business as a partnership so as to minimise tax liability is a legitimate and common practice,[707] but running a partnership at a deliberate loss, in order to set the same off against other tax liability, risks a finding that the business is not carried on 'with a view to a profit' and thus does not qualify as a partnership at all.[708]

448. Tax legislation provides that a firm's 'precedent partner'– defined as the first-named acting partner in the partnership agreement or, if there is no agreement, the partner who is named singly or with precedence over other partners in the usual name of the firm[709] – is responsible for filing a return of income and chargeable gains to the Revenue Commissioners,[710] and he or she is also the person to whom the Revenue gives notice of its determinations as to the partnership's tax affairs.[711] There are, in addition, certain other consequences of a person being a precedent partner. For example, in the event that profits for a given period are not exhausted (in the sense of being divided among the partners), the precedent partner is liable to an assessment in respect of such remaining balance, but if and when that balance (or part of it) is paid to the partner(s) entitled to it, the precedent partner may deduct therefrom the amount of such assessment paid by him or her.[712]

449. Finally, two miscellaneous points: First, a partnership may register collectively for Value-Added Tax (VAT) and income tax by filing a form TR1 and is for this purpose included in a category with sole traders, trusts and unincorporated bodies. This is in effect an instance of the law treating a partnership as if it were a separate entity, which it is not. Secondly, the template Partnership Tax Return 2008, Form 1 (Firms), is a ten-page document readily available on the website of the Revenue Commissioners at www.revenue.ie.

706. Social Welfare (Consolidation) Act 1993, ss 10 and 17.
707. *Inspector of Taxes v. Cafolla & Co.* [1949] IR 210.
708. This almost arose in *MacCarthaigh (Inspector of Taxes) v. D.* [1985] IR 73.
709. TCA 1997, s. 1007(1).
710. TCA 1997, ss 880 and 951(2). Any claim for a joint allowance must be made by the precedent partner: TCA 1997, s. 1010(9)(a).
711. TCA 1997, ss 1008(3), 1010(6), and 1012(1).
712. TCA 1997, s. 1008(4).

Chapter 2. Limited Partnerships

§1. Limited Partnerships Act

450. The Limited Partnerships Act 1907 for the first time under Irish law enabled a partnership to be formed that did not display three characteristics of a general or traditional partnership, namely: (1) the unlimited liability of every partner; (2) the implied authority of each partner to bind the firm and his or her fellow partners in all matters within the ordinary scope of the partnership business; and (3) the right of a partner, subject to contrary agreement, that each partner was entitled to participate in managing the business.[713] The Annual Report of the CRO stated that at the end of 2019, there were 2, 926 limited partnerships registered with the CRO.[714]

451. The 1907 Act did not create an internally complete, freestanding body of law. Rather, subject to the provisions of the 1907 Act, the law applicable to traditional, general partnerships (i.e., the 1890 Act and, to the extent that they are not inconsistent therewith, the rules of equity and common law relating to partnerships) apply to limited partnerships.[715] With that in mind, the following is a brief discussion of the modifications created by the 1907 Act.

§2. Personality and Liability

452. A limited partnership established under the 1907 Act must consist of one or more persons called general partners and one or more persons to be called limited partners.[716] General partners manage the firm and have unlimited liability, whereas limited partners, like company shareholders, invest in the firm and enjoy limited liability (i.e., they are only liable for the firm's debts and obligations in the amount of their capital investment), but have no default right to take part in managing the firm.[717] (If a limited partner, notwithstanding that he or she does not have a right to do so, *does* take part in the management of the firm's business, he or she shall be liable for all debts and obligations of the firm incurred while so doing as though he were a general partner.[718]) A limited partner may, however, inspect the firm's books and 'examine into the state of the partnership business, and … advise with the partners thereon'.[719]

713. Roderick I'Anson Banks: *Lindley and Banks on Partnership* 842 (18th edn., Sweet & Maxwell 2002).
714. CRO Annual Report 2019 available on www.cro.ie. The names of these partnerships are listed in Appendix 4 of that Report.
715. Limited Partnerships Act 1907, s. 7.
716. Limited Partnerships Act 1907, s. 4(2).
717. Limited Partnerships Act 1907, ss 4(2) and 6(1).
718. Limited Partnerships Act 1907, s. 6(1).
719. *Ibid.*

453. The 1907 Act (by section 7 thereof) is, in effect, superimposed onto the 1890 Act and the common law, and so it follows that a limited partnership, to qualify as such, must meet the definition of a partnership contained in the 1890 Act and discussed *supra*: It must consist of two or more persons carrying on business in common with a view to a profit. Therefore, for example, a firm intentionally incurring losses for tax purposes could not in law be a limited partnership, just as it could not be a partnership under the 1890 Act.

454. As regards management of the company, the Act provides, as a default rule subject to contrary express or implied agreement between the partners, that: 'Any difference arising as to ordinary matters connected with the partnership business may be decided by a majority of the general partners.'[720] Likewise, a limited partner has no right of veto over the introduction of a new partner into the firm.[721]

455. The 1907 Act expressly provides that a body corporate may be a limited partner. The Act is silent on whether a company may be a general partner in a limited partnership, and, therefore, it would appear that the principle applicable to traditional partnerships – that a company, because it is a legal person, maybe a partner – would appear by virtue of section 7 to apply also to limited partnerships. Therefore, by incorporating a company (such as, for example, a de facto or de jure single-member private company), the person effectively acting as a general partner may, subject to the rules of company law, cap his or her liability.

456. Every limited partnership must be registered with the Registrar of Companies, under pain of being regarded in default of that requirement as a general partnership and every limited partner being regarded as a general partner.[722] The following particulars (and a change in any of them) must be notified to the Registrar: the firm name; the general nature of the business; the principal place of business; the full name of each of the partners; the term, if any, for which the partnership is entered into and the commencement date thereof; a statement that the partnership is limited and a description of every partner as such; and the sum contributed by each limited partner and whether paid in cash or how otherwise.[723]

§3. Dissolution

457. A limited partner is not entitled to dissolve the partnership by reason of any limited partner suffering his or her share to be charged for his or her separate debt or to dissolve the partnership by notice.[724] In addition, a limited partnership shall not be dissolved by the death or bankruptcy of a limited partner, and the lunacy of

720. Limited Partnerships Act 1907, s. 6(5)(a).
721. Limited Partnerships Act 1907, s. 6(5)(d).
722. Limited Partnerships Act 1907, ss 5 and 15.
723. Limited Partnerships Act 1907, ss 8 and 9.
724. Limited Partnerships Act 1907, s. 6(5)(c) and (e).

a limited partner shall not be a ground for dissolution of the partnership by the Court, unless the lunatic's share cannot be otherwise ascertained and realised.[725]

§4. Taxation

458. All partnerships offer the benefit of being 'tax-transparent'. This means that the partnership, not having a separate corporate personality, is not itself taxed, but rather income derived by partners from a partnership is subject only to the same taxation as income from any other source. (This is unlike the situation in a company where corporate profits are subject to corporation tax and any dividends declared out of those profits are then taxed again). Limited partnerships' additional feature of not requiring limited partners to contribute to the debts and obligations of the firm beyond their capital contribution means that losses incurred by a limited partnership may be used for tax reduction purposes. For a time, a partner's share of the firm's trading losses could be set off against other taxable income, even when such losses exceeded (and sometimes far exceeded) that partner's capital contribution. The Revenue Commissioners unsuccessfully challenged that practice in *MacCarthaigh (Inspector of Taxes) v. D.*,[726] but shortly thereafter, the legislature moved to limit the amount a partner could set off against other taxable income to the amount of his or her capital contribution, rather than his or her share of trading losses.[727] Statutory Instrument 597/2019 amends certain requirements for partnerships and limited partnerships. The regulations applied Part 6 of the Companies Act 2014 (annual return requirements) to limited partnerships. The regulations also applied Part 26 of the Companies Act 2014 (which was inserted into the Companies Act 2014 by the Companies (Accounting) Act 2017 to qualifying partnerships. Part 26 applies to particular types of companies and obliges large companies, large groups and 'public interest entities' that are active in the mining and extractive industries or the logging of primary forests to prepare and file annual reports on payments made to governments with the CRO. Partnership reports are required to be filed within 11 months of the financial year end. This financial year refers to any financial year which commences on or after 1st January 2020.

725. Limited Partnerships Act 1907, s. 6(2).
726. Limited Partnerships Act 1907, s. 6(2).
727. Finance Act 1986, s. 46. *See* now Taxes Consolidation Act 1997, s. 1013.

Chapter 3. Investment Limited Partnerships Act

459. The ILP Act 1994 which has now been amended by the ILP Act 2020 created a modified form of limited partnership for businesses principally engaged in the investment of funds in property.[728] Though they are a form of limited partnership, section 4(2) of the 1994 Act 'expressly disapplies' the provisions of the 1907 Act to ILPs.[729] The passing of the 1994 Act but more importantly the more recent ILP Act 2020 is generally regarded as an extremely important initiative for the investment funds industry in Ireland.

460. The amendments to the ILP Act 1994 greatly enhance the attractiveness of the ILP structure for private equity managers and investors. The ILP can be structured to suit all major investment strategies and with enhancements under the amending legislation is promoted as a suitable vehicle for all types of private funds or indeed real asset-based funds including private equity funds, funds based on real estate, venture capital funds generally, credit and loan originated funds. It is also hoped by those involved in the fund industries that hedge fund managers may also find the Irish ILP an attractive vehicle.

461. An ILP must have, and does not come into existence until it receives, a certificate of authorisation from the Central Bank.[730] The Central Bank may impose such conditions on the authorisation of an ILP as it considers appropriate and prudent.[731] Contravention of any such condition by the ILP is an offence, and any partner in default is liable to maximum penalties of a EUR 634,869 fine and fifteen years' imprisonment. The Central Bank may also apply to the Court for an order prohibiting contravention of such a condition[732] or decide to revoke an ILP's authorisation.[733] Detailed consideration of the regulation of ILPs is beyond the scope of this work. The unusual structure of ILPs bears noting, however.

462. ILPs differ significantly from traditional partnerships, in that they 'consist of one or more general partners and one or more limited partners'.[734] The 1994 Act provides that management and conduct of the business of an ILP is a matter solely for general partners, inasmuch as that in order to maintain their limited liability status, limited partners in ILPs must not take part in the conduct of the business of the ILP, 'and in particular shall not have power to contract on behalf of the [ILP] and all letters, contracts, deeds, instruments and documents whatsoever shall be entered into by the general partner on behalf of the [ILP]'.[735] If a limited partner takes part in the conduct of the business of the ILP in its dealings with persons who are not

---

728. ILP Act (ILPA) 1994, s. 5(1)(a). *See* generally, Kevin Murphy 'Investment Limited Partnerships', Commercial Law Practitioner 1 (1994): 287.
729. *Quigley v. Harris* [2008] IEHC 403 (unreported, High Court, 28 Nov. 2008) per Laffoy J.
730. ILPA 1994, s. 3.
731. ILPA 1994, s. 7.
732. ILPA 1994, s. 34.
733. ILPA 1994, s. 29.
734. ILPA 1994, s. 5(1)(b) as amended by S.I. No. 257 of 2013.
735. ILPA 1994, s. 6(1).

partners, he or she 'shall be liable in the event of the insolvency of the [ILP] for debts of the [ILP] incurred during the period that he so participates' as if he or she were a general partner, but only in respect of debts or obligations incurred in favour of a person who reasonably believed, based upon the conduct of the partner, that he or she was a general partner.[736] Thus, from the point of view of limited partners, ILPs do not really resemble traditional partnerships regulated by the 1890 Act, or limited partnerships under the 1907 Act, but are better understood as arms-length investment vehicles.

463. The 2020 Act permits umbrella-type ILPs to be formed with multiple segregated liability compartments or 'sub-funds'. This provides asset managers with significant structuring flexibility and allows different strategies and investor types to be accommodated within one overall architecture while at the same time preserving segregation of liability (i.e., the assets of one sub-fund are not available to discharge the liabilities of other sub-funds within the same umbrella). The umbrella structure concept is well established and recognised. Umbrella structures are regularly used by asset managers. However, the ability to use an umbrella structure in an ILP is a unique feature which will provide considerable operational efficiencies and potential economies of scale.

736. ILPA 1994, s. 6(2) and 6(3).

Selected Bibliography

Deirdre Ahern, *Directors' Duties*: *Law and Practice*. Dublin: Thomson Roundhall, 2009.

Hugh Byrne & Louis McEntaggart, *The National Asset Management Agency Act 2009: Annotations and Commentary*. Dublin: Bloomsbury Professional, 2010.

Thomas B. Courtney, (gen. ed.) et al. *The Professional's Guide to the Companies Act 2014*. Dublin: Bloomsbury, 2015.

Thomas B. Courtney, *The Law of Companies*. 3rd edn. Dublin: Bloomsbury Professional, 2012.

Thomas B. Courtney, *The Law of Companies*. 4th edn. Dublin: Bloomsbury Professional, 2016.

Michael Forde &Hugh Kennedy. *Company Law*. 4th edn. Dublin: Thomson Round Hall, 2007.

Ronan Keane, *Company Law in Ireland*. 4th edn. Tottel, 2006.

Brian (G.B.) Hutchinson, *Keane: Company Law in Ireland:* 5th Edition, Thompson Roundhall 2016.

Irene Lynch Fannon, Jane Marshall & Rory O'Ferrall. Corporate Insolvency and Rescue. 1st edn. Butterworths, 1996.

Irene Lynch Fannon & Gerard Nicholas Murphy. *Corporate Insolvency and Rescue*. 2nd edn. Dublin: Bloomsbury, 2012.

Irene Lynch Fannon, *Working Within Two Kinds of Capitalism*. Oxford: Hart Publications, 2003.

Sinead McGrath, *Company Law Essential Law Texts*. Dublin: Roundhall, 2003.

Michael Twomey, *Partnership Law*. Dublin: Butterworths, 2000.

Michael Twomey & Maedbh Clancy. *Partnership Law*. Dublin, Bloomsbury, 2019.

Patrick Ussher, *Company Law in Ireland*. London: Sweet & Maxwell, 1986.

Maire R. Whelan, Mark Kennedy & Fergus O'Raghallaigh, *The National Asset Management Agency Act 2009*. Dublin: Gill and MacMillan, 2011.

Other Useful Resources

British and Irish Legal Information Institute (BAILII) – www.bailii.org.
Irish Legal Information Initiative (IRLII) – www.irlii.org.
Company Law Review Group www.clrg.org
Companies Registration Office – www.cro.ie.
Corporate Enforcement Authority – www.cea.gov.ie.
The Department of Enterprise, Trade and Employment – www.enterprise.gov.ie
The Law Reform Commission www.lawreform.ie

Selected Bibliography

Irish Statute Book – www.irishstatutebook.ie

Oireachtas – www.oireachtas.ie

The UK Government's Department for Business Innovation and Skills for comparative information on reform of Company Law. https://www.gov.uk/government/organisations/department-for-business-innovation-skills.

Enterprise Act (UK) 2002.

Companies (UK) Act 2006.

As English decisions prior to 1922 form part of Irish law and since 1922 are considered to be of persuasive authority in Irish law, the following English texts are also referred.

Paul L. Davies, *Introduction to Company Law.* 2nd edn., Clarendon Law Series, Oxford: Oxford University Press, 2002.

Alan Dignam & John Lowry. *Company Law*. Oxford: Oxford University Press, 2006.

Paul L. Davies, Sarah Worthington & Christopher Hare, *Gower Principles of Modern Company Law* 11th edn. London: Sweet and Maxwell, 2021.

Ross Grantham & Charles Rickett. *Corporate Personality in the 20th Century.* Oxford: Hart Publishing, 1998.

Louise Gullifer & Jennifer Payne, *The Law of Corporate Finance: Principles and Policy*. 2nd edn., Oxford: Hart Publications, 2015.

Leornard Sealy & Sarah Worthington. *Cases and Materials on Company Law*. 10th edn. Oxford: Oxford University Press, 2012.

Leonard Sealy & Sarah Worthington. *Cases and Materials on Company Law.* 11th edn. Oxford: Oxford University Press, 2016.

Sarah Worthington and Sinead Agnew. *Sealy and Worthington's Text, Cases and Materials in Company Law* 12th edn. Oxford University Press, 2022.

Roderick l'Anson *Lindley and Banks on Partnership.* 18th edn. London: Sweet & Maxwell, 2002.

Geoffrery Morse, *Partnership Law*. 6th edn. Oxford: Oxford University Press, 2006.

Geoffrey Morse, (ed.). *Palmer's Company Law: Annotated Guide to the Companies Act 2006.* London: Sweet & Maxwell, 2007.

Gabriel Moss, Ian Fletcher & Stuart Isaacs. *The EC Regulation on Insolvency Proceedings: A Commentary and Annotated Guide*. (Oxford University Press 2002; 2nd edn., 2009, edn., due to be published in 2016).

Christophy Paulus & Reinhard Damamm, European Preventive Restructuring: Article by Article Commentary (Beck/Hart/Nomos, 2021).

Robert R. Pennington, *Company Law*. 8th edn. Oxford: Oxford University Press, 2001.

Robert Pettet, *Company*. 2nd edn. Longman Law Series, 2005.

Reinhard Bork and Michael Veder: *Harmonisation of Transactions Avoidance Laws* (Intersentia, Antwerp, 2022)

Bob Wessels, Bruce A. Markell & Jason Kilborn, *International Co-operatioin in Bankruptcy and Insolvency Matters.* Oxford University Press, 2009.

Government Reports

The Report of the Company Law Review Group, December 1994.

Report of the Working Group on Company Law, Compliance and Enforcement, November 1998.
Report of the Company Law Review Group on the Regulation of Receivers, March 2019.
Report of the Company Law Review Group on the Protection of Employees and Unsecured Creditors, 2017.
Report of the Company Law Review Group on the Rescue of Small Companies, November 2020.
Report of the Company Law Review Group on Existing Legislative provisions regarding the provision of information to creditors generally and in particular to employees. March 2021
Report of the Company Law Review Group on the consequences of certain Corporate Liquidation and Restructuring Practices including the splitting of corporate operations from asset holding entities in group structures. December 2021.
Central Statistics Office, This is Ireland, Highlights from Census 2011 Part 1 (CS0, Government of Ireland, March 2012). 978-1-4064-2650-2.
Central Statistics Office, Census 2016, Preliminary Results, Part 1 – 2017.
Census of Population, Preliminary Results 2022. Press Release 23 June 2022.
Department of Trade and Industry (UK) Consultative Document, Modern Company Law for a Competitive Economy. 200.

Selected Bibliography

Index

The numbers here refer to paragraph numbers.

Index

Index

www.ingramcontent.com/pod-product-compliance
Lightning Source LLC
Chambersburg PA
CBHW071439230926
51846CB00001B/283
* 9 7 8 9 4 0 3 5 0 0 5 8 4 *